TEXTUAL SOURCES FOR THE STUDY OF RELIGION
edited by John R. Hinnells

Zoroastrianism

TEXTUAL SOURCES FOR THE STUDY OF RELIGION

Judaism ed. P. Alexander
Sikhism ed. Hew McLeod

Further titles are in preparation

TEXTUAL SOURCES FOR THE STUDY OF

Zoroastrianism

edited and translated
by Mary Boyce

*Emeritus Professor of Iranian Studies
in the University of London*

Manchester
University Press

Copyright © MARY BOYCE 1984

Published by MANCHESTER UNIVERSITY PRESS
Oxford Road, Manchester M13 9PL, U.K.
51 Washington Street, Dover, N.H. 03820, U.S.A.

British Library cataloguing in publication data

Zoroastrianism. – (Textual sources for the study of religion)
1. Zoroastrianism
I. Boyce, Mary   II. Series
295   BL1525
ISBN 0–7190–1064–0 (cased)
ISBN 0–7190–1091–8 (limpback)

Photoset in Plantin by
Northern Phototypesetting Co., Bolton
Printed in Great Britain by
Bell & Bain Ltd., Glasgow

CONTENTS

GENERAL INTRODUCTION

This series is planned to meet a fundamental need in the study of religions, namely that for new, reliable translations of major texts. The first systematic attempt to provide such translations was the monumental *Sacred Books of the East* in the nineteenth century. These were pioneering volumes but, naturally, are now somewhat out of date. Since linguistic studies have advanced and more materials have come to light it is important to make some of these findings of twentieth-century scholarship available to students. Books in this series are written by specialists in the respective textual traditions, so that students can work on the secure foundation of authoritative translations of major literary sources.

But it is not only that linguistic and textual studies have advanced in the twentieth century. There has also been a broadening of the perspective within which religions are studied. The nineteenth-century focus was largely on scriptural traditions and the 'official' theological writings of the great thinkers within each tradition. Religious studies should, obviously, include such materials; but this series also reflects more recent scholarly trends in that it is concerned with a much wider range of literature, with liturgy and legend, folklore and faith, mysticism and modern thought, political issues, poetry and popular writings. However important scriptural texts are in a number of religions, even the most authoritative writings have been interpreted and elucidated; their thoughts have been developed and adapted. Texts are part of living, changing religions, and the anthologies in this series seek to encapsulate something of the rich variety to be found in each tradition. Thus editors are concerned with the textual sources for studying daily religious life as exemplified in worship or in law as well as with tracing the great movements of thought. The translations are accompanied by generous annotation, glosses and explanations, thus providing valuable aids to understanding the especial character of each religion.

Books in this series are intended primarily for students in higher education in universities and colleges, but it is hoped that they will be of interest also for schools and for members of some, at least, of the religious communities with whose traditions they are concerned.

John R. Hinnells

ACKNOWLEDGEMENTS

ABBREVIATIONS

I am indebted to the following individuals for kindly allowing me to reproduce passages from their works, and to the journals, institutes or publishers concerned for also giving their consent: Dr Jal F. Bulsara; Mr H. E. Eduljee (and *Zoroastrian Studies*, Bombay); Professor R. N. Frye (and the Mediaeval Academy of America); Professor Milton Gold (and Istituto Italiano per il Medio ed Estremo Oriente); Professor J. Gwyn Griffiths (and University of Wales Press); Professor K. D. Irani (and *Parsiana*, Bombay); Mr Khojeste P. Mistree; Mr B. R. Panthaki (on behalf of the late Mr Ph. N. Tavaria); Mr Rusi B. Pastakia; Dr M. Shaki (and *Archív Orientalní*); Professor H.-P. Schmidt (and the Postgraduate and Research Institute of the Deccan College, Poona).

I am further indebted to Mr J. R. Hinnells and Dastur Dr K. M. JamaspAsa for generously making available for inclusion in this anthology the materials in 11.4.2, 3.1, 3.2, which they had already selected for their own forthcoming work, *The Parsis in British India* (to be published by Manchester University Press).

A.C. After the birth of Christ
Av. Avestan
AVN. Arda Viraz Namag
Dk. Denkard
Eng. English
GAv. Gathic Avestan
GBd. Greater Bundahishn
MP. Middle Persian
NP. New Persian
Ny. Nyayesh
OIr. Old Iranian
Pahl. Pahlavi
Riv. Rivayat
RV. Rigveda
SBE. *Sacred Books of the East*
SGV. Shkand-gumanig Vizar
Skt. Sanskrit
Vd. Vendidad
WZ. Wizidagiha i Zadspram
Y. Yasna
YAv. Younger Avestan
YHapt. Yasna Haptanhaiti
Yt. Yasht
Zor. Zoroastrian
ZVYt. Zand i Vahman Yasht
*   A doubtful meaning or a restored form. (This sign is used sparingly, and not at all in the Gatha translations, for which reference should be made to the latest editions of the text, see Bibliography A under H. Humbach and S. Insler.)

FOREWORD

Zoroastrianism is the least well known of the world religions; and compiling a collection of sources for its study has accordingly been a welcome task. For a number of reasons all the ancient texts, in Avestan and Pahlavi, have been retranslated for this anthology; but references are regularly given to other renderings, either at the end of each extract or in the bibliography, part A. Translations are particularly numerous for the Gathas, composed by the founder of the faith himself. For their interpretation not only years of specialised linguistic study are needed, but also a sound knowledge of the later holy texts, and of the forms of worship. Such competence is rarely united in a single scholar, and so the interpretation of these supremely difficult works has been a matter of shared undertaking, to which generations of scholars have by now contributed, and are still contributing. The translations of them offered here have no claim to originality, but derive from this broad tradition.

I am indebted to the general editor of the series, J. R. Hinnells, not only for inviting me to contribute to it, but also for wise comments and counsel during the preparation of the volume; and as always my thanks are due to my Zoroastrian friends, both Irani and Parsi, who have generously helped a non-Zoroastrian to gain some measure of knowledge of their venerable religion. This, despite its present relative neglect, is one which in its time has exerted more influence on the religious history of mankind than any other single faith. It has also preserved, in its traditions and worship, some immensely archaic elements, going far back beyond the distant day of its own foundation; so that for manifold reasons it richly merits study, whether for comparative purposes or simply for its own sake. To such study the present work, it is to be hoped, may serve as a modest introduction. It forms a companion volume to the writer's *Zoroastrians: their religious beliefs and practices* (see Bibliography B), in which a study of theology and observance is set in a framework of the history of the faith.

To the memory of

Dastur Khodadad Shehriar Neryosangi of Yazd

d. Ruz Amurdad Mah Farvardin (qadimi),
A.Y. 1351 = 2 July 1981 A.C.

a Zoroastrian priest staunchly faithful
through all adversity

1 INTRODUCTION

1.1 THE TEXTUAL SOURCES

1.1.1 The religious writings
1.1.1.1 The Avesta
The chief source for the teachings of Zarathushtra (known to the West as Zoroaster) is the compilation of holy works called the Avesta, a name which probably means 'The Injunction (of Zarathushtra)'. The Avesta is composed in two stages of an otherwise unrecorded Eastern Iranian language: 'Gathic' Avestan (GAv.), which in its forms is close to the language of the Indian Rigveda (which is generally assigned to the second millennium B.C.); and 'Younger' Avestan (YAv.). Gathic Avestan takes its name from the chief texts to survive in this dialect, i.e. the seventeen Gathas composed by the prophet himself. Although only this part of the Avesta is directly attributable to him, traditionally the whole Avesta is held to be inspired by his teachings; and many Younger Avestan texts are presented as if directly revealed to him by God. When Zarathushtra lived the Iranians were not familiar with writing; and for many centuries afterwards they regarded this alien art as fit only for secular purposes. All their religious works were handed down orally; it was not until probably the fifth century A.C. that they were at last committed to writing, in the 'Avestan' alphabet, especially invented for the purpose. The oldest extant ms. is dated to 1323 A.C.

1.1.1.2 The Gathas
The word 'gatha' (which exists also in Sanskrit) is variously rendered as 'hymn', 'poem', or 'psalm'. Zarathushtra's Gathas are short verse texts, cast largely in the form of utterances addressed by him to Ahura Mazda; and they convey, through inspired poetry, visions of God and his purposes, and prophecies of things to come, here and hereafter. They are full of passionate feeling and conviction, with meaning densely packed into subtle and allusive words; and in form they belong, it seems, to an ancient and learned tradition of religious poetry composed by priestly seers, who sought through study and meditation to reach direct communion with the divine. However, they are the only examples of this tradition to survive in Iran; and this literary isolation, together with their great antiquity, means that they contain many words of unknown or uncertain meaning, and have baffling complexities of grammar and syntax. All this, added to their depth and originality of thought, makes them extraordinarily difficult to translate. Only a few verses can be understood by themselves in a wholly unambiguous way; but keys to their interpretation are provided by the Younger Avesta and the Pahlavi Zand (see below), which set out clearly doctrines often only alluded to in the Gathas. Linguistically the Rigveda, being composed in a closely related sister language of comparable

antiquity, provides great help. The living tradition of the faith, especially in worship, is also an invaluable aid.

1.1.1.3 The Gathic portion of the Yasna

The Gathas were piously preserved by being made part of the liturgy of the Yasna (Y.), the 'Act of worship', which was solemnised daily. They were arranged formally in five groups, according to their five metres, and were set before and after the Yasna Haptanhaiti (YHapt.), the 'Worship of the seven Sections'. This, also in Gathic Avestan, appears to be made up of what are in essence even more ancient texts, composed to accompany the traditional offerings to fire and water, and revised in the light of Zarathushtra's teachings. So in Zoroastrian worship the Gathas, as the greatest of manthras (inspired holy utterances) guard the central rituals of the faith with their sacred power. Before and after them the four great prayers are recited, brief but very holy utterances which are constantly being said.

1.1.1.4 The Younger Avestan portions of the Yasna

The Yasna liturgy was extended over the centuries, and finally grew to have seventy-two sections. These, almost all in Younger Avestan, are of varying age and content. The Gathic texts were kept at the heart of the liturgy, being now protected in their turn by the Younger Avestan additions.

1.1.1.5 The Yashts

Some of the materials of the extended Yasna were taken from the Yashts (Yt.), hymns to the lesser divine beings of Zoroastrianism. A few of these are known as the 'great yashts', because of their length, and the poetic quality and antiquity of some of their verses, which (as Rigvedic parallels show) go back in substance to the Indo-Iranian period i.e. to at least 2000 B.C.; but even such ancient materials survive in the Younger Avestan dialect, since only the Gathic texts were exactly memorised, because of their great holiness. Other, less sacred, works were handed down in a more fluid oral transmission, that is, partly memorised, partly composed afresh by each generation of poet-priests, so that the language in which they were recited evolved with the spoken tongue. New matter was also added, so that these too are composite works, with explicitly Zoroastrian doctrines closely interwoven with older traditional matter, and with later materials.

1.1.1.6 The Vendidad

The Vendidad (Vd.) is a mixed collection of prose texts in late Younger Avestan, probably compiled in the Parthian period. Most are concerned with the purity laws, as a means of combating the forces of evil; and its name, a corruption of Av. *Vidaevadata*, means 'Against the Daevas' i.e. the evil beings. At some stage, probably during the early Islamic period, it was made part of a night celebration of the Yasna, being read aloud then in its entirety. Even today this is the only liturgical text which is not recited entirely from memory.

1.1.1.7 The Visperad

This long liturgy consists of an extended Yasna with Vendidad, the extensions being mainly additional invocations. Its name means the '(Worship of) All the Masters'; and it was solemnised especially on the seven great holy days of the faith (see 1.6).

1.1.1.8 The Nyayesh and Gah

The five Nyayesh (Ny.) are prayers for regular recitation by priests and laity alike. They are addressed to the Sun and Mithra (to be recited together, three times a day); the Moon (three times a month); the Waters and Fire. They again are composite works and contain verses from the Gathas and Yashts, as well as later material. The five Gah are texts of similar character. They are meant to form part of the prayers to be recited during each of the five divisions (gah) of the twenty-four hours, and contain invocations of the lesser divinities who watch over each of these periods (cf. 2.3.3.21).

1.1.1.9 The Khorda or Little Avesta

This name is given to selections from the above texts which, together with some Middle Persian ones, form a book of common prayer. Every Khorda Avesta contains the same body of essential prayers for everyday use, but there is some variation in their arrangement, and in the selections from the Yashts. Some have at the end a few prayers in a modern language (Persian or Gujarati). The laity have used Khorda Avestas only since the nineteenth century A.C. (when the holy texts were first printed); before then they learnt all their prayers by heart from the family priest or their parents.

1.1.1.10 The 'Great' Avesta

Under the Sasanians a canon of Avestan texts was established, grouped into twenty-one nasks (books); and it was this massive collection of holy texts which was at last committed to writing in the fifth or sixth century A.C. This 'Great' Avesta contained all the texts already described, and much else, including the life and legends of the prophet, expositions of doctrine, apocalyptic works, and books of law, cosmogony, and scholastic science. Copies were presumably placed in the libraries of the chief fire temples; but during the Islamic period these fire temples were all destroyed, through successive conquests by Arabs, Turks and Mongols, and not a single copy of the Great Avesta survives. The scope of its contexts is, however, known from a detailed summary given in a Pahlavi book, the Denkard (see below); and from this it appears that the extant Avestan texts amount to about a quarter of the whole canon. They survived because they were in constant devotional use, and so were both known by heart and set down in mss. which were frequently recopied by priests in their own homes.

1.1.1.11 Avesta fragments

Some fragments of Avestan texts survive. They include portions of the Hadhokht Nask, which appears to have been used at one time liturgically; and parts of two very cryptic and difficult works on priestly rituals, the Nirangistan and Herbadistan.

1.1.1.12 The Pahlavi Zand

Zand or 'Interpretation' is a term for the exegesis of Avestan texts through glosses, commentaries and translations. There existed of old a Zand in the

Avestan language itself, whose glosses are sometimes incorporated in the original texts; and there would have been Zands in the various languages of the diverse Iranian peoples down to the fourth century A.C. Thereafter the Sasanians, the last Zoroastrian dynasty to rule Iran, imposed their own language, Middle Persian or Pahlavi, generally. The Middle Persian Zand is therefore the only one to survive fully, and it is regarded accordingly as 'the' Zand. Middle Persian has a grammar which is so simple that it can produce ambiguities; and it is written in a difficult script, with too few letters for clarity, and the use of fossilised Aramaic ideograms. Its study therefore presents its own difficulties.

1.1.1.13 The Zand of extant Avestan texts

Almost all extant Avestan texts, except the Yashts, have their Zand, which in some mss. is written together with the Avesta. The two were often spoken of in one phrase, as Zand-Avesta, so that at first Western scholars took Zand to be a synonym for Avesta, or to refer to the language in which the holy texts are written. Where the Avesta and Zand coexist, it can be seen how priestly scholars first translated the Avestan as literally as possible, then often gave a more idiomatic Middle Persian translation, and finally added explanations and commentaries, often of ever-increasing length, sometimes with differing authorities being cited.

1.1.1.14 The Zand of lost Avestan texts

Several important Pahlavi books consist largely or in part of selections from the Zand of lost Avestan nasks, often cited by name; and by comparing these with the Zand of extant texts it becomes possible to distinguish fairly confidently the translation from the paraphrases and commentaries, and so to attain knowledge of missing doctrinal and narrative Avestan works. Among these Pahlavi books is the Bundahishn (Bd.), 'Creation', which deals not only with creation and its purposes, but also with the nature of the divine beings, and with eschatology. It exists in two recensions, known as the Iranian or Greater (because longer) Bundahishn, and the Indian Bundahishn. It has the subtitle Zand-Agahih, 'Knowledge from the Zand'. Wizidagiha, 'Selections' (from the Zand), were compiled by a leading Persian priest, Zadspram, in the ninth century A.C. (WZ.), and include materials for the life of the prophet, which existed in more than one Avestan nask. More details of his life, also taken from the Zand, are contained in the Denkard (Dk.). This, the 'Acts of the Religion', is a massive compilation of very diverse materials, made in the ninth and tenth centuries A.C. This was a period of considerable literary activity by Zoroastrian priests, in the face of the growing threat posed by Islam; but much of the matter which they then re-edited for the enlightenment of their community was very ancient in substance.

1.1.1.15 Other anonymous Pahlavi works

Much Pahlavi literature remains essentially an oral literature committed to writing, which retains many of the characteristics of oral composition. Thus most Pahlavi works are anonymous, and successive redactors felt free to add to them at will, or to rehandle them for their own purposes. It is usually impossible, therefore, to date such works effectively, since their contents may range from the very ancient to matter contemporary with the last redactor.

1.1.1.16 Pahlavi works of known authorship

A few Pahlavi works by named individuals survive, composed between the sixth and tenth centuries A.C. All, being preserved by priestly copyists, are concerned in some way with religion.

1.1.1.17 Persian Zoroastrian writings

After the tenth century even Zoroastrians abandoned composition in Pahlavi almost entirely for modern Persian, written in Arabic script with many Arabic loan words. Gradually the community was reduced by persecution to a poor and intellectually isolated minority, whose energies had to go into surviving and into preserving the core of the teachings of their faith. The Persian Zoroastrian writings, whether in prose or verse, consist therefore mainly of re-renderings of older materials.

1.1.1.18 Sanskrit, Old Gujarati and Pazand writings

In the ninth century A.C. a band of Zoroastrians left Iran to find religious freedom in Gujarat, western India, where they were known as Parsis, i.e. Persians. They adopted Gujarati as their mother tongue, and in the late eleventh or early twelfth century some of their scholar priests began translating Avestan texts from the Middle Persian Zand into Sanskrit and Old Gujarati. Some other Pahlavi texts were also translated, or were transcribed into the clear Avestan alphabet. The latter process, being a form of interpretation, was known as 'pa-zand'. Pazand texts, transcribed phonetically, represent a late and often corrupt Middle Persian pronunciation, and so present their own problems.

1.1.1.19 The Persian Rivayats

From the fifteenth to the eighteenth centuries Irani and Parsi priests corresponded sporadically on matters of ritual and observance. The Iranis' answers to Parsi questions are preserved as the 'Persian Rivayats', and shed valuable light on the religious life of the community, and especially on the operation of the far-reaching purity laws.

1.1.1.20 Modern literature

From the mid-nineteenth century, when the Parsis were prospering greatly, there is a considerable Parsi literature, in Gujarati and English, concerned with doctrines and observances. Down to this period the Zoroastrian tradition appears highly conservative and orthodox; but the community suffered severe mental and emotional shocks through the abruptness of its encounter with the world of modern thought; many of its devout members were left confused and troubled, and began to look hurriedly for new interpretations of ancient doctrines and rituals. Many Parsi devotional works, from this time onward, are unconsciously influenced therefore by Christian, Hindu or theosophical teachings, and some reformist ones incline to a simple theism, with virtually no observances. From the twentieth century there is a smaller body of

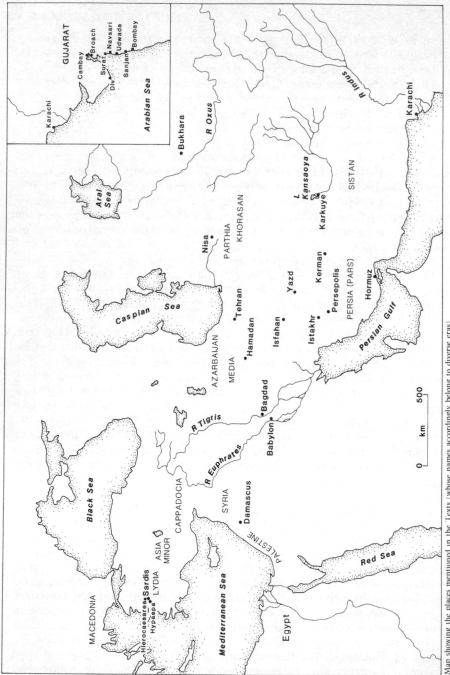

Map showing the places mentioned in the Texts (whose names accordingly belong to diverse eras)

GUJARAT

Cambay
Broach
Surat • Navsari
Div • • Udwada
Sanjan • Bombay

Karachi

Arabian Sea

Bukhara

R Oxus

Aral Sea

R Indus

Karachi

L Kansaoya

SISTAN

KHORASAN

Karkuye

Nisa

PARTHIA

Kerman

Yazd

Persepolis

PERSIA (PARS)

Hormuz

Persian Gulf

Caspian Sea

Tehran

Istakhr

Hamadan

Isfahan

AZARBAIJAN

MEDIA

Bagdad

R Tigris

Babylon

R Euphrates

500

km

0

Black Sea

CAPPADOCIA

SYRIA

Damascus

PALESTINE

ASIA MINOR

Red Sea

MACEDONIA

Hierocaesarea • Sardis
Hypaepa • LYDIA

Mediterranean Sea

Egypt

corresponding Persian writings by Iranis, in which some unconscious Muslim influence is also apparent. In the nineteenth and twentieth centuries Parsi priests began to write detailed expositions of the rituals and ceremonies of the faith, in Gujarati and English. The Pahlavi ritual texts are too technical and concise to be readily understood, and so these more recent works are valuable for the light they shed on Zoroastrian worship. This is the more important since Parsis do not admit non-Zoroastrians to their holy places.

1.1.2 Secular records
1.1.2.1. Records of the Achaemenian period (c.550–330 B.C.)
Towards the end of the second millennium B.C. the Iranian tribes moved south off the steppes, and gradually conquered and settled the land now called, after them, Iran. Eastern Iranians evidently carried Zoroastrianism with them, and eventually the western Iranians, i.e. the Medes and Persians, also adopted the faith. It became the religion of the Persian Achaemenians, whose empire (see map) was the greatest in the ancient world; and religious material occurs in their inscriptions. The Avesta itself remained, however, Eastern Iranian in substance as well as language, and there is no reference in it to these or any other Western Iranians, although the Medo-Persian magi became the best known of the Zoroastrian priests.

There are also a number of notices of the 'Persian religion' by Greek writers at this period, and after Alexander's conquest of the Achaemenian empire. This conquest appears to have done much harm to the transmission of Avestan texts, through the slaughter of priests.

1.1.2.2 Records of the Parthian period (c. 141 B.C.–224 A.C.)
The Arsacids, coming from north-east Iran, established the second Iranian empire, that of the Parthians. Their scanty written records show that they too upheld the Zoroastrian faith. There are Greek and Latin references to Zoroastrian observances at this time, and traces survive in Pahlavi literature of the Parthian transmission of religious texts. A long Parthian courtly romance, 'Vis u Ramin', contains interesting Zoroastrian material.

1.1.2.3 Records of the Sasanian period (c. 224–651 A.C.)
The second Persian empire, that of the Sasanians, is the epoch from which Zoroastrianism as an imperial faith is best known. The early kings, and their high priest, Kirder, left inscriptions; and in the fifth century Persian priests began to compile an immense chronicle, the 'Book of Kings' (MP. Khwaday Namag, NP. Shahname), whose early sections linked the Sasanian dynasty artificially with Vishtaspa, Zarathushtra's royal patron. This chronicle survives only through Arabic translations and the great Persian epic version of it by Firdausi, finished c. 1000 A.C. A number of other Sasanian works which contain some Zoroastrian matter are known only through Arabic or NP. renderings.

1.1.2.4 Notices by Muslim writers
After the overthrow of the Sasanian empire by the Muslim Arabs a number

of notices of Zoroastrians occur in Muslim histories and geographies. These are most numerous in the ninth and tenth centuries, and cease with the Mongol conquest of Iran in the thirteenth century, after which the Irani Zoroastrians become too insignificant in numbers and status to be further regarded.

1.1.2.5 Early Parsi records

In 1599 a Parsi priest completed a poem in Persian, the 'Qissa-i Sanjan'. Celebrating the history of the oldest Parsi sacred fire, it is based mainly on early oral traditions of the Parsis. From this time on Parsi records of various kinds (inscriptions, legal documents, genealogies, etc.) increase steadily.

1.1.2.6 Notices by European merchants and travellers

In the seventeenth and eighteenth centuries European merchants and travellers encountered Zoroastrians in Iran and India and wrote reports of them.

1.1.2.7 Modern Parsi and European writings

In the nineteenth century individual lay Parsis published descriptions of the traditional beliefs and practices of their co-religionists; and in this and the following century European scholars did the same for the very similar ones of the older Irani communities. These accounts make it possible to compare traditional Zoroastrianism, as it was lived down to and into modern times, with the growing diversity of beliefs and practices which has been developing since the nineteenth century.

1.2 THE RELIGIOUS BACKGROUND TO ZOROASTRIANISM

1.2.1 The means of reconstructing the Old Iranian religion

Zarathushtra has often been called a religious reformer, but he was so only in the sense that this is true of the other great founders of world religions, i.e. he evidently accepted much of the faith into which he was born, but transformed it through a new teaching. The Old Iranian faith can be reconstructed partly from comparison with closely related Vedic texts, and the Brahmanic tradition of India, partly through what clearly seem to be pre-Zoroastrian elements surviving in Zarathushtra's own revelation, or revived subsequently by his followers.

1.2.2 The physical and social background

The beliefs and observances of the Old Iranian and Vedic religions were evidently shaped by the physical and social background shared by the Indo-Iranian peoples. From perhaps 5000 to about 2000 B.C. they formed a single group, a branch of the Indo-European family of nations; and their homeland appears to have been the south Russian steppes, east of the Volga, where they lived as pastoralists, herding their cattle on foot. They moved presumably over hereditary tribal grazing grounds (such as the Airyanem Vaejah, MP. Eranvej, 'Iranian Expanse', of Zoroastrian tradition), from spring to autumn, wintering in river valleys or near the forests and mountains which bordered the plains. They lived close to their animals (a traditional Avestan term for the community is pasu-vira 'cattle-(and)-men'); and their society seems to have been divided into two main groups, priests and warrior herdsmen. Training for the priesthood began between five and seven, and maturity was reached at fifteen years of age, when all males (to judge by Brahmanic usage) were invested with a sacred cord as an act of initiation into the adult community.

1.2.3 The Old Iranian gods

The vastness of the steppes encouraged the Indo-Iranians to conceive their gods as cosmic, not local, divinities; and they apprehended a universal principle of what ought to be, Av. 'asha', Skt. 'ṛta', variously translated as 'order, righteousness, truth'. This principle should govern everything, from the workings of nature to human laws and all human conduct. It was guarded, they held, by a great triad of ethical divinities, the Lords, Av. 'Ahura', Skt. 'Asura'. The greatest of them, known to the Iranians as Ahura Mazda, 'Lord of Wisdom', was conceived, it seems, as the divine counterpart of the wise high priest, who wielded authority in the tribe through his learning and sacral powers. In the Rigveda he is reverenced, it appears, simply as 'the Asura'. Below him were the lesser Ahuras, Varuna and Mithra (Vedic Mitra), guardians respectively of the oath and covenant, who came therefore to hypostatise truth and loyalty and were active in doing his will. These two divinities seem divine counterparts of those tribal chieftains who were 'ashavan', 'possessing asha', i.e. just, upholders of the laws. Varuna as lord of the truly spoken word was venerated particularly as a creator-god. His name was not uttered in the known Iranian tradition, in which he is invoked only by cult epithets. Another powerful god, Indra, was worshipped as the divine counterpart of the warrior, an amoral being, invoked for strength, courage, and success in battle. The Indo-Iranians also venerated 'nature' and 'cult' gods. They thought of the divine beings as generally benevolent, attributing evil mainly to earth-bound devils, sorcerers and the like.

1.2.4 Worship in the Old Iranian religion

As wandering pastoralists the Indo-Iranians had no temples, and worshipped mainly in the open, without altars or images. They uttered hymns of praise and thanksgiving, and prayers, while making sacrifice and food offerings. An important rite, enacted during the Yasna, consisted of expressing the juice of an intoxicant (Av. haoma, Skt. soma), which, when consecrated, was offered to the gods and drunk ritually by the worshippers. Daily offerings were made to the hearth fire and sources of pure water; and priestly offerings to fire and water also formed part of the Yasna rituals.

1.2.5 Ancestor worship and beliefs about the hereafter

Cult of the ancestors was important, and was based on caring for the souls

(Av. urvan) of the departed by offerings of consecrated food and clothing, to benefit them in the underworld kingdom of the dead, thought to be ruled over by Yima (Skt. Yama), the first king to reign on earth and the first man to die. His kingdom was reached by perilous ways which led to the 'Chinvat Crossing', possibly a ford over an underground river, guarded by supernatural dogs. There seems also to have been a hero cult, in which the souls of the mighty dead were venerated as 'fravashis', powerful supernatural beings able to protect their descendants if duly worshipped. While the Indo-Iranians were still one people, a belief evolved that some fortunate souls were able to ascend after death to join the gods in Paradise, the 'House of Song', there to enjoy perpetual bliss. With this belief was linked the concept of resurrection of the body, which was thought, it seems, to be recreated from the dry bones a year or so after death, after which the re-embodied spirit could again experience all the pleasures of earthly existence. As the hope of Paradise grew more general the 'Chinvat Crossing' came to be thought of as a bridge between earth and heaven. If the soul succeeded in passing over this a beautiful girl appeared to lead it upward to the gods.

1.2.6 Cosmogonical and cosmological ideas

1. The Indo-Iranians had a common stock of ideas about the physical world, which Iranian priestly thinkers continued to develop, reaching ultimately a severely simple analysis of the physical world which probably owed much to the bareness of the flat landscape around them. Their speculations can be reconstructed as follows (cf. 1.5). The gods had created the world in seven stages; first the 'sky' of stone, as a huge round shell to enclose all else; second, in the lower half of this shell, water; third, earth, resting on the water like a great flat dish; then at the centre of the earth a single plant, and near it the Uniquely-created Bull, and Man, called Gayo-maretan, 'Mortal Life'; and, seventh, fire, both visible and also an unseen, vital force which gave warmth and life to the cosmos. The sun, part of the creation of fire, stood still overhead, and all was motionless and unchanging. Then the gods made a triple sacrifice: they crushed the plant, and slew the bull and man. From this beneficent sacrifice more plants, animals and men came into existence. The cycle of being was thus set in motion, with death followed by new life; and the sun began to move across the sky and to regulate the seasons in accordance with 'asha'.

2. These natural processes, it seems, were regarded as unending, so long as men did their part by offering regularly the same triple sacrifice, and by sanctifying through the daily yasna the seven creations, each of which was represented there: earth in the ritual precinct; water and fire in vessels; the stone of the sky in the pestle and mortar for the 'haoma' pressing; plants in the haoma and 'baresman' (grasses strewn beneath the sacrifice); cattle, i.e. useful animals in general, in the sacrificial beast or its products (butter and milk); and man in the officiating priest.

3. Together with this systematic analysis, linked to the yasna, more ancient

concepts survived: of high Hara (cf. Skt. Meru), a mountain peak in the centre of the earth, around which the sun was thought to circle, disappearing at night; of mighty Aredvi, a river which pours down from Hara into the sea Vourukasha and so supplies all the waters of the world; and of the Tree of All Seeds, which grows in Vourukasha. Each year its seeds are scattered over the earth with the rain. The earth itself was held to be divided into seven regions (Av. karshvar), separated by waters, or by great forests and mountains. Man lives in the central region, called Khvaniratha.

1.2.7 Social and religious developments before the time of the prophet

Even after the Indo-Iranian peoples drifted apart, developing separate languages and identities, they maintained much of their common religious tradition, evolved by countless generations of Stone Age pastoralists, and tenaciously upheld by their hereditary priesthoods. *Circa* 1700 B.C. the steppe-dwellers began to learn the use of bronze and to develop a new economy, in which the horse-drawn war chariot came to play a large part. 'Rathaeshtars', literally 'chariot-standers', began to form a new and dominant group in Iranian society: they abandoned the traditional task of helping to herd the tribe's cattle, and sought wealth and fame for themselves by fighting and raiding in the service of warrior chiefs. This was the Iranian Heroic Age, fragments of whose epic poetry survive, much recast, in the Shahname (see 1.1.2.3); and like all Heroic Ages it had its adverse side for the people at large, bringing bloodshed and lawlessness. The warrior heroes are likely to have directed their worship to the amoral Indra, rather than to the ethical Ahuras (cf. 1.2.3); but after they had become the dominant group in society the priest-poets in time made all the great gods chariot riders, and even gave Mithra a mace of bronze (cf. 2.1.1.67, 96).

1.3 ZARATHUSHTRA AND HIS TEACHINGS

1.3.1 The prophet's date and background

No firm date is known for Zarathushtra; but his Gathas suggest that he lived at a time when the Bronze Age developments were adversely affecting his own people, while they themselves, it seems, still kept to a largely pastoral economy. The word 'rathaeshtar', common in Younger Avestan, is not used by him, and his words reflect the ancient twofold social divisions of priest and warrior herdsman, he himself being a priest. Yet he speaks often of raiding, ruthlessness and bloodshed, and gives a picture of a society rent and in turmoil. The chronology of the Bronze Age changes must have varied greatly over the huge expanse of the south Russian steppes, and Zarathushtra may well have belonged to a tribe slow to be influenced by them. On this basis he may therefore be supposed to have flourished between 1400 and 1200 B.C., perhaps in some northerly region of the steppes. His teachings, though cosmic and universal, are anchored in the society which he himself knew, and the following material strands are prominent in them: cattle and cattle-herding; justice and the processes of law; kinship, friendship, and hospitality; and priestly acts of worship. For the last to be acceptable to the divine beings three things were required – right intention, truly spoken words, and correctly performed rituals – and this fact seems reflected in the threefold ethic of good thought, word and act repeatedly alluded to in the Gathas, and a ruling concept of the living faith.

1.3.2 The teachings of Zarathushtra: the divine Heptad

1. Many of Zarathushtra's teachings are clear from a combined study of the Gathas and the Zoroastrian tradition; and most are readily comprehensible by those familiar with the Jewish, Christian or Muslim faiths, all of which owe great debts to the Iranian religion. One central doctrine, however, that of the divine Heptad, has caused great difficulty to non-Zoroastrians, partly because of its uniqueness. Zarathushtra attained to this doctrine, it would seem, through meditating on the daily yasna. Iranian priests already held that behind the multiplicity of phenomena represented and consecrated at that service (see 1.2.6. 1–2) there had originally existed only one plant, animal and man; and the prophet now came to apprehend a similar original uniqueness in the divine sphere, namely that there was only one God, eternal and uncreated, who was the source of all other beneficent divine beings. For Zarathushtra God was Ahura Mazda, who, he taught, had created the world and all that is good in it through his Holy Spirit, Spenta Mainyu, who is both his active agent and yet one with him, indivisible and yet distinct. Further, Zarathushtra taught that God had made this sevenfold world with the help of six lesser divinities whom he brought into being to aid him, namely the great Amesha Spentas, 'Holy Immortals'; and they, with God himself, and/or his Holy Spirit, make up the Zoroastrian Heptad. Having aided in the task of creating the world, the Six enter as guardians into their own separate creations, being thus both transcendent and immanent. The Holy Spirit likewise enters into the 'ashavan', the just man, man being Ahura Mazda's especial creation. As transcendent Beings the Six hypostatise aspects of God's own nature, and are so close to him that in the Gathas Zarathushtra addresses Ahura Mazda sometimes as 'Thou', sometimes (when he apprehends him together with one or more of these Beings) with the plural 'You'. As immanent powers the Six are virtually identifiable with their material creations, and the word for the creation may be used to represent the divinity who informs it, and vice versa. This aspect of the doctrine of the great Amesha Spentas evidently represents an ancient, mystical way of looking at reality at a time when, it seems, 'abstract and concrete . . . appeared to the human spirit as of unified being, the abstract as the inner reality of the concrete, so that, for instance, pious devotion and the earth were the spiritual and material aspects of the same thing' (H. Lommel, in *Zarathustra*, ed. B. Schlerath, pp. 31–2). There are, moreover, subtle layers of manifold significance in the association of each divinity with his or her creation.

2. In the following table the names of the Heptad are set out in the order of the seven creations. The Avestan forms are given first, followed by the Pahlavi ones, then an approximate English rendering or renderings (since sometimes no one English word can adequately represent the meaning of the Iranian form); then the divinity's creation, together with the object or objects representing it in the yasna. In the Gathas Zarathushtra occasionally uses an epithet for one of the Six which in the tradition has become a fixed part of that divinity's name; these epithets are given in brackets. *Note:* the divinity Asha represents a hypostasis of the principle of asha, traditionally sustained by the Ahuras (see 1.2.3). In the tradition (see, e.g., 2.3.3) the members of the Heptad are often named in a different order, in accordance with their spiritual and moral dignity; and the creations are sometimes listed to correspond (see, e.g., 9.2.1).

Avestan	*Pahlavi*	*English*	*The divinity's creation and its representation*
Khshathra (Vairya)	Shahrevar	(Desirable) Power, Dominion, the Kingdom (of God)	The sky of stone (The stone pestle and mortar, and flint knife)
Haurvatat	Hordad	Wholeness, Health	Water (Consecrated water)
(Spenta) Armaiti	Spendarmad	(Holy) Piety, Devotion	Earth (The ground of the ritual enclosure)
Ameretat	Amurdad	Long Life, Immortality	Plants (The haoma, baresman, etc.)
Vohu Manah	Vahman	Good Purpose, Good Thought	Cattle (The sacrificial beast or its products)
Spenta Mainyu Ahura Mazda	Spenag Menog Ohrmazd	Holy Spirit of God; God	The Just Man (The priest)
Asha (Vahishta)	Ashavahisht, Ardvahisht	(Best) Right, Truth, Order	Fire (The ritual fire)

3. Zarathushtra speaks often also, using the same terms (khshathra, asha, etc.), of the powers or qualities which these six great Beings represent, and which every just (ashavan) person can hope, godlike, to possess. The concepts of divinity and of humanly possessed power seem frequently to blend, through the thought of that power proceeding from the divinity, who has himself actually entered into the person. This adds a further dimension to the doctrine of the immanence of the Heptad in the world; but the belief is very difficult to convey in translation, and some modern translators of the Gathas, concentrating on

the power or quality alone, fail to give a sense also of the indwelling divinity. In the versions offered in the present anthology an initial capital letter is used for these terms when the concept of the divinity appears dominant; otherwise they are given as common nouns. Only the name Mazda, 'Wisdom', is left untranslated, with the title Ahura being rendered as 'Lord'.

4. The doctrine of the Heptad is at the heart of Zoroastrian theology. Together with that of radical dualism (see 2.2.2) it provides the basis for Zoroastrian spirituality and ethics, and shapes the characteristic Zoroastrian attitude of responsible stewardship for this world. It is given tangible and visible embodiment in the yasna and all other acts of priestly worship (see 1.3.2, and cf. Boyce, *Persian Stronghold*, p. 51), and provides, through the seven holy days of obligation (see 1.6), the framework for the devotional year. Despite its ancientness the teaching has thus remained a living one for Zoroastrians themselves, kept potent through an unbroken tradition of belief, worship and practice. It was not only its total unfamiliarity, however, which made it hard for Western scholars to grasp. There was also a stumbling block created by special developments with regard to Khshathra and his creation, the sky. Zarathushtra himself evidently accepted the common ancient opinion that the sky, so mysteriously not falling (cf. 2.2.1.4), was of a hard substance, i.e. stone (see 2.2.2.5); and thus a link existed between Khshathra, lord of the stone sky, and stone weapons in the hands of 'ashavan' men as they exercised power (khshathra) in defence of the right. This link continued when stone weapons gave way generally to bronze ones; for Iranian scholar priests then defined the substance of the sky more precisely as rock crystal (cf. the crystal spheres of the Greeks), which they classified among metals. Because of the ethical aspect of the link between divinities and their creations, it was Khshathra's resulting guardianship of metals in general which came to be emphasised in the tradition; for man can do nothing to aid the distant sky, whereas metals can be worthily used in many ways: forged into weapons for just purposes; melted for judicial ordeals; minted in coins to give to the needy; made into useful tools or vessels, or beautiful ornaments to be kept always polished (cf. 11.3.1.25). So Khshathra was venerated through his aspect of lord of metals, and his guardianship of the sky was latterly overlooked; and this came to obscure the perfect correspondence between the Heptad and the seven creations. The full doctrine was recovered this century through the researches of H. W. Bailey (*Zoroastrian Problems in the Ninth Century Books*, ch. 4), R. C. Zaehner (*The Teachings of the Magi*, pp. 32–3), and the present writer (*Zoroastrians*, pp. 23–4, 41). Khshathra's link with a metallic sky is in fact clearly implied in 2.3.2.5–6 with 2.3.3.16 (where moreover his divine helpers are all sky-divinities).

1.3.3 The lesser divine beings

In the Gathas Zarathushtra invokes the two lesser Ahuras together with Ahura Mazda (by the evidently traditional phrase 'Mazda (and the other) Ahuras'), and also other beneficent ancient divinities; and the tradition makes it clear that he taught that they too were created by Ahura Mazda (cf. 2.3.1.53), being known like the Heptad as Amesha Spentas, 'Holy Immortals', or Yazatas, 'Beings worthy of worship'. A divinity very close to the Six, and like them, it seems, special to Zarathushtra's own revelation, is Sraosha, 'Hearkening'. He hypostatises men's hearkening (i.e. obedience) to God and God's hearkening to men's worship and supplications; and he is the guardian of prayer. *Note:* the hypostatising of what might now be called abstractions, but which the ancients clearly felt as forces, goes far back into Indo-Iranian times.

1.4 SOME REASONS FOR DIVERSITY IN MODERN STUDIES OF ZOROASTRIANISM

1.4.1 Concerning Zarathushtra's place and date

1. The great antiquity of the prophet meant that no authentic information survived concerning his place of birth; and this left scope for pious Zoroastrian communities to claim him for their own. Various eastern Iranian peoples (Bactrians, Sogdians, Parthians and others) shaped legends that he had been born in their territories; but it was the tradition of the Median magi, that he had lived in north-west Iran, which entered the Middle Persian Zand and so became best known. It was accepted by some Western scholars, until philologists established its impossibility. No western Iranian prophet could have spoken an eastern Iranian tongue. Nevertheless this claim is still occasionally referred to in modern books.

2. There was no means of recording absolute dates in remote antiquity. After the Seleucids had established the first fixed era in human history, beginning in 312/311 B.C., the magi in due course used this to calculate, quite erroneously, that Zarathushtra had lived *c.* 558 B.C. The modesty and apparent precision of this reckoning led some Western scholars to accept it (though it appears only in a few late sources). Others maintained from the first that a date in the sixth century B.C. was far too recent to be credible, and this view now prevails. The sixth-century date is still given, however, by some writers.

3. In the fourth century B.C. Aristotle saw his great teacher, Plato, as a re-embodiment of Zarathushtra, who, he held, had lived 6,000 years earlier. On the basis of this and other similar Greek calculations (cf. 10.2.1.1) many Parsis, especially theosophists, have placed their prophet in an impossibly remote antiquity.

1.4.2 Concerning doctrines

Christian scholars began trying to reconstruct Zarathushtra's teachings before the Avesta was known to them, and before they had made any real contact with the Zoroastrian community. Their first, respectful, hypothesis was that Zarathushtra had been an Iranian counterpart of the (idealised) Hebrew prophets, and had been sent, like them, to prepare the way for Christ. They postulated therefore that he had been a strict monotheist; and after the Avesta became known, they maintained this position by interpreting the relevant Gathic passages as implying that Ahura Mazda was the 'father' of both Spenta Mainyu and Angra Mainyu, i.e. the source of both good and evil (see 11.1.2). This 'European heresy', which was inspired by the Zoroastrian Zurvanite heresy (see 8), required the rejection of all post-Gathic Zoroastrian literature, in so far as it concerned dualism and the doctrine of the Heptad, as being grounded in error. This Western hypothesis influenced Parsi reformists in the nineteenth century, and still dominates much Parsi theological discussion, as well as being still upheld by some Western scholars.

1.4.3 Concerning practices

As part of the Western respect for Zarathushtra, it was supposed that the prophet had rejected all devotional observances except prayer. This conclusion was reached partly by interpreting the prophet's wrath against the cruelties of cattle-raiding as denunciations of blood sacrifice. Accordingly, Zoroastrian devotional practice down the ages had also to be regarded as erroneous. This Western interpretation was warmly welcomed by Parsis, who by the twentieth century had almost entirely abandoned blood sacrifice, and who by now have forgotten that their forbears ever offered it. The Iranis, living among Muslims (who still practise the rite), have been slower to reject it, though reformists among them now tend to maintain that they actually adopted it from Islam. Considerable diversity therefore exists in modern treatments of this and related matters.

1.5 THE ANCIENT IRANIAN WORLD PICTURE

Cf. 1.2.6. According to the Zoroastrian cosmogony, after the Evil Spirit's assault (cf. 2.3.4) mountains grew up from the flat earth to strengthen it; but torrential rain fell and split it into seven regions, the 'karshvars' (cf. 1.2.6.3). At the end of time it will be joined again, and once more level (cf. 10.2.1.2). The peak of Hara was held to have 360 apertures through which the sun moved on the 360 days of the year (cf. 1.7), passing twice through each, to leave half the world in darkness. Since the stars give least light of all the heavenly bodies, they were thought to be nearest to earth and farthest from heaven. Above them was the moon, then the sun (cf. 6.3.6). All water was held to have a common source, ascending from below the earth to the peak of Hara, pouring down from there on to the sea Vourukasha (cf. 2.1.7), and circulating through the seven regions before ascending again after being purified. These ancient concepts appear long after Zoroastrian scholars had revised them in the light of new knowledge, the Avestan texts being given the same divine authority as Christians accorded the 'Book of Genesis'.

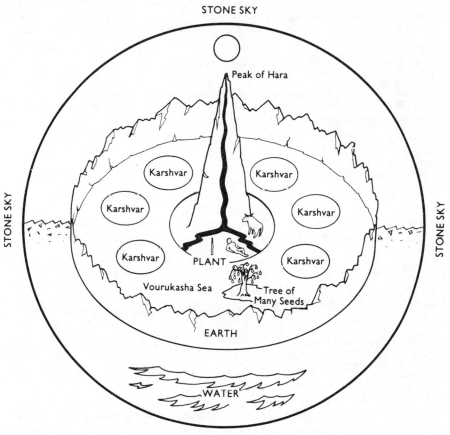

STONE SKY

STONE SKY

STONE SKY

Peak of Hara

Karshvar

Karshvar

Karshvar

Karshvar

Karshvar

Karshvar

PLANT

Vourukasha Sea

Tree of
Many Seeds

EARTH

WATER

STONE SKY

1.6 THE SEVEN HOLY DAYS OF OBLIGATION

'Gahambar' is the Middle Persian term for six of the seven obligatory Zoroastrian holy days. These appear to have been ancient seasonal festivals, refounded to honour Ahura Mazda and the six great Amesha Spentas, together with the seven creations, cf. 4.4.1. Each festival lasted originally one day, but after a calendar reform in the third century A.C. they were extended to six days each, later reduced for the gahambars to five. The seventh festival is called in Middle Persian No Roz, 'New Day', and is the greatest holy day, prefiguring annually the future 'New Day' of eternal bliss. The table shows the dates of the festivals' celebration according to the three existing calendars, Shenshai (S), Kadmi (K) and Fasli (F).

Festival's name in English	YAv or MP. name	Associated Amesha spenta	Associated creation	Celebrated dates	
				in 1980–83	in 1984–87
1. Mid-spring	Maidhyoi-zaremaya	Khshathra Vairya	Sky	S Oct. 5–9	Oct. 4–8
				K Sept. 5–9	Sept. 4–8
				F April 30 –May 4	April 30 –May 4
2. Midsummer	Maidhyoi-shema	Haurvatat	Water	S Dec. 4–8	Dec. 3–7
				K Nov. 4–8	Nov. 3–7
				F June 29 –July 3	June 29 –July 3
3. Bringing in corn	Paitishahya	Spenta Armaiti	Earth	S Feb. 18–22	Feb. 17–21
				K Jan. 19–23	Jan. 18–22
				F Sept. 12–16	Sept. 12–16
4. Homecoming (of the herds)	Ayathrima	Ameretat	Plants	S March 19–22	March 18–21
				K Feb. 19–22	Feb. 17–21
				F Oct. 12–16	Oct. 12–16
5. Midwinter	Maidhyairya	Vohu Manah	Cattle	S June 7–11	June 6–10
				K May 8–12	May 7–11
				F Dec. 31 –Jan. 4	Dec. 31 –Jan. 4
6. All Souls (precise meaning of the Av. name unknown)	Hamaspath-maedaya (Fravardigan, Gujarati Muktad)	Spenta Mainyu, Ahura Mazda	Man	S Aug. 21–25	Aug. 20–24
				K July 22–26	July 21–25
				F March 16–20	March 16–20
7. New Day	No Roz	Asha Vahishta	Fire	S Aug. 26	Aug. 25
				K July 27	July 26
				F March 21	March 21
	'Old' No Roz (Hordad Sal, celebrated on day Hordad, see 1.7.1)			S Aug. 31	Aug. 30
				K Aug. 1	July 31
				F March 26	March 26

1.7 THE ZOROASTRIAN CALENDAR

From ancient times the Iranians had a year of twelve months with thirty days each. The Zoroastrian calendar, created probably in the fourth century B.C., was distinctive simply through the pious dedication of each day and month to a divine being. The dedications are first attested through the invocation of the thirty calendar divinities in Y.16.3–6. Four days were devoted to 'Dadvah (Creator) Ahura Mazda', probably as an esoteric acknowledgement of Zurvan, who was worshipped as a quaternity (see 8.2.2). In later use the first of the four days is named for Ohrmazd, the other three for him as 'Creator', Dai (Middle Persian for Dadvah). The three Dai days are distinguished by adding to each the name of the following day, e.g. Dai-pad-Adar, 'Dai-by-(the day)-Adar'. The forms of the calendar names in current use are close to the Pahlavi ones, although the Parsis have a few slightly divergent usages. The twelve months also received dedications, which coincide with those of twelve of the days. The month names are first attested in Pahlavi.

1.7.1 The thirty days

	Avestan	Pahlavi	Parsi	English
1.	Dadvah Ahura Mazda	Ohrmazd	Hormazd	Creator Ahura Mazda
2.	Vohu Manah	Vahman	Bahman	Good Purpose
3.	Asha Vahishta	Ardvahisht	Ardibehesht	Best Truth
4.	Khshathra Vairya	Shahrevar	Sharivar	Desirable Dominion
5.	Spenta Armaiti	Spendarmad	Aspandad	Holy Devotion
6.	Haurvatat	Hordad	Khurdad	Wholeness
7.	Ameretat	Amurdad	Amardad	Immortality
8.	Dadvah Ahura Mazda	Dai-pad-Adar	Dep-Adar	Creator-by-Adar
9.	Atar	Adar	Adar	Fire
10.	Apo	Aban	Avan	Waters
11.	Hvar khshaeta	Khvarshed	Khurshed	Shining Sun
12.	Mah	Mah	Mohor	Moon
13.	Tishtrya	Tir	Tir	Dog Star (Av.), planet Mercury (Pahl.)
14.	Geush Urvan	Gosh	Gosh	Ox-soul
15.	Dadvah Ahura Mazda	Dai-pad-Mihr	Dep-Meher	Creator-by-Mihr
16.	Mithra	Mihr	Meher	Loyalty
17.	Sraosha	Srosh	Sarosh	Hearkening
18.	Rashnu	Rashn	Rashne	The Judge
19.	Fravashayo	Fravardin	Farvardin	All Souls
20.	Verethraghna	Vahram	Behram	Victory
21.	Raman	Ram	Ram	Peace
22.	Vata	Vad	Guvad	Wind
23.	Dadvah Ahura Mazda	Dai-pad-Din	Dep-Din	Creator-by-Din
24.	Daena	Din	Din	Religion
25.	Ashi	Ard	Ashishvang	Recompense
26.	Arshtat	Ashtad	Astad	Justice
27.	Asman	Asman	Asman	Sky
28.	Zam	Zamyazad	Zamyad	Earth
29.	Manthra Spenta	Mahraspand	Maharaspand	Holy Word
30.	Anagra Raocha	Anagran	Aniran	Endless Light

1.7.2 The twelve months

1. Farvardin (March/April)
2. Ardvahisht (April/May)
3. Hordad (May/June)
4. Tir (June/July)
5. Amurdad (July/August)
6. Shahrevar (August/September)

7. Mihr (September/October)
8. Aban (October/November)
9. Adar (November/December)
10. Dai (December/January)
11. Vahman (January/February)
12. Spendarmad (February/March)

Every coincidence of a month and day name was celebrated as a 'name-day' feast. There was thus one such feast in every month but the tenth, when four feasts were celebrated in honour of the Creator, Ohrmazd. The chief name-day feasts still celebrated by the Parsis are Aban and Adar. The Iranis also celebrate the festivals of Spendarmad, Tir and Mihr with special observances.

1.7.3 The five Gatha days

By the reform of the third century A.C. five extra days were added to the end of the 360 day year. These were named after the five groups of Zarathushtra's hymns. (All but the first of these are known by the opening word of the first hymn in the group. 'Gatha Ahunavaiti' is called after the Yatha ahu vairyo (Ahunvar) prayer), which precedes it in the liturgy.)

1. Ahunavad
2. Ushtavad
3. Spentomad
4. Vohukhshathra
5. Vahishtoisht

The extended gahambar of Hamaspathmaedaya is celebrated throughout these five days, cf. 4.4.1.5.

Various subsequent calendar reforms were directed at trying to stabilise the 365 day calendar in relation to the seasons. (The old 360 day one had been adjusted from time to time by the intercalation of a whole extra month.) It is these attempts which have led to the existence of three Zoroastrian calendars today.

1.8 THE ZOROASTRIAN 'WORLD YEAR'

During the Achaemenian period (sixth to fourth centuries B.C.) Persian scholar priests encountered the theory of Babylonian astronomers, that there existed a 'great year', during which all heavenly bodies completed a full cycle of their movements; and that in each 'great year' every occurrence of the preceding ones was exactly repeated, to infinity. This theory was widely adopted in antiquity, with hugely varying numbers of natural years being assigned to each 'great year'. Among the Iranians it was probably Zurvanites who first tried to reconcile these alien ideas with Zoroastrianism (see 8.1). They postulated a 'great' or 'world year' of 12,000 years (i.e. with twelve millennia corresponding with the twelve months of the calendar year). Zoroastrians could not accept the idea of an infinite repetition of historical events, but they divided the span of known human history into three millennia (i.e. 9000–12000), ushered in successively by Zarathushtra and the first two World Saviours (see 7.2). During each of these millennia, they held, the same broad pattern of events is repeated, until by the year 12000 the Third Saviour, the Saoshyant, will have accomplished the final defeat of evil and historical time will cease. This scheme of history was adopted also in due course by the orthodox, in the form whose outline is set out in 2.3. All events from Zarathushtra's day to their own were assigned to the prophet's millennium (i.e. *c.* 9000–10000). So when, subsequently, learned magi began to interest themselves in actual chronology they soon encountered difficulties as they tried to fit real events into this grand theoretic scheme.

0–3000	Ahura Mazda, with foreknowledge of the need and means to destroy evil, brought his creation into being in an invisible or spirit (menog) state. The Evil Spirit, rising from the deep, perceived this creation. He shaped the lesser evil spirits and attacked. Ahura Mazda cast him down helpless by reciting the Ahunvar prayer.
3000–6000	The Evil Spirit lay prostrate. Ahura Mazda gave material (getig) form to his creation, shaping the world in seven stages, with one plant, animal and man.
6000–8969	The Evil Spirit broke into and polluted the material world, destroying the plant, animal and man. From their seed grew all existing plants, animals and men. Yima reigned first over mankind, and all other events of Iranian myth and ancient epic took place.
8970	Birth of Zarathushtra.
9000	Beginning of his millennium. He received his revelation, and began to preach.
9012	He converted Kavi Vishtaspa.
9013–9969	A time of goodness followed by slow decline, leading to the present day.
9970	Birth of the first World Saviour, Ukhshyat-ereta (Pahl. Ushedar).
10000	Beginning of his millennium. He will lead the forces of good and overcome evil. A new time of goodness will again be followed by slow decline.
10970	Birth of the second World Saviour, Ukhshyat-nemah (Pahl. Ushedarmah).
11000	Beginning of his millennium. He will again lead the forces of good and overcome evil. A new time of goodness will again be followed by slow decline.
11943	Birth of the third World Saviour, Astvat-ereta, the true Saoshyant.
11973	He will begin the work of Frasho-kereti (Pahl. Frashegird), with resurrection of the dead, the Last Judgment, and final conquest of evil.
12000	History will end. The Kingdom (Khshathra) of Ahura Mazda will come on earth, and he will reign in bliss for ever.

1.9   CHRONOLOGICAL BACKGROUND TO THE TEXTS

1.9.1 Ancient and imperial times

Dates	General and dynastic events	Individual rulers	Religious persons and events
c. 1700-1400 B.C.	Stone Age merging into Bronze Age on S. Russian steppes, where the Iranian peoples were living as semi-nomadic pastoralists.		Cultivation of oral religious literature as represented in parts of Y.Hapt. and the 'great' yashts.
c. 1400-1200		Kavi Vishtaspa ruling over a part of the 'Avestan' people, on the steppes.	Zarathushtra was born and lived somewhere on the steppes. Composition of the Gathas.
c. 1200+	Iranian peoples moving south to conquer and settle in the land now called Iran.		Zoroastrianism spreading among the E. Iranians, who carried the faith into their new homelands. Revision of the old oral literature in the light of the prophet's teachings.
c. 614-550	Empire of the Medes, including all W. Iranian peoples.		Zoroastrianism gaining strength among W. Iranians and their priests, the magi.
550-330	Empire of the Achaemenian Persians, who ruled over all settled Iranian peoples, and many others, including the Jews, Ionian Greeks, and some Hindus and Arabs.	Cyrus the Great, 550-530. Darius the Great, 522-486. Xerxes, 486-465. Artaxerxes II, 404-358. Artaxerxes III, 358-338. Darius III, 336-330.	Zoroastrianism established by Cyrus as the Iranian religion. Temple cult of fire founded, probably under Artaxerxes II. Zoroastrian calendar created, and Zurvanism became prominent. Av. texts still being composed and transmitted orally.

Dates	General and dynastic events	Individual rulers	Religious person and events
334-326	Conquest of Iran by Alexander the Great.		Slaughter of priests leading to loss of much oral Av. literature. Intensive cultivation of Zoroastrian apocalyptic literature likely.
323-312	Iran ravaged by wars between his successors.		
312/11 B.C.	Founding of Seleucid empire, which included all Iran.		Development of local Iranian scripts. Use of writing being steadily extended.
c. 141 B.C.- 224 A.C.	Empire of the Arsacid Parthians (from N.W. Iran), which included all Iran.	Valakhsh (one of the six Vologeses, who ruled between c. 51 and 221 A.C.)	Conservation of oral Av. texts, and of local Zands, some perhaps partl written.
c. 224-651 A.C.	Empire of the Sasanian Persians, which included all Iran.	Ardashir I, c. 224-240. Shabuhr I, c. 240-270. Shabuhr II, 309-379. Vahram V Gor, 421-439. Khusrow I Anoshiravan, son of Kavad, 531-579. Hormizd IV, 579-590. Khusrow II Parvez 591-628. Yazdegird III, 632-651.	The high priest Tansar fixed the oral Av. canon. His successor Kirder organised the Zoroastrian priesthood. Many fire temples founded. The high priest Adurbad testified at a great doctrinal disputation. Invention of the Av. alphabet. By reign of Khusrow I the Avesta of 21 nasks written down, with its MP. Zand in Pahl. script.
636+	Arab conquest of Iran.		Much slaughter, and a number of instant or enforced conversions.

B

1.9.2 Zoroastrianism under alien rule
1.9.2.1 Under Arabs and Muslim Persians

Date	Secular events	Religious events
-661 A.C.	Rule of the first orthodox caliphs.	Jizya imposed on non-Muslims. Attempts at conversion sporadic. Iran still predominantly Zoroastrian.
661-750	Umayyad caliphs, ruling from Damascus.	c. 700 use of Pahlavi officially replaced by Arabic. Many Pahl. works translated into Arabic, and the originals eventually lost. Islam spreading.
750-1258	'Abbasid caliphs, ruling from Bagdad. Established largely through support of Iranian Muslims.	Antagonism between Persian and Arab yielding to antagonism between Muslim and non-Muslim. Zoroastrians still a considerable minority, and active in compiling, composing and editing Pahl. texts.
	From 869 Iranian Muslim dynasties gaining power locally under 'Abbasid overlordship.	Persecution of non-Muslims intensifying. c. 917, founders of Parsi community sailed from Persian Gulf. In 936 landed at Sanjan in Gujarat.

1.9.2.2 Under diverse Muslim, Hindu and Christian rulers

Date	Secular events in Iran	Events affecting the Irani Zoroastrians	Secular events in India	Events affecting the Parsis
1000	1037-1157 Seljuk Turks conquered Iran, and ruled it nominally under caliphs of Bagdad.	Increased harshness towards non-Muslims.	Hindu rajahs ruling in Gujarat.	1142 First Parsis settled in Navsari. Parsis gradually expanding northward along Gujarat coast.
1200				Neryosang Dhaval making Skt. and Pazand versions of Av. and Pahl. texts.
	1258 Pagan Mongols conquered Iran and overthrew Bagdad caliphate. Immense slaughter, and destruction of books.	Zoroastrian minority suffering with the rest of the population.	1297 Conquest of Gujarat by Muslim Sultans of Delhi. Most Parsis living thereafter, with the Hindus, under Muslim rule.	Jizya imposed on non-Muslims.

Date	Secular events in Iran	Events affecting the Irani Zoroastrians	Secular events in India	Events affecting the Parsis
1300	The Mongol ruler of Iran (1295-1304) adopted Islam. 1381 Timur Leng (Tamburlaine), a Muslim Turk, invaded and ravaged Iran.	Renewed zeal against non-Muslims. Zoroastrian remnant withdrawing to around desert cities of Yazd and Kerman. Some further migration to Gujarat.	1398 Timur invaded India and sacked Delhi. 1401 Independent Muzzaffarid sultanate of Gujarat established.	
1400	1404-1501 Timurids and other Turkish dynasties ruling Iran.			
		From 1478 Irani priests writing letters to Parsis, with treaties of instruction (rivayats).	1465 Sanjan besieged by Sultan's troops.	Changa Asa flourishing at Navsari. In 1495 brought the Sanjana Atash Bahram there.
1500	1501-1721 Safavids ruling Iran as Shi'ite Muslims, in general harsh towards non-Muslims. 1587-1628 reign of Shah 'Abbas, who received Europeans at his court in Isfahan.		European traders arrived off coast of Gujarat, seeking concessions. 1572 Mugul emperor Akbar conquered Gujarat. Surat developed as its chief port.	Chief Parsi priest in Navsari, Meherji Rana, invited to Delhi to take part in religious debate there. Honoured by Akbar.
1600				
		Shah 'Abbas II (1642-1667) signed an order for the forcible conversion of Zoroastrians. A massacre of the faithful at Isfahan.	1661 Bombay acquired and developed by the British, who granted complete religious freedom. Many Parsis settled there, and individuals acquired great wealth.	As Parsis worked with Europeans and acquired wealth in Surat and Bombay, more and more fire temples founded, with other pious benefactions.

Date	Secular events in Iran	Events affecting the Irani Zoroastrians	Secular events in India	Events affecting the Parsis
1700	1719 Afghan army invaded Iran. Safavids overthrown.	Zoroastrians of Kerman slaughtered by the invaders.		1728 Parsi Panchayat of Bombay founded.
	1750-1796 benevolent Zand dynasty ruling Iran.	Total amount of jizya reduced for Zoroastrian remnant in Kerman.		1759-61 Anquetil du Perron studying Av. and Pahl. with Parsis in Surat.
1800	1796-1925 Qajars ruling Iran.	Most of Qajar period a time of suffering for the Zoroastrians.	Bombay's first printing press set up by a Parsi in 1820s. 1834 British govt. took over Indian possessions of E. India Company. Honours conferred in course of time on a number of Parsis.	1829 Wilson arrived in Bombay. Parsis taking advantage of Western-type education in govt. schools in Bombay. 1851 Foundation of Zoroastrian Reform Society. 1860's Haug lecturing to Bombay Parsis. Study of Av. and Pahl. on European lines introduced in Bombay by K. R. Cama.
		1854 'Society for the Amelioration of the Conditions of the Zoroastrians in Persia' founded in Bombay. Unique Av. and Pahl. mss. sent for safety from Iran to Bombay. Schools giving Western-type education founded for Zoroastrians. 1882 Abolition of the jizya.		
1900				1885 Olcott, co-founder of Theosophical Soc., lectured to Parsis. Continuing debate among Parsis between orthodox, reformists, theosophists, rationalists etc. Lack felt of any generally acknowledged religious authority.
	1925 Last Qajar king deposed. Reza Shah Pahlavi crowned king.			

Date	Secular events in Iran	Events affecting the Irani Zoroastrians	Secular events in India	Events affecting the Parsis
		Zoroastrians moving steadily to Tehran for greater religious freedom. Influences of Parsi reform movements being felt there. 1960 First World Zoroastrian Congress held in Tehran.	1947 End of British rule in India. Founding of Republic of India and Islamic Republic of Pakistan.	Parsis split between the two republics. Some emigration, especially to London, Toronto and cities of the USA. 1970 First N. American Zoroastrian Symposium held in Toronto.
	1979 Overthrow of Muhammad Reza Shah Pahlavi. Founding of Islamic Republic of Iran.	Religious toleration granted to Zoroastrians, Jews and Christians. Some emigration.		1978 Third World Zoroastrian Congress held in Bombay.

2 TRADITION AND DOCTRINE

2.1 ANCIENT MATERIALS FROM THE YASHTS

See 1.1.1.5. All explicitly Zoroastrian elements are omitted from the texts in this section; but some Bronze Age ones, e.g. references to horse-drawn chariots, see 1.2.7, are too closely interwoven with what seems the still older material to be excised.

2.1.1 From the hymn to Mithra (Yt. 10)

This is one of the 'great yashts'. Every yasht contains repetitions of a set of words by which any act of worship can be devoted to the divinity concerned. Mithra's is: 'We worship Mithra of wide pastures, possessing a thousand ears, possessing ten thousand eyes, the divinity worshipped with spoken name'. 'Of wide pastures' is held to imply that the god gave just men, his worshippers, wide pastures in which to graze their herds safely (cf. v. 112). His 'ears' and 'eyes' are his myriad spies (cf. v. 45). Every yasht also contains repetitions of the opening words of v. 4 and the whole of v. 6, with variations only of the divinity's name. Verses 145, 4 and 5 form sections 12–14 of the prayer to Mithra, the Mihr Nyayesh, see 1.1.1.8. Ahura Berezant, 'High Lord' (v. 145), is a cult epithet of Varuna, cf. 1.2.3.

(2) A scoundrel who is false to the covenant (mithra-) destroys a whole country. . . . Never break a covenant, whether you make it with a false man or a just man of good conscience. The covenant holds for both, the false and the just. (4) For his splendour and glory I shall worship Mithra of wide pastures, with spoken words of worship, with offerings. We worship Mithra of wide pastures, who bestows peaceful dwellings, good dwellings on Iranian lands. (5) . . . May he come to us for victory, may he come to us for happiness, may he come to us for justice, he the strong, the powerful, to be worshipped, prayed to, not deceived, by all the material world – Mithra of wide pastures. (6) . . . We worship Mithra of wide pastures with haoma mixed with milk, with baresman, with skill of tongue and manthras, with word and act, with offerings and rightly spoken utterances. (7) We worship Mithra of wide pastures, right-speaking, eloquent, possessing a thousand ears, well formed, possessing ten thousand eyes, tall, with wide look-out, strong, unsleeping, wakeful, . . . (12) who ascends, the first invisible god, over Hara, before the life-giving, swift-horsed sun which first touches the beautiful, gold-tinted mountain tops. From there he, the most strong, surveys all lands dwelt in by Iranians. . . . (25) We worship Mithra of wide pastures, the profound, mighty Ahura, bestowing benefit, eloquent, gratifying supplication, lofty, of many virtues, . . . mighty of arm, . . . (26) . . . very harsh towards those deserving punishment, judging men who are false to the covenant. . . . (31) With worship in which your name is spoken, with timely prayer I shall worship you, O strong one, Mithra, with offerings. (32) May you hear our worship, Mithra! May you requite our worship, Mithra! Be seated at our worship, attend our offerings, attend them as they are consecrated, take them all into your care, deposit them in the House of Song! Grant us that boon which we ask of you, O strong one, in faithfulness to the given words: wealth, strength and victory, good life and possession of truth (asha), fair fame and peace of soul. . . . (35) We worship Mithra of wide pastures, punisher of wrong, levier of armies, of a thousand perceptions, ruling as an all-knowing ruler; (36) who sets the battle in motion, who takes his stand in the battle, who having taken his stand in the battle shatters the ranks. The wings all surge of the battle-tossed ranks, the centre of the bloodthirsty army quakes. (37) Well may he bring them terror and fear. He hurls off the wicked heads of men false to the covenant, away fly the wicked heads of men false to the covenant. . . . (39) Even their eagle-feathered arrows, flying from the bowstring of a well strung bow, pierce no wounds, because Mithra of wide pastures, enraged, provoked, unacknowledged, is hostile. Even their well sharpened, pointed, long-shafted spears, flying from their arms, pierce no wounds, . . . even their slingstones, flying from their arms, cause no wounds . . . (41) Mithra frightens these hither, Rashnu the Judge frightens them thither, . . . their protecting gods desert their ranks, because Mithra of wide pastures, enraged,

provoked, unacknowledged, is hostile. (44) We worship Mithra of wide pastures, . . . (45) for whom on every height, in every watch-post sit eight servants, watchers for the covenant, watching covenant-breakers, seeing them indeed, noting them indeed, those who first break the covenant; guarding the paths of those whom breakers of the covenant seek out, smiters of the truly just, the false. . . . (48) Then when Mithra drives forward against bloodthirsty enemy armies . . . he binds the evil hands of covenant-breaking men behind them, he destroys their sight, he makes their ears deaf. (50) We worship Mithra of wide pastures, . . . for whom Ahura Mazda . . . fashioned an abode upon high Hara, the convoluted, shining, where there is no night or darkness, no wind, cold or hot, . . . nor do mists rise upon high Hara. . . . (61) We worship Mithra of wide pastures, . . . who stands erect and watchful, the espier, mighty, eloquent, replenishing the waters, having heard the invocation, causing rain to fall and plants to grow, drawing the boundary line, eloquent, perceptive, undeceived, . . . (66) whom good Recompense (Ashi) attends, and Bounty . . . and strong manly Valour; . . . (67) . . . who comes driving in a high-wheeled chariot, spirit-fashioned . . . (68) drawn by spirit-horses, white, radiant, . . . shadowless, swifter than thought. . . . (95) We worship Mithra of wide pastures, . . . who travels the breadth of the earth, by the setting of the sun he has touched both edges of this wide, round earth with far borders. He sees all that is between earth and heaven; (96) holding in his hand his mace with its hundred bosses and hundred blades, a feller of men as he brandishes it, cast of yellow metal, strong and golden, strongest of weapons, most victorious of weapons. . . . (107) . . . He sees all deceivers. Mighty, Mithra stands forth. Strong in power he flies, with a beautiful far-shining glance he looks round with his eyes. (108) 'Who shall worship me, who deceive me? Who thinks I am to be worshipped with a good sacrifice, who with a bad sacrifice? . . .' (112) The countenance of Mithra is pleased, when he visits the land where he is well treated. Then the valleys are wide for pasture, their own cattle and men wander at will. . . . (145) Both Mithra and Ahura Berezant we worship, free from harm, just; and the stars and moon and sun. At the strewed baresman we worship Mithra, ruler of all lands!

(For an English translation of the whole yasht see I. Gershevitch, *The Avestan Hymn to Mithra*.)

2.1.2 From Yasht 19, concerning Khvarenah

Khvarenah is the hypostasis of the 'glory' or divine grace which accompanies kings and great men who are just, ashavan. It leaves Yima (see 1.2.5) when he lies (according to one source by claiming to be himself divine), and passes into the protection first of Mithra, then of Varuna (here called both Apam Napat, 'Son of the Waters', and Ahura Berezant), with their elements of fire and water. The link of the lesser Ahuras with these elements was through judicial ordeals. A man accused of breaking an oath might have his truthfulness tested through an ordeal by water, if a covenant through one by fire. The fire ordeal (cf. 4.1.5) was to be of great symbolic and practical importance in Zoroastrianism. For allusions to it in the Gathas see 2.2.6.4, 14.9, 15.6, and cf. 2.3.7.10–20.

(3) We worship mighty . . . Khvarenah . . . , (31) who for a long time accompanied shining Yima, possessed of good herds, so that he ruled over this earth of seven regions . . . ; (33) in whose kingdom there was neither cold nor heat, neither old age nor death, nor demon-created sickness, before he lied, before he brought the lying untrue word into his mind. (34) Then when he brought the lying untrue word into his mind, Khvarenah was seen to depart from him in the shape of a bird . . . . Yima wandered sad, cast into dejection he hid upon the earth. (35) . . . Khvarenah went from shining Yima . . . in the shape of a hawk. This Khvarenah Mithra of wide pastures, with listening ears and a thousand perceptions, laid hold of . . . . (49) Then the three-headed dragon rushed forward, thinking thus: 'I shall lay hold of this Khvarenah . . . . Then Fire rose up at him from behind, saying thus aloud: (50) 'Back! learn this, O three-headed dragon! If you should reach for this Khvarenah . . . , I shall blaze up, . . . I shall flame up upon your jaws. Never hereafter shall you rush forth upon the Ahura-created earth for the destruction of the creatures of asha.' Then the dragon drew his forepaws back again, forseeing an attempt on his life, for Fire was terrifying. (51) Khvarenah departed to the sea Vourukasha. Straightway Apam Napat, having swift horses, laid hold of it. And Apam Napat, having swift horses, desires this: 'I shall lay hold of this Khvarenah on the bottom of the deep sea, at the bottom of its deep bays.' (52) We worship Ahura Berezant, kingly, shining, Apam Napat having swift horses, the hero who gives help when called upon. (It is) he who created men, he who shaped men, the god amid the waters, who being prayed to is swiftest of all to hear.

2.1.3 From the hymn to Verethraghna, god of Victory (Yt. 14)

Verethraghna, later known as Vahram or Bahram, whose name means 'Victory', has the fixed epithet 'Ahura-created', i.e. he hypostatised victory in a just cause. He was venerated as a great protector, and in later times especially as guardian of travellers; his yasht is still recited particularly for those going on a journey.

(1) First Ahura-created Verethraghna approached hastening in the shape of the bold Wind. (3) Then he, most mighty, declared . . .: 'I am mightiest in strength, I am most victorious in victoriousness, I am most glorious in glory . . . . (4) And I shall overcome the enmity of all enemies. . . .' (5) For his splendour and glory I shall worship Ahura-created Verethraghna with spoken words of worship, with offerings . . . . (7) A second time Ahura-created Verethraghna approached . . . hastening in the shape of a bull, beautiful, with golden horns. . . . (11) A fourth time Ahura-created Verethraghna approached . . . hastening in the shape of a fiery camel, . . . (12) . . . stout-humped . . . splendid, tall, strong, (13) . . . whose far-seeing eye shines even in

the dark night, which tosses white foam over its head, over its strong knees and legs, which stands looking round like an all-powerful ruler . . . . (15) A fifth time Ahura-created Verethraghna approached . . . hastening in the shape of a boar, aggressive, . . . sharp-tusked, a boar which kills at a stroke, unapproachable when angry, speckle-faced, strong, nimble, rushing about . . . . (19) A seventh time Ahura-created Verethraghna approached . . . hastening in the shape of a hawk, seizing from below, tearing to pieces from above, the swiftest of birds, the quickest of flying creatures. (20) It alone of living creatures overtakes the flight of an arrow, even when it speeds well shot. It flies mantling its feathers when day begins to dawn, seeking its evening meal in evening twilight, seeking its morning meal in morning twilight. (21) It glides over the gorges of mountain ranges, it glides over the peaks of mountains, it glides over the valleys of rivers, it glides over the tops of trees, listening to the voices of birds. . . . (23) An eighth time Ahura-created Verethraghna approached . . . , hastening in the shape of a wild ram, beautiful, with backward-curving horns. . . . (47) We worship Ahura-created Verethraghna, who goes to and fro: 'Who deceives Mithra by lies? Who abandons Rashnu? On whom shall I, being powerful, bestow sickness and death?'

2.1.4 From the hymn to Ashi, goddess of Recompense (Yt. 17)

Avestan 'ashi' means 'thing attained/acquired; recompense, reward'. The old concept of Ashi appears to have been simply that of an amoral goddess of Fortune.

(6) O good Ashi, beautiful Ashi, brilliant Ashi, rich, shining with splendours! O Ashi, giving good 'khvarenah' to those men whom you attend! Fragrant is that man's dwelling in which good Ashi, the strong one, sets foot, friendly, solicitous for long succession. (7) Those men rule with possessions, with abundant stores of food, there where a couch is spread and where are other desired possessions – those whom you attend, good Ashi! Fortunate indeed is he whom you attend! And you escort me also, most mighty Ashi! (8) Their well established dwellings are rich in cattle, abundantly stocked for long inhabiting – those whom you attend, good Ashi! . . . (9) Their couches are well spread, well perfumed, well fashioned, provided with cushions . . . those whom you attend, good Ashi! (10) Their wives assuredly sit expectant on couches, (thinking) . . . : 'When will the master of the dwelling come to us? When shall we rejoice joyously in his beloved person?' – those whom you attend, good Ashi!

2.1.5 From the hymn to the Shining Sun, Hvar Khshaeta (Yt. 6)

These verses constitute also sections 11–13 of the prayer to the Sun, Khorshed Nyayesh, see 1.1.1.8.

(1) We worship the Shining Sun, life-giving, bountiful. . . . When the sun with his light brings warmth, when the sun as light brings warmth, the invisible gods stand there, a hundred and a thousand. That glory (khvarenah) of his they

gather up, that glory of his they bring down, that glory of his they distribute over the Ahura-created earth, to prosper the world of asha.... (2) When the sun rises, the Ahura-created earth is purified, the running water is purified .... (30) And if the Sun were not to rise, then demons would destroy all that is in the seven regions. Not one of the invisible gods would find a place to abide or stay in this material world. (4) He who sacrifices to the Shining Sun, life-giving, bountiful, ... in order to resist darkness, in order to resist demons born of darkness ... he rejoices all the invisible and visible gods.

2.1.6 From the hymn to the star god Tishtrya (Yt. 8)

This is another of the 'great yashts'. Tishtrya's star is identified as the Dog Star, Sirius. He is venerated as a rain-bringer, through a myth which presents him as a stallion going yearly to the 'mares' who are the waves of the sea. Yt. 8 has accordingly been recited down the ages in times of drought.

(1) We worship the star Tishtrya, the splendid, the glorious, of water-nature, strong, lofty, powerful, shining afar ... ; (5) for whom yearn sheep and cattle and men, ... (saying): 'When shall Tishtrya the splendid, the glorious, rise for us, when shall the springs of water flow anew ... ?' (20) Then Tishtrya, the splendid, the glorious, goes down ... to the sea Vourukasha, in the shape of a horse, white, beautiful, with golden ears and golden muzzle. (21) There rushes against him the demon Dearth, in the shape of a horse, black, hairless, ... horrifying. (22) Together the two fight, Tishtrya the splendid, the glorious, and the demon Dearth .... For three days and three nights the two fight. The demon Dearth overcomes him, he conquers him, Tishtrya the splendid, the glorious. (23) He drives him back ... from the sea Vourukasha. Tishtrya the splendid, the glorious calls down woe and misery on himself: 'Woe to me! ..., misery, O waters and plants! ... Men do not worship me now with worship with spoken name, as other gods are worshipped .... (24) If men should worship me ..., I should take to myself the strength of ten horses ...'. (25) ... I worship Tishtrya, the splendid, the glorious, with worship with spoken name. I procure for him the strength of ten horses .... (26) Then Tishtrya the splendid, the glorious ... goes down to the sea Vourukasha .... Those two fight at noon tide. Tishtrya the splendid, the glorious, overcomes him, he conquers him, the demon Dearth .... (29) ... He calls down prosperity on himself: 'Well is me! Well, O waters and plants! ... well shall it be, O lands! The courses of the waters shall surge out unhindered for the large-seeded corn, for the small-seeded grasses, and for the material world.' (31) He makes ... the sea surge, he makes the sea surge over .... (32) Then Tishtrya rises again from the sea Vourukasha .... Then at that time mists gather on Mount Ush-hendava, which stands in the middle of the sea Vourukasha .... (33) Then the bold ... Wind drives the rain and cloud and hail upon places, upon dwellings, upon the seven regions. (34) Apam Napat distributes to the material world those waters assigned to dwellings ....

2.1.7 From the hymn to the river goddess Aredvi Sura Anahita (Yt. 5)

Aredvi Sura Anahita, the 'pure mighty Moist One', goddess of the mythical world river (see 1.2.6.3), is celebrated in another 'great yasht'. Verses 1, 3–5 constitute part of the prayer to the Waters, Aban Nyayesh, see 1.1.1.8.

(1) Aredvi Sura Anahita, increasing corn, just, increasing herds, just, increasing possessions, just ... (3) immense, far-famed, who is as great in her immensity as all these waters which flow forth upon the earth; who, mighty, flows forth from Mount Hukairya upon the sea Vourukasha – all the edges of the sea Vourukasha are turbulent, all the middle is turbulent, as Aredvi Sura Anahita pours forth upon them .... (5) The outflow of that one sea will pour forth over all the seven regions. She pours down her waters summer and winter alike. She purifies the waters, she purifies the seed of males, the womb of females, the milk of females .... (132) Through this sacrifice, through this prayer ... descend again, O Aredvi Sura Anahita, from those stars to the Ahura-created earth, to the worshipping priest with cupped hands overflowing, for help to the libation bringer.

2.1.8 From the hymn to the fravashis (Yt. 13)

Here the concept of the mighty fravashis, seen as sharing even in the work of creation, blends with that of the shadowy 'urvan', cf. 1.2.5. Hamaspathmaedaya is the Iranian feast of All Souls, see 1.6. Yasht 13 is regularly recited at observances for the dead.

(21) I praise, invoke and sing the good, strong, holy fravashis of the just ..., (22) who arrayed sky, who arrayed water, who arrayed earth, who arrayed cattle, who arrayed sons in the womb ...; who are the givers of victory to the invoker, of a boon to the eager, of health to the sick, of good fortune to him who invokes them, worshipping, satisfying, bringing libations, just.... (49) We worship the good, strong, holy fravashis of the just who hurry homeward at the time of Hamaspathmaedaya. Then they wander there for the *whole night, desiring this help: (50) 'Who will praise us, who worship, who laud? who will treat us lovingly, who welcome us with hands full of food and clothing, with proper worship? The name of which of us will be now invoked, the soul (urvan) of which among *us will be worshipped, to which of us will that gift be given, whereby he shall have unending food for ever?' (51) Then the man who worships them with hands full of food and clothing, with proper worship, him will they bless, the contented, ... unvexed, mighty fravashis of the just. (52) To him at his dwelling there will be a herd of cattle and men.... (65) Then when the waters flow out from the sea Vourukasha ..., they go forward, the mighty fravashis of the just, many many hundreds, many many thousands ..., (66) desiring water, each for her own family.... (67) They fight in battles, each *for her own place and abode, where she had a place and abode to inhabit; even as a mighty chariot-warrior should fight, having girt on his sword belt, for his well-gotten treasure. (68) Then those of them who conquer drive off the water, each to her own family.

2.2 VERSES FROM THE GATHAS

See 1.1.1.2, and on the doctrine of the Heptad 1.3.2. Various attempts have been made to rearrange the Gathas (grouped formally in the yasna liturgy) in chronological order; but these have failed, partly because the prophet clearly added verses to some of his hymns at different times. The rearrangement here has been made simply in an attempt to present their doctrinal content as clearly as possible. The concordance with the yasna order is as follows: verses from Y. 28 = 2.2.16; 29 = 11; 30 = 2; 31 = 7; 32 = 4; 33 = 5; 34 = 6; 43 = 9; 44 = 1; 45 = 3; 46 = 13; 47 = 15; 48 = 8; 49 = 10; 50 = 12; 51 = 14; 53 = 17. On the alternating use of 'Thou' and 'You' in addressing Ahura Mazda see 1.3.2.1. The archaic 'Thou', thus unavoidable in the English translation, may serve as a reminder that the Gathas are older linguistically than the passages in 2.1, though the latter are older in content, see 1.1.1.5. As far as possible one English rendering is used consistently for the name of each member of the Heptad; but where Asha (usually translated as Truth) is rendered by Order, or Khshathra (usually as Power) by Dominion or Kingdom, the Avestan word appears in brackets, for clarity's sake.

2.2.1   Verses from Yasna 44

Literary parallels to this gatha, with rhetorical questions similarly addressed to a divine or supernatural being, exist in the Norse Edda; and the verses have been taken to represent an ancient Indo-European poetic tradition, developed to express what were felt to be solemn, divinely inspired truths. Verse 16, without the opening formula, forms part of the 'Kemna Mazda', see 3.5.1.

(3) This I ask Thee, tell me truly, Lord. Who in the beginning, at creation, was Father of Order (Asha)? Who established the course of sun and stars? Through whom does the moon wax, then wane? This and yet more, O Mazda, I seek to know. (4) This I ask Thee, tell me truly, Lord. Who has upheld the earth from below, and the heavens from falling? Who (sustains) the waters and plants? Who harnessed swift steeds to wind and clouds? Who, O Mazda, is Creator of Good Purpose? (5) This I ask Thee, tell me truly, Lord. What craftsman created light and darkness? What craftsman created both sleep and activity? Through whom exist dawn, noon and eve, which remind the worshipper of his duty? . . . (7) This I ask Thee, tell me truly, Lord. Who fashioned honoured Devotion together with Power? Who made the son respectful in heed to the father? By these (questions), O Mazda, I help (men) to discern Thee as Creator of all things through the Holy Spirit. . . . (16) This I ask Thee, tell me truly, Lord. Who will be victorious to protect through Thy teaching those who are the progeny in my house? As Healer of the world, promise to us a judge. Then let Hearkening come to him with Good Purpose, O Mazda – to him whomsoever Thou dost wish.

2.2.2 Verses from Yasna 30

Ahura Mazda has an Adversary, here called, in v. 5, 'Dregvant', the Deceitful or Wicked One, i.e. one who upholds 'drug', the lie or falsehood, opposed to 'asha'. In v. 6 he is named the Deceiver. Wicked men also are called 'dregvant', opposed to the just, 'ashavan'. 'Worst Existence' is a term for hell, i.e. a place for retributive punishment (seemingly a new concept then in religious thought). The '(House of) Best Purpose' is a name for heaven, parallel to the traditional 'House of Song' (cf. 2.2.3.8 et pass.). 'Hardest stone', v. 5., is the substance of the sky, see 1.2.6. The Daevas, v. 6, are shown by the tradition to be Indra and other warlike divinities, cf. 2.3.1.55. Fury or Wrath, Aeshma, is a great demon; for the prophet, it is suggested, he hypostatised the battle-fury of war bands, cf. 1.2.7, 1.3.1. On the Ahuras see 1.2.3, 1.3.3. Devotion 'gave body and breath', v. 7, as guardian of earth. At the last day the world will be 'made frasha-', v. 9, i.e. transfigured, made free once more from evil, made wonderful.

(1) Truly for seekers I shall speak of those things to be pondered, even by one who already knows, with praise and worship for the Lord of Good Purpose, the excellently Wise One, and for Truth . . . . (2) Hear with your ears the best things. Reflect with clear purpose, each man for himself, on the two choices for decision, being alert indeed to declare yourselves for Him before the great requital. (3) Truly there are two primal Spirits, twins renowned to be in conflict. In thought and word, in act they are two: the better and the bad. And those who act well have chosen rightly between these two, not so the evildoers. (4) And when these two Spirits first came together they created life and not-life, and how at the end Worst Existence shall be for the wicked, but (the House of) Best Purpose for the just man. (5) Of these two Spirits the Wicked One chose achieving the worst things. The Most Holy Spirit, who is clad in hardest stone, chose right, and (so do those) who shall satisfy Lord Mazda continually with rightful acts. (6) The Daevas indeed did not choose rightly between these two, for the Deceiver approached them as they conferred. Because they chose worst purpose, they then rushed to Fury, with whom they have afflicted the world and mankind. (7) With Power He came to this world, by Good Purpose and by Truth. Then enduring Devotion gave body and breath . . . . (8) Then when retribution comes for these sinners, then, Mazda, Power shall be present for Thee with Good Purpose, to declare himself for those, Lord, who shall deliver the Lie into the hands of Truth. (9) And then may we be those who shall transfigure this world. O Mazda (and you other) Lords (Ahuras), be present to me with support and truth, so that thoughts may be concentrated where understanding falters. . . . (11) O men! when you learn the commands which Mazda has given, and both thriving and not-thriving, and what long torment (is) for the wicked and salvation for the just — then will it be as is wished with these things.

2.2.3 Verses from Yasna 45

In v. 2 the Adversary is called Angra Mainyu, the 'Hostile' or 'Evil Spirit'.
This became his proper name, YAv. Anra Mainyu, Pahl. Ahriman.

(1) Then shall I speak, now give ear and hearken, both you who seek from near and you from far . . . . (2) Then shall I speak of the two primal Spirits of existence, of whom the Very Holy thus spoke to the Evil One: 'Neither our thoughts nor teachings nor wills, neither our choices nor words nor acts, not our inner selves nor our souls agree'. (3) Then shall I speak of the foremost (doctrine) of this existence, which Mazda the Lord, He with knowledge, declared to me. Those of you who do not act upon this manthra, even as I shall think and speak it, for them there shall be woe at the end of life. (4) Then shall I speak of the best things of this existence. I know Mazda who created it in accord with truth to be the Father of active Good Purpose. And His daughter is Devotion of good action. The all-seeing Lord is not to be deceived. (5) Then shall I speak of what the Most Holy One told me, the word to be listened to as best for men. Those who shall give for me hearkening and heed to Him, shall attain wholeness and immortality. Mazda is Lord through acts of the Good Spirit . . . . (8) Him shall I seek to turn to us by praises of reverence, for truly I have now seen with my eyes (the House) of Good Purpose, and of good act and deed, having known through Truth Him who is Lord Mazda. Then let us lay up supplications to Him in the House of Song. (9) Him shall I seek to requite for us with good purpose, Him who left to our will (the choice between) holy and unholy. May Lord Mazda by His power make us active for prospering our cattle and men, through the fair affinity of good purpose with truth. (10) Him shall I seek to glorify for us with sacrifices of devotion, Him who is known in the soul as Lord Mazda; for He has promised by His truth and good purpose that there shall be wholeness and immortality within His kingdom (khshathra), strength and perpetuity within His house.

2.2.4 Verses from Yasna 32

For the 'seventh region of earth', v. 3, see 1.2.6.3. The 'Bad Spirit', v. 5, is yet
another term for the Adversary. The 'karapan' (Pahl. karb) v. 12, is
generally held to be a working priest of the old religion, naturally hostile to
Zarathushtra. The 'kavi' (Pahl. kayag), v. 15, appears to be a chieftain or
princely ruler, cf. 1.2.7.

(3) But all you Daevas, and he who greatly worships you, are the seed of Bad Purpose, the Lie and Arrogance. Hateful too your acts, by which you have become known in the seventh region of earth. (4) In that you ordain those (acts) which worst men commit, they shall be called 'beloved of the Daevas', retreating from Good Purpose, departing from Lord Mazda's will and from Truth. (5) Thereby you have defrauded mankind of good life and immortality, much as you (have defrauded yourselves), you Daevas and the Bad Spirit . . . . (11) Those wicked ones who appear in grandeur as chieftains and their ladies, they too indeed have ruined life, stealing property from its inheritor. So too, O

Mazda, those who have deflected the just from best purpose. (12) Because of that teaching whereby they deflected man from the best act, Mazda declared ill things for them who with their habit of pleasure have ruined the life of the cow, because of whom the rich karapan chose the dominion (khshathra) of tyrants and the Lie, rather than Truth; (13) by which dominion the destroyers of this world beheld their riches in the House of Worst Purpose – as did those who in their greed lamented at the message of Thy manthra-maker, O Mazda, (a greed) which guarded them from beholding Truth . . . . (15) By these things the company of the karapans, and the kavis, are being ruined together with those they ensnare. They shall not be brought to those ruling over life at will in the House of Good Purpose.

2.2.5 Verses from Yasna 33

The symbolism of the pastor or herdsman, v. 6, appears to be that of the man who nurtures good purpose, since Vohu Manah, Good Purpose, is guardian of cattle. Evidently the symbols of cattle and herdsman were as powerful for the ancient Iranians as those of sheep and shepherd have been for Jews and Christians. Verses 12–14 are constantly recited, since they form the beginning of the Atash Nyayesh, cf. 4.1.1.

(1) In accord with the laws of the foremost existence, the Judgment shall thus enact the straightest dealings for the wicked as well as for the just man, and for him whose falsehood and honesty are assessed as equal. (2) Then he who shall work ill to the Wicked One, by word or thought or by his hands, or enlighten a guest in what is good – all such shall fulfil the wish and be in the affection of Lord Mazda. (3) He who is very good to the just man, Lord, whether he be a kinsman or one of the community or clan, or (simply) one serving the cow with zeal, he shall be in the pasture of Truth and Good Purpose. (4) I who sacrifice, O Mazda, shall turn from Thee lack of hearkening and bad purpose, the contempt of the family, and the lie, very near, of the community, the scoffers among the clan – and from the pasture of the cow the Worst Counsellor. (5) I am he who, at the halting (of these things), will invoke for Thee Hearkening, greatest of all. I shall attain for us here the long-lived dominion (khshathra) of Good Purpose, the paths straight in accord with truth wherein Lord Mazda dwells. (6) The priest officiating, upright through truth, embodies the Best Spirit. Thereby he is allied with that purpose by which he has learnt to perform the duties of pastor. By this I am eager, Lord Mazda, to behold and take counsel with Thee . . . . (11) Mazda, Thou who are most mighty Lord, and Devotion, and world-furthering Truth, and Good Purpose, and Power – hear You me, have mercy on me, at each apportioning of boons! (12) Arise for me, Lord! By the Most Holy Spirit, O Mazda, take to Thyself might through devotion, swiftness through good gift-offerings, potent force through truth, protection through good purpose. (13) Thou who seest afar, reveal to me for support, Lord, the incomparable things of Your kingdom (khshathra), which are the recompense (ashi) for good purpose. Instruct, O Holy Devotion, our inner

selves through truth. (14) For as gift Zarathushtra gives the breath even of his body, so that for Mazda there should be predominance of good purpose, of act and word in accord with truth, so that there should be both hearkening and dominion (khshathra).

2.2.6 Verses from Yasna 34

In v. 3 an offering is made to fire, represented by its guardian, Asha. In v. 4 the fire of the ordeal (cf. 4.1.5) seems referred to, and also the fire of the Last Day (cf. 2.2.14.9, 15.6 and 2.3.7.10–20). In v. 11 the links are implied between wholeness, immortality and devotion, and water, plants and earth.

(3) Then let us reverently give an offering, Lord, to Thee and to Truth – all creatures in Thy dominion (khshathra), whom You have nurtured by good purpose. Let salvation be granted indeed to the beneficent man among You for ever, O Mazda! (4) Then we wish Thy fire, Lord, strong through Truth, very swift, mighty, to be of manifest help to Thy supporter, but of visible harm, O Mazda, with the forces in his hands, to Thy enemy. . . . (11) Truly, both wholeness and immortality are for Thy sustinence. Through the dominion of Good Purpose, Devotion together with Truth will make grow these two enduring powers.

2.2.7 Verses from Yasna 31

The link between the Ahuras and asha, v. 4, was old, cf. 1.2.3. For Recompense, Ashi, see 2.1.4. Zarathushtra himself perceived her as an ethical divinity, who gave to each what morally he deserved. On the Ox-Fashioner, Geush Tashan, see 3.1. 'Inner Self', Daena, v. 20, was the term used by the prophet for the figure which meets the soul at the Chinvat Bridge, in the old religion simply a beautiful girl, see 1.2.5, and cf. 2.2.8.4, 13.11, 14.13, and 6.1.1.30, 2a.22–32, 6.2.125–6, 167–78.

(1) Heeding these Your commands, we teach words unheard by those who, at Lie's commands, continue to destroy the world of Truth, but the best indeed for those who shall be zealous for Mazda . . . . (3) The requital which Thou hast created through the Spirit, and promised to both parties by fire and by truth – that command for Thy worshippers, declare that, O Mazda, with the tongue of Thy mouth, for us to know that by which I may convert all the living. (4) Were I to invoke Truth, Mazda (and the other) Lords (Ahuras) would appear, and Recompense and Devotion. Through best purpose I shall seek for myself mighty power, by whose increase we might conquer the Lie . . . . (8) Truly I recognised Thee with my thought, O Mazda, to be First . . ., when with my eyes I perceived Thee to be Father of Good Purpose, real Creator of Truth, by Thy acts Lord of existence. (9) Thine was Devotion, thine the Ox-Fashioner, Thine the Spirit of great wisdom, O Lord Mazda, when Thou didst grant her (the cow) the way to go either to him who shall act as pastor or to him who shall not be a pastor. (10) Then of these two she chose for herself the cattle-tending pastor as her just lord, the herdsman of Good Purpose. One not a pastor, Mazda, has not shared in the

friendship of her who wants good heed. (11) Since, O Mazda, Thou didst fashion for us in the beginning, by Thy thought, creatures and inner selves and intentions, since Thou didst create corporeal life, and acts and words through which he who has free will expresses choices, (12) then each lifts up his voice, be he false-speaking or right-speaking, with knowledge or without knowledge, according to his heart and mind. Devotion shall plead in turn with the spirit where there is opposition. . . . (15) This I ask, Lord: what punishment shall be for him who promotes power for a wicked man of evil actions? for him who finds no other means of livelihood than harming the cattle and men of the honest pastor? . . . (19) The healer of life, having knowledge, Lord, has hearkened, he who has thought upon truth, ruling his tongue at will for the right speaking of words, when the distribution in good shall take place for both parties by Thy bright-blazing fire, O Mazda. (20) Heavenly glory shall be the future possession of him who comes (to the help of) the just man. A long life of darkness, foul food, the crying of woe – to that existence, O wicked ones, your Inner Self shall lead you by her actions. (21) By virtue of His abounding authority of power over Wholeness and Immortality and Truth, Lord Mazda will give perpetuity of communion with Good Purpose to him who is His ally in spirit and acts.

2.2.8 Verses from Yasna 48

'Saoshyant' (Pahl. 'Soshyant'), v. 12, regularly translated as 'saviour', means literally 'one who will bring benefit'. It is used, generally, for all actively good people and, particularly, for the World Saviour who is to come, cf. 2.2.9.3, 7.1, 7.2, 7.3.3, 7.3.4. 'Khshnem', v. 12, occurs also in 2.2.17.2. It has the variant 'khshnum', cf. 11.2.2.

(2) Tell me the things which Thou knowest, Lord, before the end of the course shall come for me. Will the just man, O Mazda, conquer the wicked one? For that is known as the good form of existence . . . . (4) He who makes better or worse his thought, O Mazda, he by act and word (makes better or worse) his Inner Self; she follows his leanings, wishes and likings. At Thy will the end shall be different (for each). (5) Let those of good power rule – let not those of bad power rule over us – with acts of good understanding, O Devotion! Men, let the best purification be made for the cow on earth, to nurture her for our food. (6) She (Devotion) shall indeed give us good dwelling, she (shall give) us enduring, desired strength of good purpose. Then through Order (Asha) Mazda made plants grow for her, the Lord at the birth of first life. . . . (11) When, Mazda, shall Devotion come with Order (Asha), having good dwellings, having pasturage through Power? Who will stop cruelty by bloodthirsty, wicked men? To whom will come the teaching of Good Purpose? (12) They truly shall be 'saoshyants' of the lands who follow knowledge (khshnem) of Thy teaching, Mazda, with good purpose, with acts inspired by truth. They indeed have been appointed opponents of Fury.

2.2.9 Verses from Yasna 43

Verse 3 presumably refers to the Saoshyant (cf. 2.2.8). For v. 7 ff. cf. 5.2.4.

(1) May Lord Mazda, ruling at will, grant wishes to him whosoever has wishes! I wish that enduring strength should come, in order to uphold Truth. Grant this to me through Devotion: recompenses of riches, a life of good purpose . . . (3) And may that man attain the better than good, he who would teach us the straight paths of salvation – those of the material world and of the mind, leading to the true heights where dwells the Lord; a faithful man, of good lineage, holy like Thee, O Mazda! (4) Then I shall recognise Thee as strong and holy, Mazda, when Thou wilt help me by the hand with which Thou holdest the recompenses that Thou wilt give, through the heat of Thy truth-strong fire, to the wicked man and the just – and when the might of Good Purpose shall come to me. (5) Then as holy I have recognised Thee, Lord Mazda, when I saw Thee as First at the birth of life, when Thou didst appoint rewards for acts and words, bad for the bad, a good recompense for the good, by Thy innate virtue, at the final turning point of creation. (6) At which turning point Thou, O Mazda, hast come to the world with Thy Holy Spirit, with power through Good Purpose, by whose acts the people of Truth prosper. To them Devotion proclaims the judgments of Thy will – O Thou whom none deceives. (7) Then as holy I have recognised Thee, Lord Mazda, when he (the Holy Spirit) attended me with Good Purpose, and asked me: 'Who art thou? Whose art thou? . . .' (8) Then I said to him first: 'I am Zarathushtra. Were I able, I should be a true foe to the Deceiver, but a strong support to the Just One.' (9) Then as holy I have recognised Thee, Lord Mazda, when he attended me with Good Purpose. To his question: 'Whom dost thou wish to serve?' I declared: 'Thy fire. At the offering made in reverence I shall think upon Truth, as long as I am able.' . . . (15) Then as holy I have recognised Thee, Lord Mazda, when he attended me with Good Purpose. Meditation taught the best things to be uttered. A man should not seek to satisfy the many wicked, for they declare the just to be all enemies. (16) Then, Lord, this Zarathushtra chooses for himself the Spirit, O Mazda, which is Thine, and is indeed the holiest. May Truth be embodied, strong with life. May Devotion dwell in the sun-beholding kingdom (khshathra). May He grant recompense for acts with good purpose.

2.2.10 Verses from Yasna 49

The last line of v. 10 forms part of the 'Kemna Mazda', see 3.5.1; for v. 11 cf. 6.1.2b.34–8.

(1) Truly in my lifetime I have been condemned as the greatest defiler, I who seek to satisfy with truth those who are poorly protected, O Mazda! With good apportioning of gifts come to me, support me! . . . (4) Those who with ill purpose increased with their tongues fury and cruelty, they the non-pastors among pastors, for whom evil deeds have prevailed, they having no good deeds, they serve the Daevas, which is the religion of the wicked man. (5) But he, O Mazda, is himself the sacrifice and oblation who has allied his Inner Self with

Good Purpose. Whoever belongs to Devotion is of the (same) good lineage as Truth, and as all those in Thy dominion (khshathra), Lord. . . . (10) This Thou dost guard in Thy house, O Mazda – good purpose, and the souls of the just, and reverence with which there is devotion and sacrifice – this Thou dost guard, O Thou of mighty power, with abiding strength. (11) But the wicked, of bad power, bad act, bad word, bad Inner Self, bad purpose – (departed) souls will encounter (them) with ill nourishment, they shall be rightful guests in the House of the Lie. (12) What help hast Thou, through Truth, for him who invokes Thee? What help, through Good Purpose, for Zarathushtra, who will celebrate You all, Lord Mazda, with praises, while longing for the best in Your possession?

2.2.11 Verses from Yasna 29

Here Zarathushtra links the weakness of beneficent cattle, helpless before raiders, with that of himself, weak materially, but strong if aided by the Heptad. The myth of the plaintive cow appears to be an ancient Indo-Iranian one, which he enriched with his own symbolism. On Ox-Soul and Ox-Fashioner see 3.1. Verse 7 refers, it seems, to the offerings to fire and water, cf. 1.2.4. 'Maga', v. 11, is a problem word variously rendered as 'gift, dedication, treasure, brotherhood, sacrament, task'. It undoubtedly refers to what the prophet offered mankind, and a 'magavan' is one who accepted it and became his follower.

(1) To You all the Ox-Soul lamented: 'For whom did You shape me? Who fashioned me? Fury and raiding hold me captive, cruelty and might. For me there is no pastor but You. Then appear to me with good pasturage!' (2) Then the Ox-Fashioner asked Truth: 'Of what sort is thy judge for the cow, that the ruling ones may ever grant her cattle-tending zeal by a pastor? Whom do You wish for her lord, who might repel the fury of the wicked?' (3) To him Truth replied: 'There is no help free of suffering for the cow. . . . Of those who are, he is the strongest, at whose call I soon shall come' . . . . (6) Then Lord Mazda, possessed of knowledge, spoke solemn words, heedfully: 'No master has (yet) been found, nor indeed a judge according to right. Truly the Fashioner shaped thee for pastor and herdsman.' (7) Lord Mazda, of one desire with Truth, shaped for the cow the manthra for fat and milk, the Holy One for those in need, according to His decree. 'Who has been found by thee, Good Purpose, who might give these (offerings) for mortal men?' (8) 'This one, Zarathushtra Spitama, has been found here by me, who alone has hearkened to our teachings. He wishes, O Mazda, to chant hymns of praise for Us and for Truth. So let us give him sweetness of utterance.' (9) But then the Ox-Soul lamented: 'I who have recognised my protector as powerless, his voice that of a man without strength, whereas I wished for one ruling with power – when shall one ever appear who will give him effective help?' (10) Lord, may You grant to these (my followers) strength through truth, and that power of good purpose, which gives good dwellings and peace. . . . (11) Where are Truth and Good Purpose and

Power? With Truth do You, O Mazda, in Your discernment, acknowledge me for the great 'maga'. Approach now, Lord, through our gift to You all!

2.2.12 Verses from Yasna 50

The 'steeds' of v. 7 are prayers. 'Sacrificial Offering', Izha, v. 8, is an Indo-Iranian goddess of the sacrifice. The last words of v. 11 form part of the kusti prayers, see 3.5.2.

(1) Has my soul strength over anyone for help? Who is found as protector for my cattle, who for myself, but Truth and Thee, Lord Mazda, and Best Purpose, my invocation having been heard? . . . (4) Truly, praising, I shall worship You all, O Mazda with Truth and Best Purpose and Power . . . . (6) Zarathushtra, maker of manthras, is the friend of Truth, he who lifts up his voice with reverence, O Mazda . . . . (7) Truly I shall harness for You the swiftest steeds . . . , strong through good purpose, with which, O Mazda, You together with Truth shall drive hither, should You be ready for my help. (8) With hands outstretched, O Mazda, I shall serve You all with the famed footsteps of Sacrificial Offering, truly (I shall serve) You all with truth and a faithful man's reverence, with the skilfulness of good purpose. (9) Praising, I shall approach You with these sacrifices, O Mazda and Truth, with acts of good purpose . . . . (11) Truly I shall vow myself and be, O Mazda, Your praiser as long as I shall have force and strength, O Truth! May the Creator of life accomplish through Good Purpose the true fulfilment of what is most wonderful (frasha), according to wish.

2.2.13 Verses from Yasna 46

Verse 7 begins with the words 'Kemna Mazda', and forms the major part of the 'Kemna Mazda' prayer, see 3.5.1.

(1) To what land to flee? Whither shall I go to flee? They thrust me from family and clan. The community with which I have kept company has not shown me hospitality, nor those who are the wicked rulers of the land. How then shall I propitiate Thee, Lord Mazda? (2) I know why I am powerless, Mazda: I possess few cattle and few men. I lament to Thee. Take heed of it, Lord, granting the support which friend should give to friend. Let me behold the might of Good Purpose with Truth! . . . (7) Whom, Mazda, hast Thou appointed protector for one like me, if the Wicked One shall dare to harm me? Whom but Thy Fire and Thy (Good) Purpose, by whose acts, Lord, Truth is nourished. Proclaim this teaching to my Inner Self! . . . (10) Whosoever, Lord, man or woman, will grant me those things Thou knowest best for life – recompense for truth, power with good purpose – and those whom I shall bring to Your worship, with all these shall I cross over the Chinvat Bridge. (11) Karapans and kavis by their powers yoked mankind with evil acts to destroy life. But their own soul and Inner Self tormented them when they reached the Chinvat Bridge – guests for ever in the House of the Lie!

2.2.14 Verses from Yasna 51

According to the tradition, Spitama, v. 11, was Zarathushtra's remote ancestor. Maidhyoimanha, his cousin, v. 19, was the first to accept the faith. Having then left his own people, Zarathushtra converted Kavi Vishtaspa, v. 16, cf. 5.2.5. Frashaoshtra and Jamaspa Hvogva, vv. 17, 18, were powerful lords at Vishtaspa's court, the latter his chief counsellor. The 'Good Religion', v. 17, became one of the standard names for Zoroastrianism. Verse 22 was later adapted to form the 'Yenhe hatam' prayer, see 3.3.4; 'whose' (sg.) presumably refers to a particular divinity, honoured at a rite with which this Gatha was first connected, with 'those who were and are' a traditional phrase for all divinities.

(7) Thou, Mazda, who by Thy Most Holy Spirit hast fashioned the cow, and the waters and plants, grant me Immortality and Wholeness – endurance and strength to be praised with good purpose . . . . (9) That requital which Thou wilt assign to the two parties, O Mazda, by Thy bright blazing fire and molten metal, is a sign to be given among all living beings, to destroy the wicked man, to save the just . . . . (11) What man, O Mazda, has been an ally to Spitama Zarathushtra? Who has taken counsel with Truth? With whom is Holy Devotion found? Who, upright, has declared himself for the 'maga' of Good Purpose? (12) In no such way did the corrupt Kavi show hospitality to this Zarathushtra Spitama at the earthen bridge, rejecting him when he came to that place, although his two draft animals were shivering from journeying and the cold. (13) Thus the Inner Self of the wicked man destroys for him the reality of the straight way. His soul shall surely vex him at the Chinvat Bridge, for he has strayed from the path of Truth by his acts and (the words) of his tongue. (14) Neither are karapans allies, being distant from laws and pasture. Their pleasure is from hurt to the cow by their acts and teachings, which teaching shall at the end set them in the House of the Lie. . . . (16) Kavi Vishtaspa, through Power, by the paths of Good Purpose, attained this teaching of the 'maga', which he respected with truth. – Holy is Lord Mazda. Wish therefore for Him to declare Himself to us. (17) Frashaoshtra Hvogva has shown me the desired form (of devotion) for the Good Religion . . . . (18) Glorious Jamaspa Hvogva (possesses) this teaching of might. He chooses the power of Good Purpose with Truth, in order to serve them. Lord Mazda, grant us Thy support. (19) That man, Maidhyoimanha Spitama, acquires it (i.e power?) for himself, finding it by the religion, he who ever seeks for existence (such as) the Creator, Mazda, said was the better by its acts for life. (20) All You, having the one desire, let Your salvation be granted us – truth with good purpose, words with which devotion is allied. We worship with reverence for Mazda, Who offers us support. (21) Holy is the man of piety, through understanding, words, act, Inner Self. Bounteous is Truth, and Power with Good Purpose. Lord Mazda created (all). Him shall I entreat for the good reward. (22) At whose worship Lord Mazda knows the best for me according to truth. Those who were and are, those shall I worship by their names and shall approach with praise.

2.2.15 Verses from Yasna 47

In the first verse all members of the Heptad are named. The 'him' and 'he' of vv. 1 and 2 is presumably the just man.

(1) Through the Holy Spirit and Best Purpose, by act and word in accord with Truth, They shall grant him Wholeness and Immortality – Lord Mazda, together with Power and Devotion. (2) He shall achieve the best for this Most Holy Spirit by (his) tongue, by words of good purpose, by (his) hands, through (each) act of devotion, by the one knowledge: Mazda is Father of Truth . . . . (5) And by this Holy Spirit, Lord Mazda, Thou hast promised the just man what are indeed all the best things. The wicked man shall have (his) share remote from Thy affection, since he abides by acts inspired by Bad Purpose. (6) By this Holy Spirit, Lord Mazda, Thou wilt give distribution in good to the two parties by fire.

2.2.16 Verses from Yasna 28

(1) With hands outstretched in reverence for Him, our support, for the Holy Spirit together with Truth, I by this act first entreat You all, O Mazda, for that by which Thou mayst requite the will of Good Purpose and the Ox-Soul. (2) I who shall serve You all, Lord Mazda, with good purpose, to me be granted the gifts of both worlds – of matter and mind – through Truth, whereby he might set Thy supporters in blessedness. (3) I who shall praise You in song as never before – You, O Truth and Good Purpose and Lord Mazda, and those for whom Devotion increases unassailable Power – come You at invocation to my support. (4) I who fix my mind wholly on lifting up the soul by good purpose and, with knowledge, on Lord Mazda's recompenses for acts, as long as I shall have force and strength, so long shall I look in quest of Truth . . . . (7) Give, Truth, this recompense, the boons of Good Purpose. Give, O Thou Devotion, strength to Vishtaspa and to me . . . . (8) With adoration I entreat Thee, the Best One, Lord of one desire with Best Truth, for the best things for the hero Frashaoshtra and for me, and for those to whom indeed Thou wilt grant (the House) of Good Purpose, for ever . . . . (11) Thou who guardest truth and good purpose eternally, by these, Lord Mazda, teach me through the eloquence of Thy Spirit, from Thy mouth, those things through which the foremost existence shall here come to be.

2.2.17 Verses from Yasna 53

According to the tradition, Zarathushtra gave his daughter Pouruchista (v. 3) in marriage to Jamaspa Hvogva, Haechataspa being his own grandfather. 'Poor man' in v. 9 renders Avestan 'dregush', forerunner of Persian 'dervish'. On 'khshnem', v. 2, see 2.2.8.

(1) The best wish of Zarathushtra Spitama has been heard, if Lord Mazda will grant boons in accord with truth – a good life for ever – to him and to those who have accepted and taught the words and acts of the Good Religion. (2) Then let Kavi Vishtaspa, and the son of Zarathushtra Spitama, and

Frashaoshtra accompany their knowledge (khshnem) and sacrifices continually with words and acts of (good) purpose for the veneration of Mazda, making straight the paths for the religion of the Saoshyant, which the Lord has ordained. (3) Do thou persevere, Pouruchista, descendant of Haechataspa and Spitama, youngest of Zarathushtra's daughters . . . . (4) Her indeed shall I join in marriage among you, her who shall serve father and husband, pastors and kindred. If she is just to the just, Lord Mazda will grant her the sunny heritage of Good Purpose . . . for the sake of the Good Religion, for ever . . . . (7) Then indeed there shall be reward for you all for this 'maga' . . . . If you abandon this 'maga', then there shall be the word 'woe' for you at the end . . . . (9) . . . Such, Mazda, is Thy power, by which Thou givest what is the better to the honest poor man.

2.3. PASSAGES FROM THE ZAND OF LOST AVESTAN TEXTS

The following selections are from the Greater Bundahishn, see 1.1.1.14. In them what appear to be glosses and extensions to the actual translation of the lost Avestan texts are omitted without indication. The final redaction of those texts must have taken place many generations after the composition of the Gathas, for they show scholastic developments of Zarathushtra's great vision. Thus in 2.3.1 what appears to have been Zarathushtra's own adaptation of the ancient Iranian creation myth (see 1.2.6) has been further developed through priestly speculation, notably about the 'world year' (see 1.8). The influence of the Zoroastrian calendar is also plain in 2.3.3.11 ff. (see 1.7 for it and for all the names of the divinities concerned). The myth of man's creation in 2.3.6 is probably older than Zarathushtra, while 2.3.7 sets out clearly what appear to have been his own wholly original concepts (often alluded to in the Gathas) of a Last Day and a Last Judgment, with resurrection of the body (see 1.2.5) postponed until the time when Ahura Mazda's kingdom (khshathra) will come on an earth made once more perfect, as He had created it. Middle Persian Druj (2.3.3.23–4) represents Avestan Drug, 'the Lie', cf. 2.2.2. Amahraspand (2.3.1.53–4 et pass.) is a dialect variant of Amashaspand, both representing Avestan Amesha Spenta.

2.3.1 From the Greater Bundahishn, ch. 1. About Ohrmazd, Ahriman and the spirit creation

(1–5) It is thus revealed in the Good Religion that Ohrmazd was on high in omniscience and goodness. For boundless time He was ever in the light. That light is the space and place of Ohrmazd. Some call it Endless Light. . . . Ahriman was abased in slowness of knowledge and the lust to smite. The lust to smite was his sheath and darkness his place. Some call it Endless Darkness. And between them was emptiness. (6–10) They both were limited and limitless: for that which is on high, which is called Endless Light, . . . and that which is abased, which is Endless Darkness – those were limitless. (But) at the border both were limited, in that between them was emptiness. There was no connexion between the two. Then both two Spirits were in themselves limited. On account of the omniscience of Ohrmazd, all things were within the knowledge of Ohrmazd, the limited and the limitless; for He knew the measure of what is within the two Spirits. (11–12) Then the entire kingship of the creation of Ohrmazd, in the future body for ever and ever, that is limitless. The creation of Ahriman, at the time when the future body will be, shall be destroyed. That truly is limited. (13–14) Ohrmazd by His omniscience knew that the Evil Spirit existed, what he plotted in his enviousness to do, how he would commingle, what the beginning, what the end; what and how many the tools with which He would make an end. And He created in the spirit state the creatures He would need as those tools. For 3,000 years creation remained in the spirit state. (15–17) The Evil Spirit, on account of his slowness of knowledge, was not aware of the existence of Ohrmazd. Then he arose from the deep, and came to the boundary and beheld the light. When he saw the intangible light of Ohrmazd he rushed forward. Because of his lust to smite and his envious nature he attacked to destroy it. Then he saw valour and supremacy greater than his own. He crawled back to darkness and shaped many devs, the destructive creation. And he rose for battle. (18–19) When Ohrmazd saw the creatures of the Evil Spirit, they appeared to Him frightful and putrid and evil; and He desired them not. When the Evil Spirit saw the creatures of Ohrmazd they appeared to him most profound and fully informed. And he desired the creatures and creation of Ohrmazd. (20–3) Then Ohrmazd, in spite of His knowledge of creation and the end of the affair, approached the Evil Spirit and proffered peace and said: 'Evil Spirit! Aid my creatures, and give praise, so that in recompense for that you may be immortal ...'. The Evil Spirit snarled: 'I shall not aid your creatures and I shall not give praise, but I shall destroy you and your creatures for ever and ever. And I shall persuade all your creatures to hate you and to love me.' (24–5) And Ohrmazd said: 'You are not all-powerful, Evil Spirit; so you cannot destroy me, and you cannot so influence my creatures that they will not return to being mine.' Then Ohrmazd in His omniscience knew: 'If I do not set a time for that battle of his, then ... he will be able eternally to make strife and a state of mixture for my creatures. And in the Mixture he will be able to lead my creatures astray and make them his own.' (26–7) Then Ohrmazd said to the Evil Spirit: 'Set a time, so that according to this bond we may postpone battle for 9,000 years.' For He knew that through this setting of a time He would destroy the Evil Spirit. Then the Evil Spirit, not being able to foresee the end, agreed to that pact. (28) This too Ohrmazd knew in His omniscience, that within these 9,000 years, 3,000 years will go according to the will of Ohrmazd; 3,000 years, in the Mixture, will go according to the will of both Ohrmazd and Ahriman; and at the last battle it will be possible to make Ahriman powerless, and to ward off the assault from His creatures. (29) Then Ohrmazd recited aloud the Ahunvar. And He showed to the Evil Spirit His own final victory, and the powerlessness of the Evil Spirit, and the destruction of the devs, and also the resurrection and the future body, and the freedom of creation from the Assault for ever and ever. (30–2) When the Evil Spirit saw his own powerlessness, together with the destruction of the devs, he fell prostrate and unconscious. He fell back again into hell, even as He says in the scriptures that when He had spoken one third, the Evil Spirit crouched in fear; when He had spoken two thirds, the Evil Spirit sank upon his knees; when He had spoken it all, the Evil Spirit became powerless to do evil to the creatures of Ohrmazd. For 3,000 years he lay prostrate.

(34–5) Before creation Ohrmazd was not Lord. And after creation He was Lord, seeking benefit, wise, free from harm, making reckoning openly, holy, observing all things. And first He created the essence of the yazatas, namely goodness, that spirit whereby He made himself better, since His lordship was through creation. (36–7) When He pondered upon creation, Ohrmazd saw by His clear vision that the Evil Spirit would never turn from the Assault; the Assault would not be made powerless except through creation; creation could not develop except through time; but if He created time, Ahriman's creation too would develop. And having no other course, in order to make the Assault powerless, He created time. (39–42) Then from Limitless Time He created Time of long dominion. Some call it Limited Time. . . . All that which Ohrmazd created limited, was from the limitless. Thus from the creation, when He created creatures, until the end, when the Evil Spirit will be helpless, is a period of 12,000 years. That is limited. Afterwards the creatures of Ohrmazd will join the limitless, so that they will abide in purity with Ohrmazd for ever. (44) Ohrmazd fashioned forth the form of His creatures from His own self, from the substance of light – in the form of fire, bright, white, round, visible afar. (47–9) The Evil Spirit shaped his creation from the substance of darkness, that which was his own self, in the form of a toad, black, ashen, worthy of hell, sinful as is the most sinful noxious beast. And first he created the essence of the devs, namely wickedness, for he created that creation whereby he made himself worse, since through it he will become powerless. (49–50) From the substance of darkness, which is Endless Darkness, he created lying speech. From lying speech the wickedness of the Evil Spirit was manifest. . . . From the substance of light Ohrmazd created true speech; and from true speech the holiness of the Creator was manifest. (53–4) And Ohrmazd parted Himself among the Amahraspands when He created them. . . . First He created the Amahraspands, originally six, and then the rest. Of the Amahraspands . . . He first created Vahman, through whom movement was given to the creation of Ohrmazd, . . . for the good religion of the Mazda-worshippers was with him. . . . Then He fashioned Ardvahisht, then Shahrevar, then Spendarmad, then Hordad and Amurdad. The seventh was Himself, Ohrmazd. (55) The Evil Spirit, aggressively inclined, shaped of the chief devs first Akoman, then Indar, then Savol, then Nanhaith, then Taromad, then Turiz and Zairiz; then the rest of the devs. The seventh was himself, the Evil Spirit. (59) And at creation the motherhood and fatherhood of creatures belonged to Ohrmazd; for when He nourished the creatures spiritually, that was motherhood, and when He created them materially, that was fatherhood.

2.3.2 From the Greater Bundahishn, ch. 1a. About the material creation

(1–4) When the Evil Spirit was helpless in prostration, he lay prostrate for 3,000 years. During the helplessness of the Evil Spirit, Ohrmazd created the creation materially. First, He created the Sky as a defence; second, He created Water, to defeat the demon of thirst; third, He created the all-solid Earth; fourth, He created the Plant, to help the beneficent Animal; fifth, He created the beneficent Animal, to help the Just Man; sixth, He created the Just Man, to smite the Evil Spirit together with the devs and to make them powerless. And then He created Fire and linked its brilliance to the Endless Light. (5–6) And I shall describe their nature. First, He created Sky, bright, visible, high, its bounds afar, made of shining metal. And He joined its top to the Endless Light, and created all creation within the sky, like a castle or fort in which are stored all the weapons needed for a struggle. The Spirit of the Sky accepted it as a strong fortress against the Evil Spirit, so that he will not allow him to escape. Like a heroic warrior who has put on armour so that he may be fearlessly victorious in battle, so the Spirit of the Sky is clad in the sky. And to help the sky He created joy. Now indeed in the Mixture creation abides through joy. (7–10) Second, He created Water. And to help Water He created wind and rain. Third, after Water He created Earth, round, very broad, without hill or dale . . . , set exactly in the middle of this sky. And He created in the Earth the substance of the mountains, which afterwards waxed and grew out of the earth. And to help Earth He created iron, copper, sulphur, borax, chalk, all the products of the hard earth. Beneath this Earth there is water everywhere. (11) Fourth, He created the Plant. At first it grew in the middle of this earth, several feet high, without branch or bark or thorn, moist and sweet. And it had in its essence the vital force of all plants. And to help the Plant He created water and fire; . . . through their power it kept growing. (12) Fifth, He fashioned the Uniquely-created Bull in Eranvej in the middle of the world, on the bank of the river Veh Daiti. It was white and bright like the moon, and it was three measured rods in height. And to help it He created water and plants, for in the Mixture its strength and growth are from these. (13) Sixth, He created Gayomard, bright as the sun, and four measured rods in height, on the bank of the river Daiti, where is the middle of the world – Gayomard upon the left side, the Bull upon the right side. And to help him He created sleep, the giver of repose.

2.3.3 From the Greater Bundahishn, ch. 3. The material creation, continued

(7–9) Seventh (He created) Fire, whose radiance is from the Endless Light, the place of Ohrmazd. And He distributed Fire within the whole creation. And He commanded Fire to serve mankind during the Assault, preparing food and overcoming cold.

(10) And He appointed and stationed the Amahraspands for working together during the battle of creation, so that when the Assault came each one laid hold of his own adversary in the struggle. (11–13) And I shall speak further of their nature. The first of the invisible beings is Ohrmazd. And of the physical creations He verily took mankind for His own. And His fellow workers are the three 'Dai's' (Creators), of one place, one religion, one time. All are called Creator, being the spirit from which all creation proceeds. And He created man in five parts: body, breath, soul, form and fravahr. Thus body is the physical part; breath that which is connected with the wind; soul that which, together with the consciousness in the body, hears, sees, speaks and knows; form is that which is in the station of the sun; and the fravahr that which is in the presence of Ohrmazd the Lord. For that reason He created him thus, so that when during the Assault men die, the body rejoins the earth, the breath the wind, the form the sun, and the soul the fravahr, so that the devs should not be able to destroy the soul. (14) The second of the invisible beings is Vahman. And of the physical creations he took for his own all kinds of cattle. And for aid and fellow-working there were given him Mah and Gosh and Ram. And he created cattle in five parts: body, breath, soul, form and spirit, so that during the Assault Gosh Urun may receive the seed of beneficent animals from the Moon (Mah), and with the help of the good Ram may propagate them in the world; and when they die, *the body rejoins the earth, the breath the wind, the soul Gosh Urun, the form the moon, and the spirit Vahman, so that the devs should not be able to destroy it. (15) The third of the invisible beings is Ardvahisht. And of the physical creations he took fire for his own. And for aid and fellow-working there were given him Adar, Srosh and Vahram, for that reason that during the Assault Vahram should establish and set fire within the house, and give it a stronghold. When it goes out, through Vahram it rejoins Srosh, through Srosh Adar, through Adar Ardvahisht, so that the devs should not be able to destroy it. (16) The fourth of the invisible beings is Shahrevar. And of the physical creations he took for himself metal. And for aid and fellow-working there were given him Khvar, Mihr, Asman and Anagran, so that through this fellow-working during the Assault the devs should not be able to overcome metal. (17) The fifth of the invisible beings is Spendarmad. And of the physical creations she took for herself earth. And for aid and fellow-working there were given her Aban, Din, Ard and Mahraspand. Through this fellow-working it (the earth) is kept in good order. (18) The sixth of the invisible beings is Hordad. And of the physical creations she took for herself water. And for aid and fellow-working there were given her Tir and Vad and the Fravahrs – Tir is the same as Tishtar – so that through the help of the Fravahrs she takes the water and entrusts it unseen to the Wind (Vad). The Wind guides and sends the water swiftly to the regions. By means of the clouds, with these fellow workers, she causes it to rain. (19) The seventh of the invisible beings is Amurdad. And of the physical creations she took for herself plants. And for aid and fellow-working there were

given her Rashn and Ashtad and Zam-yazad – the three Khwarrahs who are there at the Chinvat Bridge, who during the Assault judge the souls of men for their good and evil deeds.

(20–1) Innumerable other invisible beings of creation were arrayed to help them. . . . And He divided also the day into five periods (gah). And for each period He appointed a spirit: thus the spirit Havan keeps the period from daybreak as his own, the spirit Rapithwin noon, the spirit Uzerin the period till sunset, the spirit Aiwisruthrim the first part of the night, the spirit Ushahin the period till dawn. And He assigned them also to help (other divine beings); for He appointed Havan to help Mihr, Rapithwin Ardvahisht, Uzerin Burz Yazad [i.e. Ahura Berezant], Aiwisruthrim the fravahrs of the just, . . . and Ushahin Srosh. For He knew that when the Assault came, the day would be divided into these five periods. Until the coming of the Assault it was always noon. (23–4) During the noon-period Ohrmazd with the Amahraspands solemnised a spiritual yasna. During the celebration of the yasna He created all creations; and He consulted with the fravahrs of men. He bestowed the wisdom of all knowledge upon (the fravahrs of) men, and said: 'Which seems to you the more profitable, that I should fashion you for the material world, and that you should struggle, embodied, with the Druj, and destroy the Druj; and that at the end I should restore you, whole and immortal, and recreate you in the physical state, for ever immortal, unageing, free from enemies; or that you should be protected for ever from the Assault?' And the fravahrs of men saw by the wisdom of all knowledge the evil which would come upon them in the world through the Druj and Ahriman; yet for the sake of freedom in the end from the enmity of the Adversary, and restoration, whole and immortal, in the future body for ever and ever, they agreed to go into the world.

2.3.4 From the Greater Bundahishn, ch. 4. Concerning the rushing of the Assault upon creation

(10–11) Then the Evil Spirit rose up with the powerful devs to attack the lights. And he saw the Sky, which had appeared to them in the spirit state when it had not yet been created materially. Jealously he assailed it. Like a snake he rushed upon the Sky beneath the Earth and sought to cleave it. On the day Ohrmazd in the month Fravardin, at noon, he rushed in. And the Sky feared him as the sheep the wolf. Then he came to the Water, of which I said that it is set below the Earth. Then he bored into the middle of the Earth. He entered, and came to the Plant. Then he came to the Bull and Gayomard. Then he came to the Fire. Like a fly he rushed upon all creation. And he made the world at midday quite dark, as if it were black night. He made the sky dark below and above the earth. (13. . .28) And he brought a bitter taste to the Water. And he loosed noxious creatures upon the Earth. And he brought poison to the Plant, and straightway it withered. And he loosed pain and sickness upon the Bull and Gayomard. Before his coming to the Bull, Ohrmazd gave a narcotic to the Bull to eat, so that its suffering and distress would be less from his blow. Straightway it became weak and ill, and the pain left it, and it died. Before his coming to Gayomard, Ohrmazd brought sleep to Gayomard. And the Evil Spirit thought: 'I have made all the creation of Ohrmazd powerless except Gayomard.' And he loosed Astvihad upon Gayomard, with a thousand death-bringing devs. Then he came to the Fire and mingled with it smoke and darkness. And so he defiled the whole creation. Hell was in the middle of the earth where the Evil Spirit had bored through the earth and rushed in through it. So the things of the material world appeared in duality, turning, opposites, fights, up and down, and mixture.

2.3.5 From the Greater Bundahishn, ch. 5. Concerning the antagonism of the two Spirits

(1–2) Thus Ahriman is against Ohrmazd, Akoman against Vahman, Indar against Ardvahisht, Savol against Shahrevar, Nanhaith ... against Spendarmad, Turiz against Hordad and Zairiz against Amurdad, Eshm against Srosh. Falsehood and deceit are against Truthfulness, the sorcerer's spell against the holy manthra, excess and deficiency against right measure. Bad thought, word and deed are against good thought, word and deed, ... aimless lust against innate wisdom, ... idleness against diligence, sloth against (needful) sleep, vengefulness against peace, pain against pleasure, stench against fragrance, darkness against light, poison against ambrosia, bitterness against sweetness, parsimony against generosity, avarice against discriminate giving, winter against summer, cold against heat ... defilement against cleanness, pollution against purification, discontent against contentment. And other devilish spirits are against other divine spirits. ... (3) Likewise among the physical creations, hell is against the sky, drought against water, impurity and noxious creatures ... against the earth, insects against plants, hunger and thirst against beneficent animals, death and sickness and ... diverse ills against mankind, extinguishing and blowing out against fire.... The lion and predatory wolf-species are against the dog and cattle, the toad against fishes, the owl and other noxious winged creatures against birds. Wicked apostates are against just men, the whore against women, ... the demon of destruction against life-prolonging lineage.

2.3.6 From the Greater Bundahishn, ch. 14. On the nature of mankind

(2...4) When sickness came upon Gayomard, he fell upon his left side. And death entered the body of Gayomard from the left side. (Thereafter), until Frashegird, death comes to all creatures. (5–6) When in passing away Gayomard emitted seed, that seed was purified through the light of the sun. Two parts Neryosang guarded, and one part Spendarmad received, and it remained for forty years in the earth. And after forty years Mashya and Mashyanag grew up out of the earth in the form of a 'rivas' plant, with a single stem and fifteen leaves, in such a way that their hands were resting on their shoulders, and one was joined to the other, and they were of the same height and shape. (10...35) Thereafter both grew from plant bodies into human bodies, and that glory which is the soul entered invisibly into them. . . . From them were born six pairs of twins, male and female, all brothers and the sisters whom they married. . . . One of those six pairs was a man named Siyamak and a woman named Vasag; and from them were born a pair of whom the man was named Fravag and the woman Fravagen. From them fifteen pairs of twins were born, of which every pair became a race; and from them was the full populating of the world.

2.3.7 From the Greater Bundahishn, ch. 34. Concerning the resurrection

For 2.3.7.6ff. cf. the texts in 7

(4–5) Zardusht asked Ohrmazd: 'From where shall the body be reassembled which the wind has blown away, and the water carried off? And how shall the resurrection take place?' Ohrmazd answered: 'When I created the sky without pillars . . . ; and when I created the earth which bears all physical life . . . ; and when I set in motion the sun and moon and stars . . . ; and when I created corn, that it might be scattered in the earth and grow again, giving back increase . . . ; and when I created and protected the child in the mother's womb . . . ; and when I created the cloud, which bears water for the world and rains it down where it chooses; and when I created the wind . . . which blows as it pleases – then the creation of each one of these was more difficult for me than the raising of the dead. For . . . consider, if I made that which was not, why cannot I make again that which was?'

(6–9) First, the bones of Gayomard will be raised up, and then those of Mashya and Mashyanag, and then those of other people. In fifty-seven years the Soshyant will raise up all the dead. And all mankind will arise, whether just or wicked. (10...20) Then the assembly of Isadvastar will take place. In that assembly, everyone will behold his own good or bad deeds, and the just will stand out among the wicked like white sheep among black. Fire and the yazad Airyaman will melt the metal in the hills and mountains, and it will be upon the earth like a river. Then all men will be caused to pass through that molten metal. . . . And for those who are just it will seem as if they are walking through warm milk; and for the wicked it will seem as if they are walking in the flesh through molten metal. And thereafter men will come together with the greatest affection, father and son and brother and friend. (23) The Soshyant with his helpers will perform the yasna for restoring the dead. For that yasna they will slay the Hadayans bull; from the fat of that bull and the white haoma they will prepare ambrosia and give it to all mankind; and all men will become immortal, for ever and ever. (27) Then Vahman will seize Akoman, Ardvahisht Indar, Shahrevar Savol, Spendarmad . . . Nanhaith, Hordad and Amurdad Turiz and Zairiz, Truthful Utterance Lying Utterance, and the just Srosh Eshm of the bloody club. Then there will remain the two Druj, Ahriman and the Demon of Greed. Ohrmazd will Himself come to the world as celebrating priest, and the just Srosh as serving priest; and He will hold the sacred girdle in His hands. And at that Gathic liturgy the Evil Spirit, helpless and with his power destroyed, will rush back to shadowy darkness through the way by which he had entered. And the molten metal will flow into hell; and the stench and filth in the earth, where hell was, will be burnt by that metal, and it will become clean. The gap through which the Evil Spirit had entered will be closed by that metal. The hell within the earth will be brought up again to the world's surface, and there will be Frashegird in the world.

(For complete translations of the Greater Bundahishn, and also of the Indian Bundahishn, see Bibliography A under B. T. Anklesaria and E. W. West.)

3 WORSHIP, PRAYER AND CONFESSION

3.1 SELECTIONS FROM YASNA HAPTANHAITI (Y. 35–41)

See 1.1.1.3; 1.2.4. Parts of this ancient liturgy appear pre-Zoroastrian. Thus 3.1.2 was probably addressed originally to Mithra, as guardian of fire, and 3.1.4 to Varuna, as guardian of water (cf. 1.2.3, 2.1.2). The expression Ahurani, 'wives of the Ahura', used of the Waters, is paralleled by Vedic Varunani 'wives of Varuna'; and 'the Ahura' was an Iranian cult invocation of Varuna's. 3.1.5.1–2 would originally have accompanied the offering to fire of fat from the animal sacrifice. The soul of each consecrated victim, it was held, was absorbed into the divine Ox-Soul, Geush Urvan (cf. 2.3.3.14), and so helped to nourish the life of the species. To kill a beneficent animal without so consecrating it was a sin (cf. 10.5.4.10). The Ox-Fashioner, Geush Tashan, appears regularly with the Ox-Soul, apparently as a minor creator-god of the old religion. In the Zoroastrian redaction the whole liturgy is piously devoted to Ahura Mazda, with frequent mention of members of the Heptad, especially Asha, lord of fire, and with still the occasional interchange of 'Thou' and 'You' forms (cf. 2.2). The names of the Heptad in this Gathic Avestan text have not yet fully taken on fixed forms (e.g. Vohu (Good) Khshathra instead of Khshathra Vairya). The wholly Zoroastrian 3.1.3.1, beginning with 'Itha aat yazamaide', forms a much used 'baj' before eating, cf. 4.3. and 11.4.1.10.

3.1.1 From Yasna 35
(3) This we would choose for ourselves, Ahura Mazda, that through beautiful Asha we should think and say and do such acts as may be the best for both worlds. (4) For rewards for the best acts we urge the taught and untaught, the ruling and not ruling, to give peace and pasturage to the cow. (5) Truly we now devote and assign the power which is over us to Him who best exercises

power, namely to Mazda Ahura and to Asha Vahishta. . . . (6) Whatever now a man or woman knows as real, then, if it is good, let him achieve it for himself and teach it to others who may achieve it. . . . (7) Sacrifice and veneration for You, Ahura Mazda, we hold best, and pasture for the cow. That now we would achieve for You, and would teach as well as we are able. (8) Then in the society of Asha, in the company of Asha, give to all who exist the best nourishment for both worlds. (9) These spoken words, Ahura Mazda, we would now proclaim with best thought for Asha. Thee now we establish for ourselves as their revealer and teacher. (10) And for the sake of Asha and Vohu Manah and Good Khshathra, O Ahura, praises now upon praises, words now upon words, sacrifices now upon sacrifices!

3.1.2 From Yasna 36

(1) Together with this fire we first approach Thee, Mazda Ahura, who art harm then to him whom Thou mayst destine for harm. . . . The most beautiful form of forms we then devote to Thee, Mazda Ahura, these lights [i.e. fires] here below, and that yonder, the highest of the high, which is the sun. (2) Come to us as the most joyful, O Fire of Mazda Ahura, by joy of the most joyful, by reverence of the most reverent, for the greatest of decisions. (3) As Fire thou art the help of Mazda Ahura. . . . (4) With good purpose we approach Thee, with good truth, with acts and words of good doctrine. (5) We reverence, we requite Thee, Mazda Ahura. With all good thoughts, with all good words, with all good acts we approach Thee.

3.1.3 From Yasna 37

(1) Thus we now worship Ahura Mazda, who created cattle and order (asha), created waters and good plants, created light and earth and all things good. (2) By His power (khshathra) and greatness and good works Him we now worship with the best of sacrifices, we who abide with the cow. (3) Him we now worship with the Ahuric name which is pleasing to Mazda, and most holy. Him we worship with our bodies and lives. Him we worship and the fravashis of the just, men and women. (4) Asha Vahishta we now worship, the fairest, the Amesha Spenta, radiant with light, possessing all good. (5) Vohu Manah we worship, and Good Khshathra, and the Good Religion, and Good Abundance and Good Armaiti.

3.1.4 From Yasna 38

(1) This earth then we worship, together with women, this earth that bears us; and those who are Thy wives, Ahura Mazda, them we worship, excellent, accompanied by Order (Asha). (2) We worship pious zeals, energies, docilities, obediences; with these Good Recompense (Ashi), Good Prosperity, Good Abundance, Good Satisfaction, Good Bounty. (3) Then we worship the Waters welling up, coming together, flowing forth – the wives of the Ahura; you Waters beneficent and easy to cross, good to swim in and good to bathe in, the gift for

both worlds. (4) The names which Ahura Mazda created, O you good ones, he the good-creating, when he created you, by them we worship you, by them we content you, by them we reverence you, by them we thank you. (5) We call upon you the Waters, and you the milch cows, and you the mothers, giving milk, nourishing the poor, possessed of all kinds of sustinence; who are the best, the most beautiful. Down we call you, O good ones, to be grateful for and pleased by shares of the long-armed offering, you living Mothers.

3.1.5 From Yasna 39
(1) So then we worship Geush Urvan and Geush Tashan, then our own souls and those of the domestic animals which nourish us, for which we are here and which are here for us. (2) And we worship the souls of useful wild animals. (3) Thus we now worship the Good Ones, male and female, the Amesha Spentas, ever living, ever benefiting, who abide by good purpose.

3.1.6 From Yasna 40
(3) Make now, O Mazda Ahura, the laymen possessed of truth (asha), attached to truth. Make the herdsmen apt for long, zealous, firm companionship. (Make them) supportive of us (priests). (4) Thus may the family, the clan, the district to which we belong, thus may we (all) be just, O Mazda Ahura, upright through Your bestowal of that which we desire.

3.1.7 From Yasna 41
(1) We give and devote and offer praises, hymns and prayers to Ahura Mazda and to Asha Vahishta. (2) May we attain to Thy good kingdom (khshathra), Mazda Ahura, for ever.... (4) May we deserve and acquire Thy enduring support, O Mazda Ahura. May we be effective and strong through Thee.

3.2 PASSAGES FROM THE YASNA LITURGY ACCOMPANYING THE PREPARATION OF THE HAOMA OFFERING
On the extended yasna liturgy see 1.1.1.4. Although in Younger Avestan, the passages below are essentially pre-Zoroastrian in content. Baga, i.e. 'Dispenser (of Good)', is yet another epithet of Varuna's; and in the Rigveda also Varuna is said to have set soma on the mountains. Traditionalist Zoroastrians still pray to Haoma for illustrious sons; cf. 5.1.2.

3.2.1 From Yasna 9
(16) Reverence to Haoma! Good is Haoma, well created is Haoma, rightly created, properly created, healing, well formed, well working, victorious, freshly green, with pliant shoots. As it is (best) for him who drinks it, so also it is the *best provision for the soul. (17) O Green One, I call down your intoxication, your strength, victory, *health, healing, furtherance, increase, power for the whole body, ecstasy of all kinds. ... (19) This first boon I ask of you, O invincible Haoma! The Paradise of the just, light, encompassing all

C

happiness. This second boon I ask of you, O invincible Haoma! Health for this body. This third boon I ask of you, O invincible Haoma! Long life for its vital force. (22) Haoma bestows strength and powers on those who swiftly pour. . . . Haoma gives to nobly born women kingly progeny and just descendants. . . . (25) Hail to you, Haoma! Through your own strength you rule at will! Hail to you! You hearken to many words, (if) truly spoken.

3.2.2 From Yasna 10

(2) I praise with prayer, O discerning one, your mortar which holds the twigs. I praise with prayer, O discerning one, your pestle with which I pound with a man's strength. (3) I praise the cloud and rain which make your body grow on the heights of mountains. I praise the high mountains where, O Haoma, you have grown. (4) I praise the broad earth, wide, active in bringing forth, bounteous, the one who bears you, O Haoma! I praise the fields of the earth where you grow, sweet-scented, valiant. . . . May you grow, O Haoma, upon the mountain, and flourish everywhere! (5) Increase through my prayer in every root, in every shoot, in every stem. (6) Haoma grows, being praised. So the man who praises him becomes more victorious. (10) You, valiant one, created by the creator, the beneficent Baga fashioned. You valiant one, created by the creator, the beneficent Baga set down upon high Hara.

3.3 THE FOUR GREAT PRAYERS

These are embodied in the yasna liturgy, see 1.1.1.3, and are also constantly recited by Zoroastrians in their private prayers. All are named from their opening words.

3.3.1 Ahuna vairyo (Pahl. Ahunvar)
The greatest Zoroastrian prayer, composed by the prophet himself. Its recitation may at need replace all other acts of devotion. There are many translations of it, the following deriving essentially from that of S. Insler, see bibliography. The 'lord' of the last line is held to be Zarathushtra himself, cf. 2.2.11.2 ff.; on the 'poor' see 2.2.17.

As the Master, so is the Judge to be chosen in accord with truth. Establish the power of acts arising from a life lived with good purpose, for Mazda and for the lord whom they made pastor for the poor.

3.3.2 Airyema ishyo
This prayer, also in Gathic Avestan, is recited especially at weddings. Airyaman, yazata of Friendship and of healing, has a part at the Last Day, see 2.3.7.10–20.

May longed-for Airyaman come to the support of the men and women of Zarathushtra, to the support of good purpose. The Inner Self which earns the reward to be chosen, for it I ask the longed-for recompense of truth, which Lord Mazda will have in mind.

3.3.3 Ashem vohu
Most devotions end with this prayer, which seems a manthra designed to concentrate the mind on 'asha'. It again is variously translated.
Asha is good, it is best. According to wish it is, according to wish it shall be for us. Asha belongs to Asha Vahishta.

3.3.4 Yenhe hatam
This prayer, regularly recited at the end of litanies, is a somewhat awkward remodelling of Y. 51.22 (= 2.2.14.22).
Those Beings, male and female, whom Lord Mazda knows the best for worship according to truth, we worship them all.

3.4. THE CREED (FRAVARANE), Y. 12

This, also part of the extended yasna, takes its name from its first word (fravarane, 'I profess'). Its kernel was probably the profession of faith required in early times of a convert. It appears to have evolved into Younger Avestan, and then to have been put back, piously but not wholly accurately, into Gathic Avestan; the words omitted in (1) are Gathic quotations. (8) and (9), forming in themselves a shorter creed, are constantly recited as part of the 'kusti' prayers, see 3.5.

(1) I profess myself a Mazda-worshipper, a follower of Zarathushtra, opposing the Daevas, accepting the Ahuric doctrine; one who praises the Amesha Spentas, who worships the Amesha Spentas. To Ahura Mazda, the good, rich in treasures, I ascribe all things good, . . . to the Just One, splendid, glorious, . . . whose is the cow, whose is truth, whose is the light. . . . (2) Spenta Armaiti, the good, I choose for myself. Let her be mine! I renounce the theft and raiding of cattle, and harm and destruction for Mazda-worshipping homes. (3) To those who are worthy I shall grant movement at will and lodging at will, those who are upon this earth with their cattle. With reverence for Asha, with offerings lifted up, that I avow: henceforth I shall not, in caring for either life or limb, bring harm or destruction on Mazda-worshipping homes. (4) I forswear the company of the wicked Daevas . . . and the followers of Daevas, of demons and the followers of demons, of those who do harm to any being by thoughts, words, acts or outward signs. Truly I forswear the company of all this as belonging to the Drug, as defiant (of the good); (5) even as Ahura Mazda taught Zarathushtra in each instance, at all deliberations, at all encounterings at which Mazda and Zarathushtra spoke together. . . . (7) By the choice of the Waters, the choice of the Plants, the choice of the beneficent Cow, the choice of Ahura Mazda who created the Cow, who created the Just Man, by the choice of

Zarathushtra, the choice of Kavi Vishtaspa, the choice of Frashaoshtra and Jamaspa, the choice of each of the Saoshyants, bringing about reality, just – by that choice and doctrine am I a Mazda-worshipper. (8) I profess myself a Mazda-worshipper and follower of Zarathushtra, having pledged myself to and avowed the faith. I pledge myself to the well thought thought, I pledge myself to the well spoken word, I pledge myself to the well acted act. (9) I pledge myself to the Mazda-worshipping religion, which throws off attacks, which causes weapons to be laid down . . . , which is just, which of all faiths which are and shall be is the greatest, the best, the fairest, which is Ahuric, Zarathushtrian.

3.5 THE KUSTI PRAYERS

A Zoroastrian should pray five times in the twenty-four hours, at the beginning of each 'gah' (see 1.1.1.8; 2.3.3.21), standing in the presence of fire (i.e actual fire, a lamp, sun or moon). Unless he is already wholly clean, he should first make ablution, washing face, hands and feet (cf. 11.4.1.1). The basic ritual of prayer, then and at all other times (cf. 11.4.1.1,2,7), is to untie and retie the sacred cord, the 'kusti'. This passes three times round the waist over the sacred shirt, the 'sudra', and is knotted back and front. As the wearer unties it and so loses its protection he recites the Kemna Mazda. He reties it to the Middle Persian prayer known as 'Ohrmazd Khoday', to be found in all Khorda Avestas (see 1.1.1.9), followed by other short Avestan prayers, including Y.12=3.4.8–9. The sacred cord is worn by men and women alike, in contrast probably to Old Iranian usage (cf. 1.2.2).

3.5.1 The Kemna Mazda

Y. 46.7 (= 2.2.13.7), + Y.44.16 (= 2.2.1.16) without its opening formula, + Vd. 8.21 as follows: 'Protect us from the foe, O Mazda and Spenta Armaiti! Begone, daevic Drug! Begone the one of Daeva-origin, begone the one of Daeva-shaping, begone the one of Daeva-begetting! Begone, O Drug, crawl away, O Drug, disappear, O Drug! In the north shall you disappear. You shall not destroy the material world of Asha!', + Y. 49.10 (= 2.2.10.10), third line: 'Reverence with which there is devotion and sacrifice.'

3.5.2 Ohrmazd Khoday

Ohrmazd is Lord! Ahriman he keeps at bay, he holds him back. May Ahriman be struck and defeated, with devs and drujs, sorcerers and sinners, kayags and karbs, tyrants, wrongdoers and heretics, sinners, enemies and witches! May they (all) be struck and defeated! May evil rulers not exist, (or) be far away! May enemies be defeated! May enemies all not exist, (or) be far away! O Ohrmazd, Lord! I am contrite for all sins and I desist from them, from all bad thoughts, bad words and bad acts which I have thought, spoken or done in the world, or which have happened through me, or have originated with me. For those sins of thinking, speaking and acting, of body and soul, worldly or spiritual, O Ohrmazd! I am contrite, I renounce them. With three words I distance myself (from them). [Av.] With satisfaction for Ahura Mazda, scorn for Angra Mainyu! The true achievement of what is most wonderful, according to wish! [= end of Y. 50.11 = 2.2.12.11]. I praise Asha! Ashem vohu. Yatha ahu vairyo (twice). Ashem vohu.

(Text and an English translation in B. N. Dhabhar, *Zand-i Khurtak Avistak* 3–5, and *Translation of Zand-i Khurtak Avistak*, 5–8.)

3.6 THE HAMAZOR

A frequently performed religious ceremony is the 'jashn' (NP. jashan, Parsi jasan). This can be solemnised in any 'clean' place, such as a Zoroastrian house; and according to its intention it can be an act of worship, thanksgiving or supplication, which still among traditionalist Iranis ends with the Hamazor. The celebrating and the serving priests offer their hands to each other, palm to palm. The serving priest then turns to exchange this greeting with the leading member of the congregation, and it is then generally exchanged among those present. Each worshipper, as he takes another's hand between his own, utters the words 'Let us be one in strength, in righteousness!'. The Hamazor was also traditionally exchanged when people met at the festival of No Roz (see 1.6).

3.7 THE BENEDICTION, OR PRAYER FOR HEALTH (TAN-DOROSTI)

This Middle Persian benediction is recited, with special variants for particular occasions, at the end of all formal ceremonies, and also at family observances. The following version is taken from an Irani Khorda Avesta.

In the name of God, the bestower, the giver, the benevolent! May there be health and long life, complete Glory giving righteousness! May the visible yazads and the invisible yazads and the seven Amashaspands come to this fair offering. May this household be happy, may there be blessing! May there be happiness among the people of the religion of Zardusht! We beseech you, Lord, to grant to the present ruler, to all the community, and to all those of the Good Religion, health and fair repute.... May so-and-so, and his wife [or, her husband], and children live for a thousand years! Keep them long happy, long healthy, long just! Keep them thus, keep them caring for the deserving! Keep them living and abiding for many years and countless hours! A hundred thousand thousand blessings upon them! May the year be auspicious, the day fortunate, the month propitious in all these years and days and months! For many years keep them worthy to perform worship and utter prayers, to give charity and offerings, being just. May they have health to fulfil all their duties!

May they be liberal, kind and good! May it be so, may it be more so, may it be according to the wish of the Yazads and the Amashaspands!

3.8 FROM A GENERAL CONFESSION, PATET I KHWAD

The original meaning of 'patet' appears to be 'expiation'. In later use it is 'confession' (cf. 4.3.3; 10.6.2.6; 11.4.1.9). Four general confessions survive, all in Pazand (see 1.1.1.18). Though late in form they appear to represent an old tradition. 'Patet i khwad' is to be said on one's own behalf. One of the other patets is for recital on behalf of the dead.

(1) In the name of the Creator! Whoever refrains from deliberate sin, and makes use of this confession, will be free from sin. . . . (3) Before the Creator Ohrmazd, before the Amahraspands, before the Good Religion of the Mazda-worshippers, before Mihr and Srosh and Rashn, before the invisible and visible yazads, before the religious judge and dastur, before the fravahr of Zardusht of immortal soul, before my own being and conscience and soul, and before the good people here assembled, I repent, am contrite and do penance. . . . (5) For the sins which I have committed against Ohrmazd the Lord, and against men and all manner of men . . . ; against Vahman, and against cattle and all manner of cattle . . . ; against Ardvahisht, and against fire and all manner of fires . . . ; against Shahrevar, and against metal and all manner of metals . . . ; against Spendarmad, and against earth and all manner of earth . . . ; against Hordad, and against water and all manner of water . . . ; against Amurdad, and against plants and all manner of plants, I repent, am contrite and do penance. . . . (7) For not worshipping the sun, for not worshipping the moon, for not worshipping fire, for not keeping Rapithwin [i.e. No Roz] holy, for not keeping the gahambars holy, for not keeping Fravardigan holy, I repent, am contrite and do penance. (8) For any sin which I have committed against those in authority, judges, dasturs, high priests . . . , against father and mother, sister and brother, wife and child, kith and kin, dwellers in my house, friends and all others nearly connected with me, I repent, am contrite, and do penance. (9) For talking while eating and drinking, I repent. For walking unshod, I repent. . . . For deceit and slander, for image worship, for uttering falsehoods, I repent. . . . For any acts of unnatural intercourse, I repent. For arrogance, contempt, mockery, vengefulness, lust, I repent. (10) For all that I ought to have thought, and did not think, ought to have said and did not say, ought to have done and did not do, I repent, am contrite and do penance. For all that I ought not to have thought and did think, ought not to have said and did say, ought not to have done and did do, I repent, am contrite and do penance. (11) . . . For all the sins which the wicked Hostile Spirit brought into existence to assail the creatures of Ohrmazd, and which Ohrmazd declared to be sins, through which men become sinners and must go to hell – if any stand to my account, I do penance for them. . . . (13) This penance I have performed to atone for sin and to obtain my

share of reward for good deeds done, and for love of my soul; to bar the way to hell and to open the way to heaven. With this intention I have performed it, that I may sin no more, but do meritorious acts, some to atone for sins, as far as is needful, some (purely) for love of righteousness. I am opposed to sin, I assent to virtue, I am grateful for good fortune, and I do not repine at the assaults of evil. As to atonement for sins which I have not been able to expiate, I am readily prepared to atone for them during the three nights after death. Should I chance to depart this life without having done penance, if one of my close relatives does penance for me, I assent to this. (Pazand text in E. K. Antia (ed.), *Pazend Texts*, 146–52; Pahlavi retranscription in B. N. Dhabhar (ed.), *Zand-i Khurtak Avistak*, 78–84; translations by Dhabhar, *Translation of Zand-i Khurtak Avistak*, 149–56; R. C. Zaehner, *The Teachings of the Magi*, 120–3; J.-P. Asmussen, *Xvastvanift*, 90–98 (with Pahlavi text).)

4 RULES AND OBSERVANCES

4.1 THE CULT OF FIRE

4.1.1 Atash Nyayesh

See I.1.1.8. The cult of the hearth fire was common to the Indo-Iranians and probably to the Indo-Europeans, i.e. it goes back to remote prehistory. Traditionally, Zoroastrians have maintained ever-burning hearth fires, cf. 10.6.1, 4.2.3, 11.4.1.6. For Iranians fire was linked with justice and hence with 'asha' (cf. 1.2.3), and Zarathushtra enjoined praying in its presence (cf. 2.2.9.9). The daily prayers (see 3.5) regularly include the Atash Nyayesh, which begins with Y. 33 = 2.2.5.12–14, but also contains the following evidently even more ancient verses.

(7) Worthy of worship are you, worthy of prayer! Worthy of worship may you be, worthy of prayer, in the dwellings of men! . . . (13) Fire gives command to all for whom he cooks the evening and the morning meal. From all he solicits a good offering, and a wished-for offering, and a devotional offering. . . . (14) Fire has looked at the hands of all who pass by: 'What does friend bring to friend, the one going forth to the one sitting still? . . .'. (16) 'May a herd of cattle attend you, a multitude of men! May an active mind attend you, and an active spirit! May you live joyfully all the nights which you live! This is the blessing of Fire on one who brings him fuel, dry, sought out to burn brightly.

4.1.2 On purifying polluted fire, from Vendidad 8

'Nasa', i.e. corpse or carrion, when used of something being cooked, refers to the flesh of a daevic creature, one not belonging to the creation of Vohu Manah. It could include lizards, frogs, etc., eaten perhaps by the aboriginal

people of Iran. The following passage is highly condensed and contains rare words; but the ritual it describes is still often carried out in traditionalist villages in Iran (see Boyce, Persian Stronghold, 186–90), and is the basis for purifying fires to be consecrated for a temple fire (cf. 11.4.2.3). Temple fires appear to have been first instituted under the Achaemenians in the early fourth century B.C.; there is no Avestan word for a fire temple, but 'appointed place' (daitya gatu, MP. dadgah) is a phrase applied to one. Section 81 was perhaps added, therefore, in the Parthian period. There are three grades of temple fires, the highest being the Atash Bahram. This is regarded as the greatest earthly representative of cosmic fire, the seventh creation, hence 'the sacred centre to which every earthly fire longs to return' (Darmesteter, SBE. IV, 115 n. 2). On the observance of taking embers from each hearth fire yearly to grow cold in the presence of a temple fire see Boyce, op. cit., 72–3. For the dialogue form of the text see 1.1.1.1.

(73) 'Creator of the corporeal world, Most Holy Spirit, just! If Mazda-worshippers, walking or running, riding or driving, come upon a fire on which carrion (nasa) is being cooked, . . . what should they, the Mazda-worshippers, do?' (74) Then said Ahura Mazda: '. . . they should slay the cooker of carrion, they should remove the pot, they should remove the container of bones. (75) From that fire you should kindle afresh *blazing tinder, or twigs which nourish fire, so that by taking up the *fire-sustaining tinder one may bear (it) away and separate (it), so that the (polluted) fire may go out as swiftly as possible. (76) The first time, as much (*blazing tinder) as a man can hold, that he should lay down on the earth, a good span away from the fire on which carrion was cooked. (From this) he should (again) bear away (*blazing tinder) and separate it, so that the (second) fire may go out as swiftly as possible. (77) The second time, as much (*blazing tinder) as a man can hold . . . (78) The ninth time, as much (*blazing tinder) as a man can hold, that he should lay down on the earth . . . , so that the (eighth) fire may go out as swiftly as possible. (79) If (then), O Spitama Zarathushtra, one duly brings (to the ninth fire) fuel of sandalwood or gum benzoin or aloe or pomegranate, or of any other sweet-smelling plants, (80) from whichever and to whichever side the wind shall carry the fragrance of the fire, from that side and to that side Fire, son of Ahura Mazda, will turn, slaying thousands of invisible demons born of darkness, wicked, slaying twice as many sorcerers and witches.' (81) 'Creator of the corporeal world, Most Holy Spirit, just! If a man brings a carrion-burning fire (thus purified) to an appointed place, how great will be that man's reward after the separation of body and consciousness?' Then said Ahura Mazda: 'As great as if in this material life he had brought 10,000 (pure) embers to an appointed place.'

4.1.3 Two Greek accounts of sacred fires from the Parthian period
After Alexander's conquest of Asia Minor, sacred fires founded under the Achaemenians were evidently still tended by local Zoroastrian communities surviving there under Greco-Roman rule, cf. 10.3.3.8. It is custom to let

lesser sacred fires 'sleep' under hot ashes between the times of prayer. Dry wood laid on such ashes catches fire naturally. The 'tiara' had side flaps which could be used to cover nose and mouth, preventing the breath reaching sacred objects.

4.1.3a Strabo (d. 25 A.C.)

In Cappadocia (for there the sect of the magi, who are also called fire-kindlers, is large) . . . they . . . have fire temples, noteworthy enclosures; and in the midst of these there is an altar, on which there is a large quantity of ashes and where the magi keep the fire ever burning. And there, entering daily, they make incantations for about an hour, holding before the fire their bundle of rods and wearing round their heads high turbans of felt [= the tiara], which reach down over their cheeks far enough to cover their lips. (*Geography*, XV.3.15)

4.1.3b Pausanias (second century A.C.)

Those of the Lydians who are popularly called Persians have temples, at the city called Hierocaesarea and at Hypaepa. In each of these temples there is an inner chamber, and in this an altar upon which are some ashes of a colour unlike that of ordinary ashes. A magus enters the chamber, bringing dry wood which he places on the altar. After this he first puts a tiara upon his head and next intones an invocation to some god or other. The invocation is in a barbarian tongue, and quite unintelligible to Greeks . . . . This, without the application of a light, inevitably causes the wood to catch fire and break out into a bright flame. (*Description of Greece*, V.27.3; text by C. Clemen, *Fontes historiae religionis persicae*, 62–3; trans. W. S. Fox and R. E. K. Pemberton, 'Passages in Greek and Latin literature relating to Zoroaster . . .', 67–8.)

4.1.4 A Muslim description of the fire at Karkuye in Seistan, thirteenth century A.C.

This great temple probably did not survive the Mongol conquest of Iran, later in the thirteenth century. Rustam was a legendary hero of the remote past. 'House of Fire' renders the Pahlavi term for what non-Zoroastrians call a 'fire temple'. Still today a priest tending an Atash Bahram uses a metal implement for the wood.

. . . Karkuye, an ancient city in Sagistan, where are two great domes, of which men say that they have been there since the time of mighty Rustam. On the top of the two domes are two horns, so curving towards one another that they resemble the two horns of a bull. . . . Beneath the two domes is a House of Fire. . . . The fire in this house never goes out. It has servitors, who take over from one another in turn the tending of the fire, while the priest murmuring prayers sits with his attendants twenty paces distant from the fire. (The priest serving the fire), his mouth and nostrils covered, takes up a short length of tamarisk wood with a pair of silver tongs, and casts it in the fire, doing so whenever the fire is sinking, one piece of wood after another. The magi regard this as one of the greatest fire temples. (Qazvini, *Kosmographie*, ed. F. Wüstenfeld, II. 163; from the German trans. of G. Hoffmann, *Auszüge aus syrischen Akten persischer Märtyrer*, 296–7.)

4.1.5 The use of fire in judicial ordeals

Cf. 2.1.2. There were reckoned to be thirty-three kinds of judicial ordeal by fire, cf. 5.2.6.4. In the most severe the accused was cast into a vessel of molten copper, or had molten metal poured on his breast, cf. 5.2.6.5; or (as below) had to walk through blazing fire. If he was innocent, Mithra and the other divine beings, it was believed, would save him; if guilty, he perished. The mildest form, practised down to the nineteenth century A.C., required the accused to swallow a drink containing sulphur (sogand), whose fieriness was largely symbolic, while swearing a solemn oath in the presence of fire (cf. 10.6.2.8). The following incident is from 'Vis u Ramin', see 1.1.2.2. The Parthian king justly suspects that Vis, his wife, and Ramin are lovers.

The king said: 'Can you pledge yourself on oath that there is no bond between you and Ramin?' Vis answered him and said: 'Do not seek to frighten me with oaths and pledges. An innocent person is not dismayed by oaths . . .'. The king said: 'What would be better than this, or worthier of your purity? Take an oath, and you will have freed yourself from slander. . . . Now I shall kindle a blazing fire and burn on it much musk and aloe wood. There in the presence of pious people of the land, swear at that fire a solemn oath . . . .' (2) The king at once summoned the priests. . . . He made countless gifts to the fire temple, . . . of gold coins and royal gems, of land and mills and many orchards, fleet steeds of Tukhar and untold sheep and oxen. He brought embers from the fire temple and made a huge fire in the public square. He fed it with sandal and aloe wood, mixed with camphor and musk . . . . (3) From the palace roof . . . Vis and Ramin watched the fire reaching up to the Pleiades. . . . Then Vis looked at Ramin and said to him: '. . . he wants me now to prove my innocence in the presence of the whole city and army. He will say to me: "Pass through the fire. Make your chastity known to the world, so that great and small may know of it, for they are suspicious of Vis and Ramin". Let us flee before he summons us, so that belief in my virtue may remain in his heart.' . . . Like devs they hid their faces from mankind, disguised as women they fled away. (From sections 54 and 55 of the text, published successively by M. Minovi and M. Mahjub; there is a complete English translation by G. Morrison.)

4.2 CONCERNING HUMAN 'NASA' AND THE PROPER DISPOSAL OF THE DEAD

Much Zoroastrian observance is linked with purity laws. Some of these go back to Indo-Iranian times, but they were reinforced by Zoroastrian dualism,

*and greatly extended. Death was held to be brought by Angra Mainyu (cf.
2.3.4.13–28), and so a corpse was wholly unclean. It was therefore not to be
brought into contact with any of the vulnerable good creations. The stone
tower or 'dakhma' for exposure of the dead (see 11.4.3) appears to have been
evolved relatively late. After the polluting flesh has been devoured the sun-
dried bones are 'clean'.*

4.2.1 From Vendidad 5

(1) 'A man dies there, down in the valleys of rivers. A certain bird flies up
from the tops of mountains, down into the valleys of rivers. It eats of the corpse
(nasa) of that dead man. Then that bird flies up from the depths of valleys to the
heights of mountains. It flies to some tree, whether of hard wood or soft wood. It
spits on it, and passes dung and water on it. (2) A man goes there, from the
depths of valleys to the heights of mountains. He comes upon the tree on which
that bird (perched). He wants fuel for fire. He fells it, he hews it, he chops it, he
kindles it for Fire, son of Ahura Mazda. What is his punishment?' (3) Then said
Ahura Mazda: 'Dead matter carried by dog or carried by bird, carried by wolf
or carried by the wind or carried by flies does not make a man sinful. (4) Indeed,
if dead matters carried by dog or carried by bird . . . were to make a man sinful,
straightway my whole material world would become affrighted of soul and
condemned of body, because of the quantity of these corpses which have lain
upon the earth.'

4.2.2 From Vendidad 6

(26) 'If walking or running, riding or driving, these Mazda-worshippers
come upon a corpse in flowing water, what would you have them do?' (27) Then
said Ahura Mazda: 'Let them halt, Zarathushtra, with taking off of shoes, with
taking off of clothes. . . . Let (them) go forward, let (them) lift the body out of
the water – up to the shins in water, up to the knees in water, up to the waist in
water, up to a man's height in water. . . . (29) Let them lift (it) from the water,
let them lay (it) on dry land. They shall not sin against the waters by casting
into them bones nor hair nor spittle nor excrement nor blood.' . . . (44) 'Where
shall we carry the body of a dead man, where lay it down?' Then said Ahura
Mazda: 'On the highest places, so that corpse-eating beasts and birds will most
readily perceive it. (46) There these Mazda-worshippers must fasten down this
corpse by its feet and hair, using a piece of metal or stone or horn. Otherwise
corpse-eating beasts and birds will come to drag these bones away to the waters
and plants.' . . . (49) 'Where shall we carry the bones of a dead man
(thereafter), where lay them down?' (50) Then said Ahura Mazda: 'A receptacle
should be made out of reach of dogs and foxes and wolves, not to be rained on
from above with rain-water. (51) If these Mazda-worshippers have the means,
(let it be placed) on stones or chalk or *clay. If they have not the means, let it
(the skeleton) be laid down upon the earth, being its own couch, being its own
cushion, exposed to the light, seen by the sun.'

4.3 ON 'TAKING THE BAJ'

This characteristic Zoroastrian practice consists of saying an Avestan prayer (NP. baj) before performing a wide variety of daily acts (see 10.5.4.2), performing the act in silence, and then 'leaving the baj' by saying another Avestan prayer. Nowadays only some old Irani priests maintain this exacting observance strictly. The following passages, from the Shahname (see I.1.2.3), refer to the reign of the Sasanian king Khusrow Parvez (591–628 A.C.). In 1, one of his envoys speaks of the Zoroastrian faith to the Byzantine emperor. In 2, gifts have been brought to Khusrow by the emperor's envoy, 'Niyatus'. In 3, Khusrow, in prison, prepares to meet death in purity of body and soul. For further examples of 'taking the baj' see 6.3.2.2; 11.4.1.10.

4.3.1

(It is) the faith of Gayomard, the path and way of Tahmuras, which tell us that the Lord of the world is One, and that there is no wisdom but serving Him. If a nobleman be wise and devout, then unless, barsom in hand, he has taken the baj, he will not taste even a drop of water, though thirst is driving him to dream of water. . . . His 'qibla' is the highest element [i.e. fire], which is above water, earth or air.

4.3.2

When Khusrow viewed (the gifts) and read the letter, he marvelled at that wealth. To his minister the king then said: 'These Grecian robes, jewel-adorned, are not fit wear for a Persian, for they are the raiment of Christian priests. If there are crosses on our robes we shall be conforming to Christian usage . . .'. His counsellor thus replied to Khusrow: 'O king! raiment does not make the faith. Even if you have dealings with Caesar, your faith is that of the prophet, Zardusht.' . . . (2) Next day Khusrow had his throne prepared, and set the royal crown on his head. The banquet was made ready within the rose garden. Then he bade them summon the Greeks. Niyatus came with the other Greeks, and they took their seats at table. . . . Khusrow descended from the audience-throne and, wearing the jewel-adorned Grecian robe, strode, smiling, to take his place at table. Bindoy hastened, barsom in hand; the ruler of the world received it and privily murmured prayers with his nobles. When Niyatus saw this, he flung down his food and left the table in agitation, saying: 'Baj and Cross together are an insult to Christ through Caesar!' . . . (3) Khusrow Parvez was perturbed at hearing this and said' 'Let none dare hide the faith of God! From Gayomard and Jamshid to Kay Kobad there was no word of Christ. Heaven forfend that I should abandon the faith of my forefathers, chosen and pure lords of the earth, and go over to the faith of Christ — not take the baj at table and become a Christian!' . . . Niyatus said: 'World-ruling king! Look not for wisdom from a Greek who has drunk wine! Rest content with the faith of your forefathers. A wise man does not turn from his own religion.'

4.3.3

Khusrow Parvez said to him: 'Wretch! what is your name? Your mother has cause to weep over you!' 'They call me Mihr-Hormizd,' he answered, 'a stranger in this city, lacking friend or comrade.' Then said Khusrow: 'My time has come! And at the hand of a worthless traitor . . .'. A page stood before him, and to this page he said: 'Go, my companion! Fetch a bowl of water, and musk and perfume, and most clean, fair robes.' The page heard his command, though the boy did not understand his inner meaning. The small servitor left his presence and brought the king a golden bowl and ewer, water and robes. Khusrow made haste to use them. Perceiving a barsom, (first) he took the baj. It was not a time for talk or idle words. When the king had put on the robes he murmured a confession of his sins. He wound a fresh scarf around his head so that he should not see his assassin's face. Mihr-Hormizd went, dagger in hand, and fastened the door of the king's chamber. Swiftly he approached and putting aside the robes pierced the heart of the king of the world. (Shahname, ed. Beroukhim, Vol. IX, p. 2761, ll. 1510 ff.; p. 2793, ll. 2085 f.; p. 2934, ll. 445 f.; English verse rendering by A. G. and E. Warner, Vol. VIII, p. 277, pp. 308–11; Vol. IX, p. 34.)

4.4 FESTIVALS

The framework of the Zoroastrian devotional year is formed by the seven holy days of obligation, see 1.6. Not to celebrate these with worship and merrymaking, and by refraining from all but essential work (cf. 10.6.2.5), was a sin that 'went to the Bridge', i.e. counted at Judgment Day. The greatest of these festivals is No Roz, 'New Day', which as the last of them is an annual prefiguration of Frashegird and the 'new day' of eternal happiness. The number seven is prominent in its observances, as is the holy colour white (see 4.4.2). There was also a traditional fire festival in late autumn, see 4.4.1.3; and with the creation of the Zoroastrian calendar, 'name day' feasts were founded for individual yazatas, see 1.7.2. In the following extracts Arabicised forms of names have been replaced by Middle Persian ones.

4.4.1 From 'On the festivals in the months of the Persians'
This account was written by the great Muslim Persian scholar Al Biruni, c. 1000 A.C. He is known to have had access to Zoroastrian sources, as well as knowledge of the Zoroastrianism of his own day. He describes the festivals as they were after the second Sasanian calendar reform, in consequence of which from the early sixth to the early eleventh centuries A.C. the extended Hamaspathmaedaya (= Fravardigan, '(the days) of the Fravashis') was celebrated at the end of Aban Month, instead of Spendarmad, see 4.4.1.5.
(1) (p. 219) Ardvahisht Month. On the 3rd, or Ardvahisht Day, there is a feast, Ardvahishtagan, so called on account of the identity of the name of the

month and the day. . . . Ardvahisht is the genius of fire and light; both elements stand in relation to him. God has ordered him to watch over these elements, . . . to distinguish truth from falsehood, the true man from the liar. . . . The 26th, or Ashtad Day, is the first day of the third Gahambar; it lasts five days, the last of which is the last day of the month. In these days God created the earth. This Gahambar is called Paitishahim-Gah. The six Gahambars, each of which lasts five days, have been established by Zardusht. (2) (p. 220) Hordad Month. The sixth day, or Hordad Day, is a feast, Hordadagan . . . Hordad is the genius instructed to watch over the growth of creation, of the trees and plants, and to keep off all impure substances from water. . . . (3) (p. 221) . . . This feast was called Adar-jashn, that is, the feast of the fires that are found in the human dwelling-places. It was the beginning of winter, therefore people used to make great fires in their houses, and were deeply engaged in the worship and praise of God; also they used to assemble for eating and merriment. They maintained that this was done for the purpose of banishing the cold and dryness that arises in winter-time, and that the spreading of the warmth would keep off the attacks of all that which is obnoxious to the plants in the world. In all this, their proceeding was that of a man who marches out to fight his enemy with a large army. . . . (4) (p. 222) Mihr Month. . . . On the 16th, or Mihr Day, there is a feast of great importance, called Mihragan. The name is identical with that of the month; it means 'love of the spirit'. According to others, Mihr is the name of the sun. . . . This is indicated by the custom of the kings of crowning themselves on this day with a crown on which was worked an image of the sun. . . . It has become a custom in the house of kings, that at the time of dawn a valiant warrior was posted in the court of the palace, who called at the highest pitch of his voice: 'O ye angels [i.e. yazads], come down to the world, strike the devs and evildoers and expel them from the world!' . . . (5) (p. 224) Aban Month. . . . The last five days of this month . . . are called Fravardigan. During this time people put food in the halls of the dead and drink on the roofs of the houses, believing that the spirits of their dead during these days come out from the places of their reward or their punishment, that they go to the dishes laid out for them, imbibe their strength and suck their taste. They fumigate their houses with juniper, that the dead may enjoy its smell. The spirits of the pious men dwell among their families, children, and relations, and occupy themselves with their affairs, although invisible to them. . . . The first day of the 'extra' days is the first day of the sixth Gahambar, in which God created man. It is called Hamaspathmae-daem-gah. (6) (p. 225) Dai Month. The first day . . . and the month are both called by the name of God. . . . On this day the king used to descend from the throne of the empire, to dress in white garments, to sit on white carpets in the plain, to suspend for a time the duties of the chamberlains and all the pomp of royalty, and exclusively to give himself up to the consideration of the affairs of the realm and its inhabitants. Whosoever, high or low, wanted to speak to him in any matter went into his presence and addressed him, nobody preventing him from doing so. Besides, he held a meeting with the small landowners and farmers, eating and drinking with them, and then he used to say: 'Today I am like one of you. I am your brother; for the existence of the world depends on that culture which is wrought by your hands, and the existence of this culture depends upon government; the one cannot exist without the other.' . . . The 8th, 15th and 23rd days of this month are feast days on account of the identity of the names of these days with that of the month. . . . (7) (p. 229) Spendarmad Month. On the 5th, or Spendarmad Day, there is a feast on account of the identity of the names of the month and the day. . . . Spendarmad is charged with the care of the earth and with that of the good, chaste and beneficent wife who loves her husband. In past times this was a special feast of women, when the men used to make them liberal presents. This custom is still flourishing at Isfahan, Ray, and the other districts of Fahla. . . . (8) (p. 230) The Zoroastrians have no fasting at all. He who fasts commits a sin, and must, by way of expiation, give food to a number of poor people. . . . The Persians divide all the days of the year into preferable and lucky ones, and into unlucky and detested ones. . . . (9) (p. 215) Fravardin Month. . . . No Roz . . . is a 'preferable' day because it is called Hormazd, which is the name of God, who has created, formed, produced and reared the world and its inhabitants, of whose kindness and charity nobody could describe even a part. . . . (10) (p. 219) The 17th is the day of Srosh. . . . This day is a blessed day in every month, because Srosh is the name of that angel who watches over the night. . . . He is the most powerful of all angels against the devils and sorcerers. Thrice in the night he rises above the world; then he smites devils and drives off the sorcerers; he makes the night shine brilliantly by his appearance. (From Al-Biruni, *The Chronology of Ancient Nations*, ed. and trans. E. Sachau.)

4.4.2 On the celebration of No Roz at court

This account too is by a Muslim scholar, written on the basis of Zoroastrian sources in the late ninth century A.C.

(1) (pp. 97–8) When the King . . . had donned his attire and joined his assembly there came to him a man, pleasant of name, experienced in luck, joyful of face and quick of tongue. He stood facing the King and said: 'Give me leave to come in.' 'Who are you? asked the King. . . . The man replied: '. . . My name is Khujaste (Fortunate One); with me the new year approaches; I have brought good news and greetings and a message for the King.' So the King said: 'Give him leave!' and to the man he said: 'Come in.' (2) (p. 98) Then he put before the King a table of silver, containing cakes baked of different kinds of seed: of wheat, barley, millet, sorghum, peas, lentils, rice, sesame, beans and kidney beans. From each sort seven grains were taken and put on the table's sides while in the middle of it they put seven branches of trees which were deemed auspicious . . . and whose aspect was thought a blessing, such as the willow, the olive, the quince tree and the pomegranate tree. . . . Besides, they put on this table seven white earthen plates, seven white dirhams of the year's coinage, and a new dinar. . . . All this the King accepted while the messenger

called on his head eternal life, unceasing kingdom, bliss and power. (3) (pp. 98–9) All this day the King abstained from discussing any matter, fearing lest something unpleasant should come of it and head the whole year. The first thing brought before the King was a vase of gold or silver containing white sugar with fresh Indian nuts pared, and bowls of silver or gold. . . . On each of the No Roz days they set a white falcon flying. Among other things which it was thought propitious to begin this day with was a mouthful of pure fresh milk and fresh cheese; all the Kings of Persia took it as a blessing. . . . (4) (pp. 99–100) Twenty-five days before No Roz they built in the inner court of the King's house twelve columns of sun-dried brick. One column was sown with wheat, one with barley, another with rice, the other ones with lentils, beans . . . millet, sorghum . . . . And the harvest thereof was never gathered but with songs and music and mirth, which happened on the sixth day after the beginning of No Roz. . . . (5) Among the presents which the kings of different nations gave to the Persian kings were the rarest wonders of their lands. . . . Ministers, chief scribes and private courtiers gave gold and silver bowls set with jewels and bowls of silver enriched with gold. Great men and nobles gave falcons, eagles, . . . hawks, lynxes and saddles with their apparel. . . . Wise men gave their wisdom; poets, their verses; jewel dealers their jewels. . . . People of the middle class gave dinars and dirhams of the year's coinage put in a lemon, a quince or an apple. And a clerk stood there, inscribing the name of every donor as well as the reward of all those whom the King rewarded for their present. (From E. Ehrlich, 'The celebration and gifts of the Persian New Year according to an Arabic source,' *Dr J. J. Modi Memorial Volume*, 95–101.)

4.4.3 Celebration of the festival of No Roz, from Vis u Ramin

There once lived a king who in his sovereign rule did as he pleased and had fair fortune. . . . How joyous was the festival which he celebrated in the spring! All the illustrious were there . . . , the king seated among the nobles like the moon among stars. . . . The wine-filled cup passed among them, . . . blossoms scattered from the trees like coins showered upon the fortunate. . . . To one side minstrels sang to the wine, to the other nightingales sang to the rose. . . . Joyous as was the king's celebration, others were no less so. . . . Each had left his house for the fields, carrying with him the means for enjoyment. From every garden and meadow and stream different kinds of song could be heard. . . . Each set a crown of wild tulips on his head, each had the glowing ember of wine in his hand. One group had pleasure in racing their horses, another in listening to music and in dancing. . . . All had gone out to make merry, they turned the earth's surface into a bright brocade. (From section 8; for bibliography see 4.1.5.)

5 THE LIFE AND LEGEND OF ZARATHUSHTRA

5.1 PASSAGES FROM YOUNGER AVESTAN TEXTS

5.1.1 From the hymn to the fravashis (Yt. 13)

Cf. 2.1.8. Much of this yasht consists of veneration of the fravashis of great men and women of early generations of the faithful, following that of the prophet himself. Verse 95 (cf. 2.1.2) shows the interweaving, characteristic of the liturgical texts, of explicitly Zoroastrian with still more ancient material.

(87) We venerate the recompense (ashi-) and the fravashi of just Spitama Zarathushtra, (88) the first who thought what was good, the first who said what was good, the first who did what was good; the first priest, the first warrior (rathaeshtar-), the first herdsman; ... (89) ... who first in the material state praised Asha, reviled the Daevas, confessed himself a Mazda-worshipper ..., opposed to the Daevas, accepting the Ahuric doctrine ...; (92) whom the Amesha Spentas, all of one desire with the Sun, longed for ... as master and judge of the world, and as praiser of the greatest and best and most beautiful Asha.... (94) 'Hail to us! A priest is born to us, who is Spitama Zarathushtra! With offerings and strewn baresman Zarathushtra will worship us. Henceforth the good Mazda-worshipping religion will spread over the seven regions of earth. (95) Henceforth Mithra of wide pastures will further all ruling councils of the lands and pacify the lands that are in turmoil. Henceforth mighty Apam Napat will further all ruling councils of the lands and restrain the lands that are in turmoil.' And we venerate the recompense and fravashi of Maidhomanha, son of Arastya, who first listened to the word and teaching of Zarathushtra...; (97) and we venerate the fravashi of just Saena, son of Ahumstut, who was the first to have a hundred priestly pupils ...; (98) ... and we venerate the fravashi of just Isatvastra, son of Zarathushtra ... and of just Urvatatnara, son of Zarathushtra, ... and of just Hvarchithra, son of Zarathushtra, ... (99) ... and of just Kavi Vishtaspa.

5.1.2 From Yasna 9

Cf. 3.2. The first to press haoma is said to have been Yima, followed by two great heroes of ancient Indo-Iranian and Iranian tradition.

(1) At the time of haoma-pressing, Haoma came to Zarathushtra as he purified the fire round about and chanted gathas. Then Zarathushtra asked him: 'Who are you, O man, the fairest whom I have seen of all the material world?' ... (2) Then answered Haoma: '... I am Haoma, just, invincible....' (12) Then said Zarathushtra: 'What man, O Haoma, was fourth to press you for the material world? What reward was granted him, what boon came to him?' (13) Then answered Haoma: 'Fourth among men Pourushaspa pressed me for the material world. This reward was granted him, this boon came to him, that

to him you were born, O upright Zarathushtra of the house of Pourushaspa, opposing the Daevas, accepting the Ahuric doctrine. (14) Famed in Airyanem Vaejah, Zarathushtra, you were the first to utter the 'Ahuna vairyo'. . . . (15) You made all Daevas hide beneath the earth, O Zarathushtra, who before that rushed about this earth in human shape, you who became the strongest, mightiest, most vigorous, swiftest, and most victorious of the creatures of the two Spirits.'

5.2 PASSAGES FROM THE ZAND OF LOST AVESTAN TEXTS (PRESERVED IN THE DENKARD AND WIZIDAGIHA I ZADSPRAM)

See 1.1.1.14. The Denkard gives a longer version of the prophet's life, taken from more than one Avestan nask; but some incidents are dealt with in greater detail in Wizidagiha i Zadspram. Again, what appear to be glosses and expansions of the actual translation of the Avestan text are omitted here.

5.2.1 On the prophet's miraculous birth, from Denkard 7, ch. 2

(3) As the Religion says: when Ohrmazd created the *creation of Zardusht, then (first) was his Glory. Then the creation of Zardusht *sped down from before Ohrmazd to the Endless Light; from the Endless Light it sped down to the sun; from the sun it sped down to the moon; from the moon it sped down to the stars; and from the stars it sped down to the fire in the house of Frahim-ruvanan-Zoish. From that fire it sped upon Zoish's wife, at the time when she bore the daughter who became Zardusht's mother. (4) People said: 'In the house of Frahim-ruvanan-Zoish a fire is burning which needs no fuel.' (6) And it is revealed that, because the devs were harmed by that Glory, they brought three hostile armies upon the land in order to assail that girl, namely winter and much plague and powerful foes. And they put it into the minds of the people of the land that this harm had come to the land through the girl's witchcraft, so that the people of the land accused the girl of witchcraft, and fiercely demanded of her parents that she should be sent out of the land. (7) And the girl's father, among his many pleas concerning the unjust accusation of witchcraft against the girl, said this to the people of the land: 'When this girl was born in my house, all the light which shone from the fire blazed up, and then settled on her. (8) In the dark night when this girl sits in the innermost room where there is no fire, and they keep making the fire blaze high in the hall, there where this girl sits is brighter than where the fire is kept blazing high, through the light which shines from her person. Anyone who possesses so much glory cannot have been a witch.' (9) Yet, through the prompting of the devs, the wicked kayags and karbs of the land were not content. (So) her father ordered the girl to go to *Patiritarasp, the father of Purushasp, whose house was in the land of the Spitamas. (10) And the girl obeyed her father's order. The trouble which the

devs brought about, wretchedly, by driving the girl into exile, the yazads by their miraculous power made the cause of her going to become the wife of Purushasp, father of Zardusht. (13) The Glory (thus) came to (the house of) Purushasp.

(14) And it is thus revealed that the Creator Ohrmazd caused the fravahr of Zardusht to pass miraculously into the parents of Zardusht through the hom plant. (15) The Religion further says that at the end of the 3,000 year period of spiritual existence, before the Assault, the Amahraspands formed Zardusht. And they installed his fravahr, having mouth and tongue and power of speech, and the body of a man. (16) Then for the (next) 3,000 years Zardusht appeared in visible characteristics as having the same form as the Amahraspands. (17) At the end of (these) 3,000 years ... (19) Ohrmazd discoursed with Vahman, Ashavahisht, Shahrevar, Spendarmad, Hordad and Amurdad. (20) 'If we send Zardusht to the material world with mouth and tongue and power of speech, and the body of a man, then an ordinary lineage will be attributed to this Just Man of mine. Let us form him within water and earth and plants and cattle.' (22) Then the Amahraspands formed a stem of hom, tall as a man, fair, fresh in colour; and they bore Zardusht's fravahr to that stem. (23) And when of the (first) 3,000 years of material existence, from the time of the Assault, only *thirty-three years remained, then Vahman and Ashavahisht went forth. (28) The hom was grafted to a tree, in the top of that tree. It grew, fresh and green. (29) ... Vahman and Ashavahisht went to Purushasp, there in the cattle pasture of the Spitamas. And they directed his thoughts towards fetching that hom. (30) According to the divine wish and bounty, Purushasp then went forth, ... he saw the hom as it grew on that tree.... (31) Then Purushasp thought: 'I must reach it. But I cannot get up to the hom. I must fell the tree.' ... (32) Lo, a great miracle was manifested. (33) The hom descended from the crown to the middle of the tree. Then Purushasp climbed up to it ... and he cut it all. (35) Purushasp carried the hom stems to his noble wife, and said to her: 'Look, Dugdov! Cherish these stems until they have fulfilled their task'. ...

(37) As the Religion says: then when Ohrmazd fashioned the creation of Zardusht which was his bodily substance, then the creation of Zardusht sped from before Ohrmazd to Hordad and Amurdad, and to the clouds. (38) Then the clouds let rain-water fall, ever anew, drop by drop, perfect, warm, to the joy of cattle and men ... Through it grasses sprang up, of all kinds, at a season when other grasses were bent and dry. And the bodily substance of Zardusht passed from that rain-water into those grasses. (39) And it is revealed that, in order that the bodily substance of Zardusht should reach his parents, then at the prompting of those Amahraspands Purushasp drove to the grasses six white golden-eared cows. (40) And lo, a great miracle was manifested. The Religion says: of those cows two which had not born a calf became with milk. And the bodily substance of Zardusht passed from the grasses to those cows, and was blended with the cows' milk. (41) And Purushasp drove the cows back; and

Purushasp said to Dugdov: 'Dugdov! These two cows which have not born a calf have become with milk. Milk these two cows.' (42) Then Dugdov stood up and took the pot ... and milked them. And the bodily substance of Zardusht was in the milk. (46) It is revealed that Purushasp then asked Dugdov for the hom. And he poured it and mixed it with the cows' milk into which Zardusht's bodily substance had entered. Thus Zardusht's fravahr and his bodily substance came together. (47) And it is revealed that after the hom and the milk had been mixed together and consecrated to Ohrmazd, Purushasp and Dugdov drank them. And thus the Glory, fravahr and bodily substance of Zardusht were united in his parents. (48) Then the pair ... lay together, desiring a son. (52) And that man was conceived who was the just Zardusht.

5.2.2 On the miracles of the prophet's infancy and boyhood, from Denkard 7, ch. 3

(1) About the miracles made manifest after the birth of the most fortunate of beings until his coming to consultation with Ohrmazd. (2–3) This is revealed, that he laughed at birth, (3) at which Purushasp said: 'O Dugdov! this man-child saw the coming of glory and the coming of blessedness, when he laughed at his birth. . . . (8) It is revealed that by sorcery the karb Durasrab so implanted in Purushasp's mind fear of Zardusht, and so destroyed Purushasp's understanding, that from fear he of his own accord consulted the karb about killing Zardusht. . . . (9) The karb growled that the way was to collect much firewood and to lay Zardusht in the middle of it, and to kindle fire, so that he would be burnt with the wood. (10) But lo, a great miracle was manifest to many, as the Religion says: the fire did not spread to the brushwood, the fire did not take hold of the brushwood. At dawn his mother ran, seeking her son, and came to him . . . , and took him and laid him on her right arm. . . . (11) It is revealed that Purushasp then spoke to the karb Durasrab about the fire not burning Zardusht, and asked again how to kill him. The karb growled to Purushasp that the way was to lay Zardusht on a narrow path and to drive a herd of cattle along that path so that the cattle would trample him underfoot. And Purushasp did this. (12) And a great miracle was thus manifest to many, as the Religion says: a bull came along who was the leader, fierce and big as an elephant. It ran to him. The whole day long it took pity on him, keeping the other cattle away from him. It was the first to come, the last to go. At dawn his mother ran, seeking her son, and came to him . . . , and took him and laid him on her right arm.

Other attempts are made to kill the child, with a herd of horses, and in the lair of a she-wolf. He continues to be miraculously saved, till Purushasp desists. He grows up, and stories are told of his grace and wisdom in boyhood.

5.2.3 On his tying on the kusti, and entering on his religious quest, From Wizidagiha i Zadspram, ch. 13, 16, 20

(1) It is thus revealed that when Zardusht was fifteen years old the sons of

Purushasp asked their father for their shares, and Purushasp divided their shares between them. Among the clothes there was a kusti, doubled, four fingers' breadth thick, to be wound three times round the waist. Zardusht chose it and tied it on. This was one of the guides of Vahman, who had come into his mind at birth. It tied his thoughts fast against all that was not fitting, and made him fervent for what was fitting. (2) This too is revealed that when he was twenty years old, he departed against his parents' will, leaving his home . . . (3) He came to a group of people who were famed locally for great knowledge. And he questioned them: 'What greatly advantages the soul?' And they said: 'To feed the poor, to give fodder to cattle, to carry wood to fire, to make the hom-libation to water, and to worship many devs with the Word, the Word which is called religion.' Then Zardusht fed the poor, and gave fodder to cattle, and carried wood to fire, and prepared the hom-libation for water. But never did Zardusht worship any dev whatsoever with the Word.

Various other incidents are then told to illustrate the prophet's quest for wisdom and righteousness.

5.2.4 His receiving enlightenment, from Wizidagiha i Zadspram, ch. 21, 22

For some of the following narrative cf. Y. 43 = 2.2.9, and Y. 30 = 2.2.2.

(1) It is thus manifest that after the passing of the thirtieth year from his birth. . . . (2) . . . Zardusht went at dawn to the bank of the river Daiti, to make the hom-libation. . . . When he came up from the water . . . he saw Vahman, the Amahraspand, in the shape of a man, fair, bright and radiant. . . . He wore a garment like silk . . . which was as light itself. And he was nine times taller than Zardusht. And he questioned Zardusht: 'Who are you? Whose are you? What is your chief desire? In what are you diligent?' And he answered: 'I am Spitaman Zardusht. My chief desire, in both existences, is righteousness. . . . And my wish is to become aware of the aim of the two existences. And I shall practise as much righteousness as they show me in the pure existence.' And Vahman bade Zardusht: 'Go forward to the assembly of divine beings.' Zardusht took ninety steps to the nine steps of Vahman. And when he had taken ninety steps, he saw the assembly of the seven Amahraspands. And when he came to within twenty-four feet of the Amahraspands, he no longer saw his own shadow on the ground, because of the great light of the Amahraspands. . . . Zardusht paid homage. And he said: 'Homage to Ohrmazd! homage to the Amahraspands!' And he went forward, and sat in the place of seekers after enlightenment. (5) Then Ohrmazd . . . showed the duality of the original principles and declared the difference between all their operations, saying: 'Of these two spirits he who was wicked, that is Ahriman, chose the worse actions; the Holy Spirit, (I who am) Ohrmazd, chose righteousness . . .'.

After further Gathic paraphrases there follow brief accounts of Zoroaster's consultations with the other members of the Heptad, lasting ten years.

5.2.5 On his conversion of Vishtaspa, from Denkard 7, ch. 4

(65) After the last question of the ten years of consultations Zardusht departed alone, at the counsel and command of Ohrmazd, to the court of Vishtasp and the ordeal of that terrible contest. (66) . . . Vishtasp, through his great wisdom, rightness of thought and spiritual beliefs, would have been ready to listen to Zardusht's words in order to judge of his prophethood; (69) but even before he could hear Zardusht's words and recognise his nature, Vishtasp was turned against Zardusht, through slander and sorcery, by the persuasions of . . . the kayags and karbs. Then he consigned Zardusht to imprisonment and torture . . . . (69) And lo, through the strength of Zardusht, who, alone, fought a terrible battle against evil, a great miracle was manifest to King Vishtasp and his retainers, when they found him alive and full of glory, despite hardship and fetters and other afflictions and prolonged starvation. . . .

Zarathushtra then works miracles from his prison, among them a cure of the king's favourite war-horse.

(71) Further, through his spiritual insight he was able to tell and make known the thoughts of King Vishtasp and his fellow countrymen, and many other hidden things. . . . (73–74) . . . Then in order to vindicate the faith, and to reveal its truth and wisdom, and to remove all doubts from King Vishtasp, . . . the Creator Ohrmazd sent Vahman, Ardvahisht and holy Fire as messengers to Vishtasp, to make known the truth of Zardusht's prophethood, and the will of Ohrmazd that Vishtasp should accept the Mazda-worshipping Religion and make it current in the world. (75) The miracle was revealed to the people of the land of Vishtasp when the Amahraspands descended from sky to earth and entered the dwelling of Vishtasp. . . . (77) The Fire of Ohrmazd said in a man's voice: 'Fear not, illustrious Kay Vishtasp, for you have no cause for dread. . . . (78–9) This is the message we bring you: accept then, most justly and wisely, the vision which Spitaman Zardusht has expounded in purity. (80) Chant the Ahunvar, praise perfect righteousness and deny all worship to the Devs. For Ohrmazd desires that you should adhere to this Religion, and the Amahraspands desire it . . .'. (87) And it is revealed that when Vishtasp accepted the Religion and praised righteousness, the devs in hell were troubled. And the demon Eshm rushed to the land of the Hyons and to the scoundrel Arjasp, who was the greatest tyrant of that age. And he bellowed with the ugliest of voices in the land of the Hyons and incited them to war.

5.2.6 A brief account of subsequent events, from Denkard 7, ch. 5

(1) About the miracles made manifest after the accepting of the Religion by Vishtasp, up to the departure of Zardusht of revered fravahr to the Best Existence, seventy-seven years after his birth . . . : (2) This is revealed that when Zardusht proclaimed the Religion in the dwelling of Vishtasp, it was plain to see that joy showed among sheep and cattle and fires, and the spirits of dwellings . . . . (4) And another miracle was the establishing by Zardusht with regard to decisions and judgments of the means for making known the innocent

and guilty – ordeals and tests in obscure cases, which are said in the Religion to be of thirty-three kinds. (5) The disciples of Zardusht made use of these thereafter, until the downfall of Iranian rule. One of them was applied by pouring molten copper on the breast. It is widely known in the world how Adurbad i Mahraspand, of blessed fravahr, was proved right in this way in the test concerning (the doctrines of) the Religion. . . . (7) And much is revealed from the Religion concerning the victory of Vishtasp over Arjasp the Hyon. . . . (12) And another miracle was the coming indeed to Vishtasp of the reward announced by the Amahraspands for his accepting the Religion: he, the prosperous ruler, saw his son Pishyotan immortal, not aging, needing no sustinence, mighty of body and perfect in strength, full of glory, powerful, victorious, equal to the yazads. Pishyotan was taken to the fortress of Kang and ruled there, as Ohrmazd had destined for him.

According to the Zand, Zarathushtra himself met death while solemnising an act of worship, stabbed by a 'karb', i.e. a priest of the old religion.

(Text and French translation of the Denkard passages in M. Molé, *La légende de Zoroastre*, 14 ff.; text and English summary of the Zadspram passages in B. T. Anklesaria, *Vichitakiha-i Zatsparam*, xc ff., 70 ff.)

5.3 KAVI VISHTASPA AND THE EARLY WARS OF THE FAITH

5.3.1 Verses from Yasht 19

Cf. 2.1.2. The hostility aroused in neighbouring tribes by Vishtaspa's conversion figures largely in Zoroastrian tradition (cf. 5.2.5.87, 6.7), with Av. Arejataspa, Pahl. Arjasp, king of the Hyaonas (Hyons), as the chief foe.

(83) We worship the mighty Khvarenah of the Kavis . . . (84) which impelled Kavi Vishtaspa to think according to the Religion, to speak according to the Religion, to act according to the Religion, so that he professed this Religion . . . , (85) he who became the arm and support of this Ahuric, Zarathushtrian Religion; (86) who when it was at a stand and in bonds led it out of bondage and established it in a seat of honour. . . . (87) Mighty Kavi Vishtaspa became victorious over Tanthryavant of bad religion, and the Daeva-worshipping Peshana, and the wicked Arejataspa, and other evil, slanderous Hyaonas.

5.3.2 From an epic fragment, the 'Memorial of Zarer'

This was transmitted by Parthian minstrels (as Parthian words in it show), but survives in a Pahlavi version written down probably in the ninth century A.C., with a parallel account in the Shahname. It has the anachronisms of an immensely long oral tradition (writing of letters, huge armies, war elephants, etc.). Spendodad (Av. Spentodata, NP. Isfandiar), Vishtaspa's eldest son, is the great hero of Zoroastrian epic tradition, as his brother Pishyotan, NP. Pishotan (see 5.2.6.12, 7.3.3.19–22, 10.5.1.2, 5) is of the apocalyptic one.

Their fravashis, and that of Zarer (Av. Zairivairi) are venerated in Yt. 13, cf. 5.1.1.

(1–4) When King Vishtasp, with his sons and brothers, nobles and retinue, received from Ohrmazd the pure faith of Mazda-worship, then the news reached Arjasp, lord of the Hyons .... He was much perturbed; and he sent Vidrafsh the sorcerer and Namkhvast son of Hazar, with 20,000 chosen warriors, on an embassy to the land of the Iranians, [bearing a letter]. ... (10) In the letter it was thus written: 'I have heard that Your Majesty has received from Ohrmazd the pure religion of Mazda-worship. If you do not renounce it, it will assuredly be the cause of great harm and distress to us. (11) If it please Your Majesty to relinquish this pure faith and to become (again) of the same religion as ourselves, then we shall serve you as our lord, and every year we shall give you much gold and silver, many good horses, and many kingly thrones. (12) But if not ..., then we shall attack you, and we shall consume what is green and burn what is dry, and carry off captive man and beast from your land. And we shall set you to toil in bondage, in much misery.' (13) When King Vishtasp heard those words he was greatly distressed. (14–16) Then the brave and mighty captain, Zarer, ... said to King Vishtasp: 'If it please Your Majesty, I shall give command how to answer this letter.' King Vishtasp bade him answer the letter. (17–18) And the brave and mighty captain, Zarer, ordered this answer to be made: 'From King Vishtasp, ruler of the Iranians, to Arjasp, king of the Hyons, greeting! First, we shall not relinquish this pure faith and we shall not become (again) of the same religion as you. ... Next month we shall meet you in mortal combat, at the White Forest ..., there where there are no high mountains and no deep lakes. On that level plain let the decision be for our brave horsemen and foot warriors. (20–1) You shall approach from your side, we from ours, until we see one another. And we shall show you how devs are struck down at the hands of yazads.' (22) ... Vidrafsh the sorcerer and Namkhvast son of Hazar took the letter, bowed to King Vishtasp, and departed. (23–4) Then King Vishtasp bade his brother Zarer order (signal) fires to be kindled on the mountain tops. 'Alert the land, and alert heralds to proclaim: "Except for mobads who worship and tend Water and the Atash Bahram, let no man, from ten-year-old to eighty-year-old, remain at home. (25) So act that next month you present yourselves at the court of King Vishtasp. ..."' (26) Then all men heard the heralds' proclamation and went in a body to the court of King Vishtasp. And they sound *bagpipes and blow flutes and raise the clarion of great trumpets. (27) And he reviews his army, and the elephant-drivers pass on their elephants, and the camelteers on their camels, and the charioteers on their chariots. (28) And many are the mighty *swords, and many the quivers full of arrows, and many the bright suits of armour, and many the four-times-tempered coats of mail. (29) The army on the march from the Iranians' land is so great that the tumult goes up to heaven, the reverberation down to hell. (30) Along the road where they pass they so cut up the way that they mix (its dust) with the water, so that for a month the water cannot be drunk. (31) For fifty days there is no light. No bird finds a resting-place unless it perches on the mane of a horse or the tip of a spear or a mountain's lofty peak. Day is dark as night through the dust and haze. (32) Then King Vishtasp ordered his brother Zarer: 'Pitch your tent, so that the Iranians too will pitch their tents, and we may indeed know if it is night or day.' (33) Then Zarer left his chariot and pitched his tent, and the Iranians pitched their tents, and the dust and haze settled, and the stars and moon showed in the sky. . . . (35–9) Then Vishtasp . . . summons Jamasp, the Chief Minister, to his presence and says: 'I know you to be wise and brave and sage. . . . And you know even this, what will happen tomorrow in that terrible "Battle of Vishtasp", and which of the sons and brothers of me, Kay Vishtasp the King, will live, which die.' (40) Jamasp, the Chief Minister, says: '. . . If it please Your Majesty . . . to swear by the Glory of Ohrmazd the Lord, and by the Mazda-worshipping Religion, and by the soul of your brother Zarer . . . that you will not strike nor kill me, nor even banish me, then I shall tell what will take place in the "Battle of Vishtasp".' (42) Then King Vishtasp says: 'I swear . . .'. . . . (45) Then Jamasp, the Chief Minister, says: 'Happier is he who was not born of his mother, or, being born, died. . . . (46) Tomorrow when hero meets hero, wild boar against wild boar, many a mother who now has a son will become sonless, many a son will lack a father, and many a father a son. . . . (47) Many an Iranian horse will gallop riderless, seeking its master among those Hyons, and will find him not. . . . (49) And of your sons and brothers, two and twenty will die.' (50) When King Vishtasp heard these words, he fell from his throne to the ground. . . . (53) Then Jamasp says: 'May it please Your Majesty to rise from the dust and be seated again on the royal throne! For what is to be, will be, and that which I have said will come to pass.' (54) King Vishtasp does not rise and does not look up. (55) Then it is the mighty captain, brave Zarer, who goes and says: 'May it please Your Majesty to rise from the dust and be seated again on the royal throne! For tomorrow I shall go and I shall slay with my own might 15,000 Hyons'. (56) King Vishtasp does not rise and does not look up. [*Other champions follow, each promising to slay great numbers of the foe, but each is unheeded.*] (61) Then it is the brave hero Spendodad who goes and says: 'May it please Your Majesty to rise from the dust and be seated again on the royal throne! For tomorrow I shall go, and I swear by the Glory of Ohrmazd the Lord and by the Mazda-worshipping Religion, and Your Majesty's soul, that I shall not leave alive a single Hyon from the battle.' (62) Then King Vishtasp rises and takes his place again on the royal throne. . . . (68) Then Kay Vishtasp the King declares: 'If all the sons and brothers and nobles of me, Kay Vishtasp the King, . . . were to die, even then I would not relinquish this pure religion of Mazda-worship, even as I have received it from Ohrmazd.'

There follows an account of the heroic battle, as a series of single combats, ending at last with Spendodad victorious, as he has foretold, in a field of tragic carnage.

(Text in J. M. Jamasp-Asana, *Pahlavi Texts*, 1–17; trans. A. Pagliaro, *Il Testo Pahlavico Ayatkar-i-Zareran*; E. Benveniste, *Le Mémorial de Zarer*; D.

Monchi-Zadeh, *Die Geschichte Zarer's*.)

6 THE FATE OF THE SOUL AT DEATH, AND A VISION OF HEAVEN AND HELL

6.1 THE FATE OF THE SOUL, FROM YOUNGER AVESTAN TEXTS

6.1.1 From Vendidad 19

The 'beautiful one' of (30) is the Daena of the just man, cf. 2.2.7 and 6.1.2a.22–3. In Vd. 13.9 there is a reference to two dogs which guard the Bridge, cf. 1.2.5.

(26) Zarathushtra said to Ahura Mazda . . . : (27) 'O Creator! where shall the rewards be, where shall the rewards be adjudged, where shall the rewards be concluded, where shall the rewards be reckoned up, which a man earns for his soul in the material world?' (28) Then said Ahura Mazda: 'After a man is dead, after his time is over, after the wicked demons, evil of thought, rend him completely, at dawn of the third night, the Radiant One (the Dawn) grows bright and shines, and Mithra, having good weapons, shining like the sun, arises and ascends the mountains which possess the bliss of Asha. (29) The demon named Vizaresha ('He who drags away'), O Spitama Zarathushtra, leads the bound soul of the wicked man, the worshipper of demons. . . . It (the soul) goes along the paths created by time for both the wicked and the just, to the Mazda-created Chinvat Bridge. . . . (30) There comes that beautiful one, strong, fair of form, accompanied by the two dogs. . . . She comes over high Hara, she takes the souls of the just over the Chinvat Bridge, to the rampart of the invisible yazatas. (31) Vohu Manah rises from his golden throne. Vohu Manah exclaims: "How have you come here, O just one, from the perilous world to the world without peril?" (32) Contented, the souls of the just proceed to the golden thrones of Ahura Mazda and the Amesha Spentas, to the House of Song, the dwelling-place of Ahura Mazda, the dwelling-place of the Amesha Spentas, the dwelling-place of the just.'

(Following, for 28 and 29, the translation of Bruce Lincoln, 'Mithra(s) as Sun and Saviour', p. 512.)

6.1.2a From Hadhokht Nask, ch. 2

See 1.1.11. The quotation in (3–6) is from Y. 43 = 2.2.9.1.

(1–2) Zarathushtra asked Ahura Mazda: 'Ahura Mazda, Most Holy Spirit, Creator of the material world, just! When a just man dies, where dwells his soul that night?' (3–6) Then said Ahura Mazda: 'It sits at the (corpse's) head, chanting Gatha Ushtavaiti, invoking for itself the wished-for things: "May Lord Mazda, ruling at will, grant wishes to him whosoever has wishes!" On this night the soul feels as much joy as all that it had felt in life.' (7 ff.) 'On the second night, where dwells the soul?' 'It sits at the head . . .'. (12 ff.) 'On the third night where dwells the soul?' 'On this night also it sits at the head . . . . (18–20) At the end of the third night, the dawn appearing, it is as if the soul of the just man were amid meadows and breathing in sweet scents. It is as if a wind blew on it from the most southerly quarter, from the most southerly quarters, fragrant, more fragrant than any other wind. (21) Then it is as if the soul of the just man breathed that wind in its nostrils. "From where blows this wind, which is the most fragrant wind that I have ever breathed in my nostrils?" (22–3) As that wind blows on him, his own Daena appears in the form of a maiden, beautiful, queenly, white-armed, . . . in shape as beautiful as the most beautiful of creatures. (24) Then the soul of the just man said to her, inquiring: "What girl are you, the most beautiful in form of all girls that I have ever seen?" (25) Then his own Daena answered him: "Truly, youth of good thoughts, good words, good acts, good inner self (daena), I am your very own Daena." (26) "And who has loved you for that stature and goodness and beauty . . . , as you appear to me?" (27) "You have loved me, youth of good thoughts . . . . (28–9) When you would see another who *mocked, and *worshipped devils, and *practised oppression, and *crushed plants, then you would seat yourself and chant the Gathas, and worship the good Waters and the Fire of Ahura Mazda, and show hospitality to the just man, whether he came from near or far. (30) Then you would make me, who was beloved, more beloved, who was beautiful, more beautiful, who was desired, more desired. (31–2) You would set me, who was sitting in a high place, in a higher place, by this your good thought, . . .". (33–4) First the soul of the just man advanced a step, he set it in "Good Thought". Second, he advanced a step, he set it in "Good Word". Third, he advanced a step, he set it in "Good Act". Fourth, he advanced a step, he set it in Endless Light. (35–6) Then a just man, who had died before, said to him, inquiring: "How, O just one, did you die? How did you depart from the dwellings with cattle . . . , from the material world to the spirit world, from the perilous world to the world without peril? How has long happiness come to you?" (37) Then said Ahura Mazda: "You shall not question him. He whom you question has come hither on a grim, fearful, calamitous road, that is, the separation of body and consciousness. (38) Let there be brought to him as food some spring butter, that is the food after death for a man of good thought, good word, good act, good inner self; that is the food after death for a woman of excellent thought, excellent word, excellent act, well instructed, ruled by a master, just." '

6.1.2b From Hadhokht Nask, ch. 3

The quotation in (2) is from Y. 46 = 2.2.13.1. For (33–8) cf. Y. 49 = 2.2.10.11.

(1) Zarathushtra asked Ahura Mazda: 'Ahura Mazda . . . When a wicked man dies, where dwells his soul that night?' (2) Then said Ahura Mazda: 'Truly, O just Zarathushtra, it scuttles about there near the (corpse's) head,

chanting the Gatha Kam nemoi: "To what land to flee? Whither shall I go to flee?" On this night the soul feels as much distress as all that it had felt in life.' (3–16) 'On the second night . . .'. (17) 'At the end of the third night, O just Zarathushtra, the dawn appearing, it is as if the soul of the wicked man were in a *wilderness and breathing in stenches. (18) It is as if a wind blew on it from the most northerly quarter, from the most northerly quarters, foul-smelling, more foul-smelling than any other wind. (20) Then it is as if the soul of the wicked man breathed that wind in its nostrils. "From where blows this wind, the most foul-smelling wind that I have ever breathed in my nostrils?" (21–33) First the soul of the wicked man advanced a step, he set it in "Bad Thought" . . . . Fourth, the soul of the wicked man advanced a step, he set it in Endless Darkness. (34) Then a wicked man, who had died before, said to him, inquiring: "How, O wicked one, did you die? (35) How, O wicked one, did you depart from the dwellings with cattle . . . How has long woe come to you?" (37) Then snarled Anra Mainyu: "You shall not question him . . . . (38) Let there be brought to him as food poisonous and poisonous-smelling things, that is the food after death for a man of bad thought, bad word, bad act, bad inner self; that is the food after death for a harlot of exceeding bad thought, exceeding bad word, exceeding bad act, ill-instructed, not ruled by a master, wicked." '

6.2 THE FATE OF THE SOUL, FROM PAHLAVI SOURCES

6.2.1 From the Menog i Khrad, ch. 2
This, the book of the 'Spirit of Wisdom', is a compilation of the later Sasanian period, which contains much ancient material.

(110–13) Do not trust in life, for in the end death will overcome you, and dog and bird will rend your corpse, and your bones will lie on the ground. (114) And for three days and nights your soul will sit at the body's head. (115) And on the fourth day at dawn, accompanied by the just Srosh and the good Vay and mighty Vahram, and opposed by Astvihad and the worse Vay and the demon *Vizarsh . . . it will reach the high and terrible Chinvat Bridge, to which everyone comes, just or wicked. (116) And there many adversaries wait, (117) (such as) Eshm with bloody club, malevolently, and Astvihad, who swallows all creatures and is never sated. (118) And to mediate there are Mihr and Srosh and Rashn. (119–20) In the weighing Rashn the just, who holds the balance for souls, never makes it dip to one side, neither for the just nor for the wicked, neither for a lord nor for the ruler of a land. (121) He does not swerve by as much as a hair's breadth, and has no regard for persons. . . . (123) When then the soul of the just man crosses that bridge, the bridge becomes as if a mile wide, (124) and the just soul crosses accompanied by the just Srosh. (125–6) And his own good acts will come to meet him in the form of a girl, more beautiful and fairer than any girl in the world. . . . (158) When a wicked person dies, then for three days and nights his soul scuttles about near the evil head of that wicked one. (159) It weeps, saying: 'Whither shall I go and whom shall I now take as refuge?' (160) And it sees with its eyes, during those three days and nights, all the sins and wickednesses which it has done in the world. (161–2) On the fourth day the demon Vizarsh comes and binds the wicked man's soul in the harshest way, and, in spite of opposition by just Srosh, leads it to the Chinvat Bridge. (163) Then just Rashn will discover that wicked person's soul in its wickedness. (164) Then the demon Vizarsh will seize that wicked person's soul and will beat and torment it scornfully and wrathfully. (165) And the wicked person's soul will cry out with loud lamentation, and will weep and utter many pleas, entreatingly, and make many desperate struggles in vain. (166) And since his struggles and entreaties are of no avail at all, and no good being nor yet devil comes to his aid, the demon Vizarsh drags him evilly to . . . hell. (167) And then a girl approaches, not like other girls. (168–9) And the wicked man's soul says to that hideous girl: 'Who are you, than whom I have never seen a girl more hideous and hateful?' (170–1) And answering him she says: 'I am no girl, but I am your own acts, O hateful one of bad thought, bad word, bad act, bad inner self. (172–3) For when indeed while in the world you saw someone who worshipped the yazads, you sat down and worshipped the devs, and served the devs and she-devils. (174–5) And when indeed you saw someone providing shelter and hospitality for good people, and giving them gifts, whether they came from near or far, then you despised and humiliated good people, and did not give them gifts and indeed barred your door. (176–7) And when you saw someone giving true judgment and not taking bribes, and bearing true witness, and holding pious discourse, then indeed you sat down and gave false judgment, and bore false witness, and held wrongful discourse. (178) I am this your bad thought, bad word and bad act, which you have thought and said and done.' (For the text and a translation of the whole work see E. W. West, *The Book of the Mainyo-i-Khard*.)

6.2.2 From the Dadestan i denig, Question 20

This, the 'Religious Judgments', is a collection of answers given by Manushchihr, Zoroastrian high priest in the ninth century A.C., to questions put to him by members of his community.

(3) The [Chinvat] Bridge is like a sword . . . , one of whose surfaces is broad, one narrow and sharp. With its broad side, it is so ample that it is twenty-seven poles wide; with its sharp side, it is so constructed that it is as narrow as a razor's edge. (4) When the souls of the just and the wicked arrive, it turns on that side which is required for them. (5) Through the great glory of the Creator, and at the command of him who is the true judge and protector of the Bridge, it becomes a broad crossing for the just . . . ; for the wicked it becomes a narrow crossing, just like a razor's edge. (6) The soul of a just person crosses the Bridge, and its way is pleasantness. . . . (7) When that of a wicked person sets foot on the Bridge, because of the . . . sharpness it falls from the middle of the Bridge and tumbles down. (Text, T. D. Anklesaria, *The Datistan-i-dinik*, 44–5; translation,

E. W. West, *SBE*, XVIII, 48–9; J. C. Pavry, *The Zoroastrian doctrine of a future life*, 94–5.)

6.3 A VISION OF HEAVEN AND HELL, FROM ARDA VIRAZ NAMAG

The fravashi of 'just Viraza' is among those venerated in Yt. 13 (cf. 5.1.1). The 'vision of the home of the dead' is a widely attested type of mantic composition in the oral literatures of the world. This ancient Zoroastrian version of it was evidently retold down the generations, and was finally used, in a Pahlavi version of probably the ninth century A.C., to strengthen the faithful against the assaults of Islam. Chapter 1 tells how the religious leaders (dasturs) resolve to send the most self-disciplined and just member of the community in spirit to the other world, to verify the teachings of the faith; and how the lot falls to Viraz. – His vision has been shown to be the ultimate source of Dante's Divine Comedy.

6.3.1 From AVN., ch. 2
The service for consecrating the 'dron' (unleavened bread) is the most elaborate form of 'baj' before eating, cf. 4.3. 'Zand' here means the colloquial tongue.

(2) Then Viraz stood before the Mazda-worshippers, his arms folded across his breast, and said to them: 'Is it permitted that I should offer worship for departed souls, and take food, and make my will? Thereafter give me the wine and narcotic.' The dasturs bade him do so. (3) Then the dasturs of the faith chose . . . a place thirty steps away from all good things, and Viraz washed his hair and body, and put on fresh clothes and scented himself with sweet scent. He spread a new, clean carpet on a prepared couch, and sat down on the clean carpet of the couch, and consecrated the dron, and remembered departed souls, and partook of food. Then the dasturs of the faith filled three golden bowls with wine and narcotic . . . ; and they gave the first bowl to Viraz with the word 'good thought', and the second with the word 'good word', and the third with the word 'good act'. He drank the wine and narcotic, and while still conscious said the prayer after food, and fell asleep upon the carpet. (4) For seven days and nights the dasturs of the faith . . . , scattering incense upon the ever-burning fire, recited religious prayers in Avestan and Zand. They solemnised the nask and chanted the Gathas, and kept watch during darkness. (His) seven sisters sat round Viraz's carpet, and recited Avesta for seven days and nights. Those seven sisters, with all the Mazda-worshippers and the dasturs of the faith, and herbads and mobads, never in any way relaxed their watch.

6.3.2 From AVN., ch. 3
The 'Peak of the Law' is another name for the peak of Mount Hara, where

*the departed soul is judged. Towards the end of (2) Hordad and Amurdad are
especially thanked as the givers of food.*

(1) The soul of Viraz went from his body to the Peak of the Law and the
Chinvat Bridge; and after seven days and nights it returned and entered his
body again. Viraz arose as if he were rising from a sweet sleep, thinking good
thoughts and serene. And when those sisters, together with the dasturs of the
faith and the Mazda-worshippers, saw Viraz, they were joyful and glad. And
they said: 'You are welcome, Viraz, messenger of us Mazda-worshippers! You
are come from the land of the dead to this land of the living!' And the herbads
and dasturs of the faith bowed before Viraz. (2) Then when Viraz perceived this
he came forward and bowed and said: 'Hail to you from Ohrmazd the Lord and
the Amahraspands; and hail from just Zardusht Spitaman; and hail from just
Srosh and Adar Yazad and the Glory of the Mazda-worshipping Faith; and hail
from the . . . blessed souls, and hail from the other divine beings of Paradise
who are in goodness and peace.' Then the dasturs of the faith said: '. . . Hail to
you also! All that you have seen, tell us truthfully!' Then Viraz said: '. . . let it be
ordered that first food should be given to him who is hungry and thirsty, and
then questions be asked of him.' Then the dasturs of the faith said: 'Good!' And
food . . . was brought; and they consecrated the dron, and Viraz took the baj
and ate, and made offering, and left the baj; and he uttered praises to Ohrmazd
and the Amahraspands, and gave thanks to the Amahraspands Hordad and
Amurdad, and recited the benediction. And he directed that a learned and very
intelligent scribe should be brought; and they brought a trained and intelligent
scribe, and he sat down before him. And all that Viraz related, he wrote down
accurately and clearly and in detail.

6.3.3 From AVN., ch. 4

(1) And he ordered him to write thus: On that first night the just Srosh and
Adar Yazad came to meet me. And they bowed to me and said: 'You are
welcome, just Viraz, even if it is not yet your time for coming.' I said: 'I am a
messenger.' Then the victorious, just Srosh and Adar Yazad took my hands.
Setting the first step in 'Good Thought', and the second step in 'Good Word',
and the third step in 'Good Act', I reached the Chinvat Bridge . . . created by
Ohrmazd.

6.3.4 From AVN., ch. 5

(1) Then the Chinvat Bridge became nine spear-lengths wide, and in company
with just Srosh and Adar Yazad I crossed over easily and happily. . . . And I,
just Viraz, saw righteous Rashn, who held the bright golden scales in his hand,
and weighed the just and the wicked. (2) Then just Srosh and Adar Yazad took
my hands and said: 'Come! that we may show you heaven and hell, and the light
and ease and comfort and happiness . . . of heaven, the reward of the just. And
we shall show you the darkness and distress and discomfort and evil . . . in hell,
and the punishments of various kinds which demons and devils and sinners

inflict. And we shall show you the place of the true and that of false. And we shall show you the reward for firm believers in Ohrmazd and the Amahraspands.

6.3.5 From AVN., ch. 6

The 'future body', tan i pasen, is that which will be made immortal at Frashegird, cf. 2.3, 2.3.7.

(1) I came to a place and saw the souls of a number of people who were in Hammistagan. And I asked the victorious just Srosh and Adar Yazad: 'Who are these, and why are they here?' Just Srosh and Adar Yazad said: 'This is called Hammistagan, "The Place of the Motionless Ones"; and until the future body these souls will remain in this place. They are the souls of those people whose goodness and evildoing were equal. Say to the people of the world: "Do not consider the most trifling good act to be *trouble or vexation, for everyone whose good acts outweigh his bad ones goes to heaven, and everyone whose bad ones weigh more, to hell, even if the difference is only three tiny acts of wrongdoing; and those for whom both are equal remain until the future body in this Hammistagan. Their punishment is cold or heat from changes in the atmosphere. And they have no other affliction.'

6.3.6 From AVN., ch. 7–10

(1) Then I took the first step to the star station, to 'good thought' . . . the second step was to the moon station, to 'good word' . . . the third step was to the sun station, to 'good act' . . . . (2) The fourth step I took up to the light of heaven, which is all bliss. And the souls of the departed came to meet us, and saluted and blessed us. And they spoke thus: 'How have you come, O just one? From that perilous world, full of wickedness, you have ascended to this world which is free from peril and adversity. Taste of ambrosia, for here you will know peace for a long while.'

6.3.7 From AVN., ch. 11

(1) Then Vahman the Amahraspand arose from his golden throne, and took my hand; and with the words 'good thought', 'good word', 'good act' he led me into the presence of Ohrmazd and the Amahraspands and the host of the blessed; among them were the fravashis of Zardusht Spitaman, and Kay Vishtasp, and Jamasp, and Isadvastar son of Zardusht, and other upholders and leaders of the faith. And Vahman said: 'Behold, Ohrmazd'. And I wished to bow before Him. And He said to me: 'Hail to you, just Viraz, you are welcome. From that perilous world you are come to this pure place of light.' And He gave command to just Srosh and Adar Yazad: 'Take Viraz, and show him the place and reward of the just, and also the punishment of the wicked.' (2) Then just Srosh and Adar Yazad took my hands, and led me on from place to place.

6.3.8 From AVN., ch. 12

(1) I came to a place and saw the souls of generous people, who walked adorned and were above all other souls in all brightness. And Ohrmazd ever honoured the souls of the generous, which were bright and tall and strong. And I said: 'Happy are you, who are the soul of a generous person, exalted thus above other souls.' And it seemed to me praiseworthy. (2) And I saw the souls of those persons who in the flesh had chanted the Gathas and performed acts of worship, and professed the Good Religion of the Mazda-worshippers which Ohrmazd had taught to Zardusht. And when I advanced, they were in garments adorned with silver and gold, the most embellished of all garments. And it seemed to me very praiseworthy.

6.3.9 From AVN., ch. 14

(1) . . . And I saw the souls of 'warriors', who went in the highest happiness and joyfulness of mind, and in kingly garments. And the well made caparisons of those heroes were made of gold, studded with jewels, very glorious, richly adorned; and they were in chariots with wondrous bodywork, in much splendour and strength and victoriousness. And it seemed to me praiseworthy. . . . (2) And I saw the souls of 'herdsmen', in a brilliant place and glorious raiment, as they had stood before the spirits of Water and Earth and Plants and Cattle, and blessed them. And they utter praise and thanks and gratitude, and their position is great, and they occupy a good place. And it seemed to me praiseworthy. (4) And I saw the souls of those 'artisans' who in the world had served their lords and masters, as they sat upon daises which were well carpeted, large, brilliant and shining. And it seemed to me very praiseworthy.

6.3.10 From AVN., ch. 15

(1) . . . And I saw the souls of those who love good, the intercessors and peace-seekers, from whom there ever shines a light like that of the stars and moon and sun; and, possessed of joy, they ever walked in the atmosphere of light. (2) And I saw the foremost existence of the just, light, with all ease and plenty, and many fragrant flowers of all colours, all in blossom – radiant, full of glory and every happiness and joy, from which none knows satiety.

6.3.11 From AVN., ch. 53

(1) Then just Srosh and Adar Yazad took my hands, and brought me into a desolate place on the Peak of the Law, beneath the Chinvat Bridge; and they showed me hell in the midst of that desolate place, in the earth beneath the Chinvat Bridge. From that place there rose up the weeping and lamentation of Ahriman and the demons and she-devils and also the many souls of the wicked, concerning which I thought: 'The seven regions of the earth would shake, if they should hear that lamentation and weeping.' I was affrighted and entreated just Srosh and Adar Yazad: 'Do not bring me here! Turn back!' (2) Then just

D

Srosh and Adar Yazad said to me: 'Fear not! for there will never be any dread for you here'. And just Srosh and Adar Yazad went on before; and behind went I, just Viraz, fearlessly, further into that dark hell.

6.3.12 From AVN., ch. 54

(1) And I saw the blackest hell, dangerous, fearful, terrible, holding much pain, full of evil, foul-smelling. Then I thought that it seemed like a pit, to whose bottom a thousand spears would not reach; and if all the firewood which is in the world were placed on the fire in the most evil-smelling, darkest hell, it would never give out fragrance. Again, as (close) as eye to ear, and as many as the hairs on a horse's mane, so (close) and many in number are the souls of the wicked therein. Yet they see not, and hear no sound from one another. Each one thinks: 'I am alone.' And they suffer gloom and darkness and stench and fearfulness and torment and punishment of diverse kinds, so that he who has been one day in hell cries out: 'Are not those nine thousand years yet fulfilled, that they do not release us from this hell?'

6.3.13 From AVN., ch. 55

(1) Then I saw the souls of the wicked, who endure diverse punishments, such as snow and bitter cold, and the heat of swiftly blazing fire, and foul stench . . . , and many other evils in that terrible place . . . ; and they ever suffer torment and punishment. (2) And I asked: 'What sin had these bodies committed, whose souls suffer such heavy punishment?' (3) Just Srosh and Adar Yazad said: 'These are the souls of those wicked people who committed many mortal sins in the flesh, and extinguished Vahram fires, and destroyed bridges over swiftly flowing streams, and spoke falsely and untruthfully, and often gave false witness. And their desire was anarchy; and because of their greediness and miserliness, and lust and anger and envy, innocent and just people were slain. They acted very deceitfully; and now their souls must endure such heavy torment and punishment.'

6.3.14 From AVN., ch. 56

(1) Then I saw the souls of those whom serpents bit and ever devoured. And I asked: 'Whose souls are those?' And just Srosh and Adar Yazad said: 'These are the souls of those wicked people who in the flesh denied the yazads and the religion'.

6.3.15 From AVN., ch. 57

(1) And I saw the souls of women whose heads were cut off and separated from their bodies, and their tongues kept up an outcry. And I asked: 'Whose souls are those?' Just Srosh and Adar Yazad said: 'These are the souls of those women who in the flesh made much lamentation and mourning, and beat their heads and faces'.

6.3.16 From AVN., ch. 58

(1) There I saw the soul of a man whom they were carrying off to hell, dragging him, and they beat him continually. And I asked: 'What sin was committed by this body?' Just Srosh and Adar Yazad said: 'This is the soul of that wicked man who in the flesh often washed his hair and face, and his dirty hands, and other impurity from his limbs, in large stretches of standing water and in springs and streams; and he injured the Amahraspand Hordad.'

6.3.17 From AVN., ch. 100

(1) Then I saw the Evil Spirit, death-dealing, destroyer of the world, whose religion is evil, who ever mocked and scorned the wicked in hell, and said: 'Why were you eating the bread of Ohrmazd and doing my work? And not thinking of your Creator, but fulfilling my wish?' Thus he ever shouted very mockingly at the wicked.

6.3.18 From AVN., ch. 101

(1) Then just Srosh and Adar Yazad took my hands and bore me out of that black place, dangerous and fearful, and carried me to the Endless Light and the assembly of Ohrmazd and the Amahraspands. (2) When I wished to do homage before Ohrmazd . . . He said: 'You are welcome, just Viraz, messenger of the Mazda-worshippers! Go to the material world and as you have seen and understood, tell it truly to those who dwell therein. For I who am Ohrmazd am with you. Each man who speaks what is sound and true, I recognise and know him. Tell this to the wise.' When Ohrmazd spoke in this way, I remained astonished, for I saw light, but I saw no one; and I heard a voice, and I knew that this was Ohrmazd. (3) And He, the Creator Ohrmazd, holiest of divine beings, said: 'Speak, just Viraz, to the Mazda-worshippers of the world, saying: 'One is the path of righteousness, the path of the original doctrine, and all other paths are no paths. Take you that one path of righteousness, and turn not from it in prosperity, nor in adversity, and go not by any other path. Practise good thoughts, good words and good acts; and remain in that same faith which Spitaman Zardusht received from Me, and Vishtasp made current in the world. . . . Well is it with you, just Viraz! Depart in your prosperity; for whatever purity and purification you (men) perform and keep, and all which you keep lawfully, and the pure and holy acts of worship which you perform in like manner, mindful of the yazads, I know it all'. (4) When I heard those words, I made deep obeisance to the Creator Ohrmazd. Then just Srosh conveyed me triumphantly and valorously to this carpeted place. May the Glory of the Good Religion of the Mazda-worshippers be victorious! (Text, with a complete English translation, by H. Jamaspji Asa and M. Haug, *The Book of Arda Viraf*.)

7 APOCALPYTIC TEXTS

7.1 ON THE COMING OF THE SAOSHYANT, FROM Yt. 19

Cf. 2.1.2. On making the world transfigured, frasha, i.e. bringing about Frasho-kereti, Frashegird, cf. 2.2.2. On the 'Living One' i.e. the Saoshyant cf. 2.2.9.3, 17.2. His name derives from Zarathushtra's words: 'May truth be embodied!' (2.2.9.16). Vispa-taurvairi is his virgin mother, cf. 7.2. Lake Kansaoya is the Hamun lake in south-east Iran, with which the legend of the Saoshyant evidently became associated in pre-Achaemenian times.

(10) . . . Ahura Mazda created many and good creatures . . . (11) in order that they shall make the world wonderful, . . . in order that the dead shall rise up, that the Living One, the Indestructible, shall come, the world be made wonderful at his wish. . . . (88) We worship mighty Khvarenah . . . , (89) which will accompany the victorious Saoshyant and also his other comrades, so that he may make the world wonderful. . . . (92–3) When Astvat-ereta comes out from Lake Kansaoya, messenger of Mazda Ahura, son of Vispa-taurvairi, brandishing the victorious weapon which . . . Kavi Vishtaspa bore to avenge Asha upon the enemy host, then he will there drive the Drug from the world of Asha. (94) He will gaze with eyes of wisdom, he will behold all creation, . . . he will gaze with eyes of sacrifice on the whole material world, and heedfully will he make the whole material world undying. (95) His comrades – those of the victorious Astvat-ereta – advance, thinking well, speaking well, acting well, upholding the Good Religion; and they will utter no false word with their tongues. Before them will flee ill-fated Aeshma of the bloody club. Asha will conquer the evil Drug, hideous, dark. (96) Aka Manah will also be overcome, Vohu Manah overcomes him. Overcome will be the falsely spoken word, the truly spoken word overcomes it. . . . Haurvatat and Ameretat will overcome both Hunger and Thirst. . . . Anra Mainyu of evil works will flee, bereft of power.

7.2 ON THE THREE WORLD SAVIOURS, FROM THE ZAND

This elaboration of the hope in the coming Saviour was presumably the work of scholar-priests, seeking to fill in the millennia of the 'world year' (see 1.8) with recurring cycles of events. Triplication is characteristic of Zoroastrianism, three being an auspicious number. Pahl. Kayansih = Av. Kansaoya.

(1) There were born to Zardusht three sons and three daughters. (The sons) were Isadvastar, Urvatatnar and Khvarshedchihr. . . . The three daughters were named Fren, Srit and Puruchist. . . . (2) Then there were three (other) sons of Zardusht . . . , namely Ushedar, Ushedarmah and the Soshyant. . . . As He

says: 'Three times Zardusht approached his wife, Hvovi. Each time his seed fell to the ground. The yazad Neryosang took all the light and power of that seed, and . . . it was consigned to Lake Kayansih, in the care of the Waters. . . . It is said that even now three lamps are seen shining at night in the depth of the lake. (3) And for each, when his own time comes, it will be thus: a virgin will go to Lake Kayansih to bathe; and the Glory (of Zardusht) will enter her body, and she will become with child. And so, one by one, the (three) will be born thus, each at his own time. (Put together from GBd. XXXV.56–60 and XXXIII.36–38; for the text with complete English translation see Bibliography A under B. T. Anklesaria.)

7.3 ON THE SEVEN AGES OF THE WORLD, AND THE COMING OF THE SAVIOURS, FROM THE ZAND OF VAHMAN YASHT

There are no ancient yashts to any of the Heptad; but some were eventually created, presumably after the introduction of the Zoroastrian calendar (see 1.7). Vohu Manah (Vahman), who had led the prophet to enlightenment (cf. 2.2.9, 5.2.4), was linked with prophetic wisdom; and it seems that at some stage (very possibly in the troubled period after Alexander's conquest) a text was put together in his honour out of ancient prophetic and apocalyptic materials. All that remains of this is its Zand. In this the 'prophecies' have been extended through the Parthian and Sasanian periods, down into Islamic times; and what may once have been lamentations over Macedonian conquerors, 'devs with dishevelled hair', have been adapted to the Arabs.

7.3.1 From ZVYt., ch. 3
For the kings named here see 1.9.1.

(6) Ohrmazd, the Holy Spirit (Spenag Menog), Creator of the material world, just, put the wisdom of all knowledge, in the form of water, into the hand of Zardusht . . . (7) And Zardusht drank of it, and the wisdom of all knowledge passed into Zardusht. (8) For seven days and nights Zardusht dwelt in the wisdom of Ohrmazd. . . . (11) And on the seventh day and night He took back the wisdom of all knowledge from Zardusht. (12) Zardusht supposed that he had beheld things in a pleasant dream sent by Ohrmazd. . . . (14) Ohrmazd said to Spitaman Zardusht: 'What have you beheld . . .?' (15–19) Zardusht said to Him: '. . . I beheld a tree on which there were seven branches: one of gold, one of silver, one of copper, one of brass, one of lead, one of steel and one of blended iron.' (20–1) Ohrmazd said: 'Spitaman Zardusht! this is what I declare. The trunk of the tree which you beheld is the worldly existence which I, Ohrmazd, created. The seven branches which you beheld are the seven times which are to come. (23) That of gold is the reign of King Vishtasp, when I and you shall confer about the religion and King Vishtasp will receive the religion. . . . (24) That of silver is the reign of Kay Ardashir [= the

Achaemenian Artaxerxes II], who will adorn the whole world, and make the religion current. (26) That of copper is the reign of Valakhsh the Arsacid, who will remove from the world the schisms which will exist. (25) That of brass is the reign of Ardashir [= the Sasanian Ardashir I], who will array and set right the world, and of King Shabuhr, who . . . will propagate salvation to the ends of the earth. . . . (27) That of lead is the reign of King Vahram Gor, who will make visible the spirit of joy, and Ahriman with his sorcerers will rush back to the darkness and gloom of hell. (28) That of steel is the reign of King Khusrow, son of Kavad, who will hold back from this religion the accursed Mazdak, son of Bamdad, adversary of the faith, together with other schismatics. (29) That of blended iron is the evil rule of devs with dishevelled hair, the seed of Eshm, at the end of your millennium, O Spitaman Zardusht!'

7.3.2 From ZVYt., ch. 4

The men in black from Khorasan are the supporters of the 'Abbasids (see 1.9.2.1), whose reign saw the irreversible eclipse of Zoroastrianism in Iran.

(1) Zardusht said: 'Creator of the material world, Holy Spirit! What will be the signs of that tenth century?' (2–3) Ohrmazd said: '. . . During that basest of times a hundred, a thousand, ten thousand kinds of devs with dishevelled hair will arrive, the seed of Eshm. (4) Those men of basest lineage will rush from the region of Khorasan upon the land of Iran, with banners uplifted and trappings all of black. . . . (7) Since they will burn and destroy many a thing – the houses of householders, the villages of villagers – prosperity and greatness, husbandry, fidelity to the faith, moderation, security, joy – all the things which I, Ohrmazd, created, and the pure religion of Mazda-worship, and the Vahram Fires which are established in their appointed places, all will come to naught. . . . (8) The large district will become a single town, the large town a single village, the large village a single household. . . . (10–11) These devs with dishevelled hair are deceivers . . . and of very bad religion. No treaty or pact . . . is to be made with them, . . . and the treaty which they make, they do not keep. (12) Through deceit and greed and misrule they will destroy these Iranian lands which I, Ohrmazd, created. (13) In that time, Spitaman Zardusht, all men will become deceivers, and great covenants will be altered. (14) Honour and affection and love for the soul will depart from the world. . . . (16) When your millennium will be at an end, Spitaman Zardusht, the sun's rays will be very level and low-slanting, and year and month and day will be shorter. (17) And the earth, Spendarmad, will contract. . . . (18–20) Crops will not yield seed, . . . and plants and bushes and trees will be small . . . ; and people will be born very stunted, and will have little skill or energy. . . . (41) . . . All people will worship greed and be of false religion. (42–6) It will not be possible for an auspicious cloud and a just wind to bring rain at its due time and season. Clouds and fog will darken the whole sky. A hot wind and a cold wind will come and carry off all fruits and grains of corn. The rain too will not fall at its due time, and it will rain noxious creatures rather than water. And the water of rivers and springs

will shrink and have no increase. (47–8) Camel and ox and sheep will be born much smaller and less sturdy. They will carry lighter loads, their fleece will be shorter, and their hides thinner. Their milk will not increase, and they will have little fat. The draft-ox will have small strength, and the swift horse will have little power and be able to carry little at a gallop. (49) At that harsh time, O Spitaman Zardusht, the people who wear the kusti at their waists will desire death as a boon, because of the evil demands of misrule and the many false judgments which they will encounter, by which their lives will become not worth living. . . . (57) The earth, Spendarmad, will open wide her mouth, and all jewels and metals will become visible. . . . (58) And lordship and rule will pass to non-Iranian slaves. . . . (60) They will rule so wrongfully that it will be all the same in their eyes, whether they kill a good and just man or a fly. . . . (66) That wicked Evil Spirit will be very oppressive and tyrannical, then when it becomes needful to destroy him.'

7.3.3 From ZVYt., ch. 6, 7

Chihrmiyan is a by-name of Pishyotan, Vishtaspa's immortal son, cf. 5.3.2.

(1) Zardusht asked Ohrmazd: 'O Ohrmazd! Holy Spirit, Creator of the material world, just! From where will they restore this Good Religion of the Mazda-worshippers? And by what means will they smite these devs with dishevelled hair, the seed of Eshm?' . . . (2) Ohrmazd replied: 'O Spitaman Zardusht! when the devs with dishevelled hair, the seed of Eshm, appear . . . Ushedar son of Zardusht will be born at Lake Frazdan (some call it Lake Kayansih). . . . (3) At thirty years of age he will come to confer with Me, Ohrmazd. . . . (19) And I, the Creator Ohrmazd, shall send Neryosang Yazad and the just Srosh to the fortress of Kang, . . . to Chihrmiyan, son of Vishtasp, the true restorer of the royal Glory of the religion, that they may say: "O illustrious Pishyotan! go forth to these Iranian lands which I, Ohrmazd, have created!" . . . (22) And illustrious Pishyotan will go forth, with 150 just men who are the disciples of Pishyotan. . . . They will advance with good thoughts, good words, good acts. They will consecrate the Hadhokht and Bayan services for Fire and the Waters, and they will praise Me, Ohrmazd, with the Amahraspands. . . . (27) And I, the Creator Ohrmazd, . . . shall bid the Amahraspands say to all the spiritual yazads: "Go forth! come to the aid of illustrious Pishyotan!" (28) Mihr of wide pastures and valiant Srosh and just Rashn and mighty Vahram and victorious Ashtat and the Glory of the Mazda-worshipping Religion will come at the command of Me, who am the Creator. . . . (30) They will smite the devs, who are the seed of darkness. . . . (39) Illustrious Pishyotan will reach these Iranian lands which I, Ohrmazd, created. . . . When the wicked see him, being of the seed of darkness, contemptible, they will be shattered.

7.3.4 From ZVYt., ch. 9

The coming of the second Saviour, Ushedarmah, has been omitted here. It repeats that of the first, except that the sun stands still for longer, etc.

(1–2) As regards Ushedar, ... at thirty years of age he will come to a conference with Me, Ohrmazd, and receive the Religion. When he departs from the conference, he will call to the swift-horsed sun: "Stand still!" (3–4) For ten days and nights the swift-horsed sun will stand still. When this happens, all the people of the world will abide in the Good Religion of the Mazda-worshippers. . . . (11) And then . . . through Ushedar creation will progress and grow stronger . . . ; (23) and then deceit and opposition will depart from this world. And thereafter the Soshyans will make creation pure again, and there will be the resurrection, and the final body.' (Text with complete English translation by B. T. Anklesaria, *Zand-i Vohuman Yasn*; complete pioneer English translation by E. W. West, *SBE*. V, 189–235.)

7.4 ON YIMA'S VAR, FROM VENDIDAD 2

According to the scholastic working out of the apocalyptic tradition, all events which took place at the beginning of history will have their resolution at Frashegird; and one happening then will be the opening of Yima's var, whose inhabitants will join in the final triumph of the good. The legend concerning the var is accordingly included in this section. It goes back, seemingly, to Indo-Iranian times (cf. 1.2.5, 2.1.2); but in western Iran, perhaps under the Medes, (see 1.9.1), it appears to have been contaminated by Mesopotamian legends about the flood and ark. This has produced a curious confusion, so that the 'var' (lit. 'enclosure, enclosed place') is both Yima's ancient subterranean kingdom and a fabricated place of refuge from a natural disaster. Eventually, having been given a Zoroastrian framework, the story was incorporated in the Vendidad.

(1) Zarathushtra asked Ahura Mazda: 'Ahura Mazda, Most Holy Spirit, Creator of the material world, just! To which man did you first speak, Ahura Mazda, other than to me, Zarathushtra? To whom did you first teach the Ahuric, Zarathushtrian religion?' (2) Then said Ahura Mazda: 'To fair Yima, possessed of good herds, O just Zarathushtra. . . . To him I taught the Ahuric, Zarathushtrian religion. (3) Then to him I said . . . : "Fair Yima, son of Vivahvant, make ready to recite and propagate my religion!" Then fair Yima answered me, O Zarathushtra: "I was not born nor taught to remember and propagate the religion." (4) Then to him I said, O Zarathushtra, I who am Ahura Mazda: "If, Yima, you are not ready to recite and propagate my religion, then increase my world, then enlarge my world. Then shall you make ready to be protector and guardian and watcher over my world." . . . (6) Then I, Ahura Mazda, gave him two tools, a golden goad and a gold-adorned whip. . . . (8) Then three hundred winters passed under Yima's rule. Then this earth became full for him of flocks and herds and men and dogs and birds and red burning fires. And the flocks and herds and men found no place (any more) upon it. (9)

Then I proclaimed to Yima: "Fair Yima, son of Vivahvant! Full is the earth, with the thronging of flocks and herds and men. . . . And the flocks and herds and men find no place (any more) upon it." (10) Then Yima went forth, to the light, to the south, along the path of the sun. He drove this earth on with the golden goad, he struck it with the whip, saying: "Beloved Spenta Armaiti! Go forth and stretch yourself for the bearing of flocks and herds and men." (11) Then Yima extended this earth by one-third more than it was before. Here the flocks and herds and men made a home for themselves, according to their wish and desire. . . . (12) Then six hundred winters passed under Yima's rule. Then this earth became full for him . . . . (15) Then Yima extended this earth by two-thirds . . . . (16) Then nine hundred winters passed under Yima's rule. Then this earth became full for him . . . . (19) Then Yima extended this earth by three-thirds. Here the flocks and herds and men made a home for themselves, according to their wish and desire . . . . (20) The Creator held an assembly together with the invisible yazatas, He, Ahura Mazda, being renowned in Airyanem Vaejah of the good Daiti. (21) Then to that assembly came shining Yima, possessed of good herds, together with the best of men, he being renowned in Airyanem Vaejah of the good Daiti. (22) Then said Ahura Mazda to Yima: 'Fair Yima, son of Vivahvant! Bad winters will come to the material world, therewith one harsh destructive winter. Bad winters will come to the material world, therewith the cloud will snow abundantly with snow, from the highest mountains to the depths of the Aredvi. (23) Then, O Yima, only a third part of the cattle will escape, whichever will be in the remotest places, whichever will be on the summits of mountains, in the valleys of rivers. . . . (24) Before that winter the land will have well cared-for pasture. Water in abundance will carry this away. Then after the melting of the snow, O Yima, it will be a marvel for the material world if here is seen the footprint of a sheep. (25) Then make that "var" with each of its four sides a stadium-length. At the same time fetch seed of small cattle and large cattle and men and dogs and red burning fires. Then make that "var", a stadium long on each of its four sides, to be a dwelling place for men, . . . an abiding place for cattle. (26) At the same time let water flow along a course half a stadium in length. At the same time lay out meadows. At the same time put up houses . . . . (27) At the same time fetch the seed of all men and women who are the tallest, best and fairest upon earth. At the same time fetch the seed of all kinds of cattle which are the largest, best and fairest upon earth. (28) At the same time fetch the seed of all flowers which are the . . . most fragrant upon earth. At the same time fetch the seed of all foods which are the most delicious . . . upon earth. Have these in pairs, imperishably, for as long as there shall be men in the "var". (29) Let there not be the . . . hump-backed there, . . . not the mad, . . . nor the leper set apart, . . . nor those with any other marks which are the mark of Anra Mainyu set in men. (30) . . . Fetch into the highest *section (of the "var") the seed of a thousand men and women, into the middle one six hundred, into the lowest one three hundred. Go over the "var" with the golden goad, touch the "var" lightly. For light *put in a door, a window, ...' (31) Then Yima thought: 'How shall I make the "var" of which Ahura Mazda has spoken to me?' Then Ahura Mazda said to Yima: 'Fair Yima, son of Vivahvant! Trample this earth asunder with your heels, thrust it apart with your hands . . .'. (32) Then Yima did as Ahura Mazda wanted of him. . . . (39) 'Creator of the material world, just! which will be these luminaries, O just Ahura Mazda, which will give light there in the "*var" which Yima made?' (40) Then Ahura Mazda said: 'Self-governing luminaries, not everlasting. Once (in a year) they are seen setting and rising – stars and moon and sun. (41) And those (in the "var") regard a year as a day. After every forty years each human pair will give birth to twins, a female and a male; and so with the animal species. And those men lead the best of lives in the "var" which Yima made.' (42) 'Creator of the material world, just! Who shall there propagate the Mazda-worshipping religion, in this "var" which Yima has made?' Then said Ahura Mazda: 'The raven, O Spitama Zarathushtra'. (43) 'Creator of the material world, just! Who is the lord and judge of its inhabitants?' Then said Ahura Mazda: 'Urvatatnara, O Zarathushtra.'

8 A ZOROASTRIAN HERESY: ZURVANISM

This is the only considerable Zoroastrian heresy, evolved probably by Persian magi in the late fifth century B.C. It was a monism, based on a new exegesis of Y. 30 = 2.2.2.3, whereby Ahura Mazda and Angra Mainyu were seen as twin sons of Time, Zurvan (a minor divinity of late Younger Avestan texts). The earliest reference to it, by the Greek historian Theopompus, shows it linked with a special version of the 'world year'. The heresy was, it seems, adopted as the true orthodoxy by the late Achaemenian kings, and was adhered to by their Persian successors, the Sasanians; but its teachings have nevertheless to be pieced together from scattered sources. Because the Zurvanites regarded Ahura Mazda as Creator of all things good, under the remote Zurvan, they were able to worship together with the orthodox in full orthopraxy, using the same liturgies; and this seems to have prevented serious schism. The heresy disappears after the tenth century A.C.

8.1 A CITATION FROM THEOPOMPUS (BORN c. 380 B.C.)

Theopompus says that, according to the Magians, for three thousand years alternately the one god will dominate the other and be dominated, and that for another three thousand years they will fight and make war, until one smashes up the domain of the other. In the end Hades shall perish and men shall be happy; neither shall they need sustenance nor shall they cast a shadow, while the god who will have brought this about shall have quiet and shall rest, not for a long while indeed for a god, but for such time as would be reasonable for a man who falls asleep. Such is the mythology of the Magians. (Trans. J. Gwyn Griffiths, *Plutarch's De Iside et Osiride*, ch. 46, pp. 193–5.)

8.2 VERSIONS OF THE MYTH OF ZURVAN AND HIS TWIN SONS

8.2.1 From an Armenian source

This is probably derived from a lost Pahlavi document of the fourth century A.C.

(1) Behold what (Zardusht) said concerning the begetting of Ormazd and Ahriman. When nothing at all yet existed, neither heaven nor earth nor any other creature which is in heaven or on earth, there existed the great god Zurvan, whose name is to be interpreted as 'fate' or 'fortune'. For one thousand years he offered sacrifice in order that he might perhaps have a son who would be called Ormazd, and who would make the heavens and earth and all which they contain. (2) For one thousand years he offered sacrifice. Then he pondered in his heart and said: 'Shall I truly have profit of these sacrifices, and shall I have a son called Ormazd? Or do I strive thus in vain?' And even while he reflected in this manner, Ormazd and Ahriman were conceived in the womb: Ormazd through the offered sacrifice, Ahriman through the doubt. (3) When he became aware of this, Zurvan said: 'Lo, two sons are in the womb. Whichever of them appears swiftly before me, him I shall make king.' Ormazd, being aware of their father's purposes, revealed them to Ahriman. . . . (4) And Ahriman, having heard this, pierced the womb and came forth and presented himself to his father. And Zurvan, beholding him, knew not who he might be, and asked 'Who are you?' And he said: 'I am your son.' Zurvan answered him: 'My son is fragrant and bright, and you, you are dark and noisome.' And while they spoke thus, Ormazd, being born at the due time, bright and fragrant, came and presented himself before Zurvan. And Zurvan, beholding him, knew that he was his son, Ormazd. And taking the rods which he held in his hand, and with which he had offered sacrifice, he gave them to Ormazd and said: 'Until now it is I who have offered sacrifice for you. Henceforth it is you who will offer it for me.' (5) And while Zurvan was giving the rods to Ormazd and blessing him, Ahriman, having drawn near to Zurvan, said to him: 'Have you not made this vow, that whichever of my two sons shall first come before me, him I shall make king?' And Zurvan, that he should not violate his oath, said to Ahriman: 'O false and injurious one! The kingship shall be granted you for nine thousand years; and I shall establish Ormazd as ruler over you. And after nine thousand years Ormazd shall reign and do all that he will wish to do.' (6) Then Ormazd and Ahriman set to fashioning the creatures. And all that Ormazd created was good and straight, and all that Ahriman made was evil and crooked. (From the

Armenian Christian apologist Eznik of Kolb; French translation by J. P. de Menasce, see Zaehner, *Zurvan*, text F 1.)

8.2.2 From a Christian Syriac treatise of the late sixth century A.C.

The three additional gods are thought to be hypostases of Avestan attributes of Zurvan: arshokara, 'who makes virile'; frashokara, 'who makes splendid'; *zarokara, 'who makes old'. Zurvan was thus worshipped as a quaternity.

Zardusht, the Persian magus, he also founded a school in Persia, at the time of king Bashtasp [i.e. Vishtasp]. He drew many pupils to himself, who, being blind in spirit, readily agreed with him in his errors. He taught first of all the existence of four gods, Ashoqar, Frashoqar, Zaroqar and Zarvan; but he did not say what were their undertakings. Then he admitted of two other gods, Hormizd and Ahriman, saying that both of them had been begotten by Zarvan. Hormizd is wholly good; Ahriman is wholly bad. These are the gods who made this world. The good god created the good creatures, and the evil god created the evil creatures. (From the French translation of J. Bidez and F. Cumont, *Les mages hellénisés*, Vol. II, 100; cf. Zaehner, *Zurvan*, 439–40.)

8.2.3 From the Second 'Ulema-i Islam, probably twelfth century A.C.

A Persian Zoroastrian text, see 1.1.1.17.

(1) . . . Six hundred years after Yazdegird (III) certain learned men of Islam put several questions to one versed in the Religion. . . . They asked: 'What do you say about the resurrection? Do you believe in it or not?' The Mobadan mobad replied: 'We believe in the resurrection. The Day of Judgment shall be.' (2) Then the learned men of Islam asked: 'How has the world been created? . . .'. The religious dasturs of the time replied: '. . . It is thus revealed in the religion of Zardusht that except Time all other things have been created. Time is the Creator. Time has no bound . . . . It has always been and shall ever be. And no one endowed with wisdom will say whence Time has come. Yet despite all its greatness there was none who called it Creator. Why? Because it had not yet made the creation. (3) Then it created fire and water. When it brought them together, Ohrmazd came into existence. Time was both Creator and Lord with regard to the creation it had made. (4) Ohrmazd was bright, pure, fragrant, beneficent, and He had power over all good things. Then when He looked into the lowest depth, He saw Ahriman 96,000 miles away, black, foul, stinking and maleficent. Ohrmazd marvelled, for this was a terrible enemy. When Ohrmazd saw that enemy He thought, 'I must utterly root out this enemy'; and He planned what and how many instruments (were needed). Then He began. Whatever Ohrmazd did, He did with the help of Time. . . . Ohrmazd made manifest Time of Long Dominion, which has the measure of 12,000 years. (5) If someone says, 'Since (Time) possessed all this mastery, why then did it create Ahriman?' we said in the beginning that both Ohrmazd and Ahriman came into existence from Time. Every group speaks of this in a different way. One party says that it (Time) created Ahriman so that Ohrmazd

should know that Time has power over all things. . . . Another says: 'What pain or pleasure has Time from the evil of Ahriman or the goodness of Ohrmazd?' Another group says that it (Time) created Ohrmazd and Ahriman so that it might mingle good and evil, in order that things of diverse kinds might come into existence.' (M. R. Unvala, *Rivayat II*, 80–2; trans. Dhabhar, *Rivayats*, 449–53, and Zaehner, *Zurvan*, 409–12.)

9 DOGMATIC PASSAGES FROM NINTH-CENTURY PAHLAVI BOOKS

Dogmatic works of the Islamic period are characterised by the words 'one must be without doubt', and similar phrases, as the writers strove to stiffen their co-religionists against Muslim proselytising and persecution.

9.1 FROM 'SELECTED PRECEPTS OF THE ANCIENT SAGES'

9.1.1 A brief catechism

For the opening words of the catechism proper cf. 2.2.9.7.

(1) In conformity with the revelation of the religion the ancient sages – those with first knowledge of the faith – have said that each man or woman who attains the age of fifteen should know these things: 'Who am I? Whose am I? From where have I come? To where shall I return? Of what stock and lineage am I? What is my duty on earth, and what my spiritual reward? Am I come from the spiritual world, or was I (simply) of this world? Do I belong to Ohrmazd or to Ahriman? To the yazads or to the devs? To the good or to the bad? Am I a human being or a dev? How many are the paths, and which is my religion? Where lies my profit, where my loss? Who is my friend, who my foe? Is there one first principle or are there two? From whom is goodness, from whom badness? From whom light and from whom darkness? From whom fragrance and from whom stench? From whom justice and from whom injustice? From whom compassion, from whom pitilessness?' (2) . . . by the path of wisdom one must know without doubt: 'I am from the spiritual world, I was not (simply) of this world. I was created, I did not (simply) exist. I belong to Ohrmazd, not to Ahriman. I belong to the yazads, not to the devs, to the good, not to the bad. I am a human being, not a dev, a creature of Ohrmazd, not of Ahriman. My stock and lineage is from Gayomard. My mother is Spendarmad, my father Ohrmazd. My humanity is from Mahre and Mahryane, who were the first offspring and seed of Gayomard. (3) And fulfilling my duty and obligations means to believe that Ohrmazd is, was, and evermore shall be, that His kingdom is eternal, and that He is infinite and pure; and that Ahriman will

cease to exist and be destroyed; and to hold that I myself belong to Ohrmazd and the Amahraspands; and to keep from thought of Ahriman and the devs.'

9.1.2 A list of man's duties on earth

(4) Man's first (duty) on earth is to profess the religion and to practise and worship according to it; not to turn from it, but to have belief in the Good Religion of the Mazda-worshippers ever in mind; to distinguish profit from loss, sin from virtue, goodness from badness, light from darkness, Mazda-worship from dev-worship. (5) Second, he should take a wife and beget earthly progeny. He should be diligent in this and not neglectful of it. (6) Third, he should turn the soil into ploughground and cultivate it. (7) Fourth, he should treat domestic animals properly. (8) Fifth, a third of his days and nights he should attend the priests' school and inquire after the wisdom of just men; a third of his days and nights he should work and create prosperity; and a third of his days and nights he should eat and take pleasure and rest. (9) He should have no doubt about this, that profit is from virtue and harm from sin; that 'my friend is Ohrmazd, my enemy Ahriman'; and that the path of religion is one. (10) There is one path of good thoughts, good words and good acts, that of the light and purity and infinity of the Creator Ohrmazd, who ever was and shall be. (11) And there is one path of evil thoughts, evil words and evil acts, that of the darkness and finiteness and total evil and death and badness of the wicked Evil Spirit, who once was not in this creation, and who again will not be in the creation of Ohrmazd, and who in the end will be destroyed. (12) And this truly one must not doubt, that there are two first principles, one the Creator and one the Destroyer. (13) The Creator is Ohrmazd, from whom is all goodness and all light. (14) And the Destroyer is the wicked Evil Spirit, who is all badness and deals in death, the lying Druj. (15) And about these several things one must not doubt: that except for the Soshyant and the seven heroes (who will help him) all men are mortal; (16) and that the soul will be severed (from the body) and the body will decay. One must not doubt the judgment after the three nights, . . . the crossing of the Chinvat Bridge, the coming of the Soshyant, the raising of the dead and the future body. (17) . . . One must preserve the doctrines of the ancient faith, and maintain one's thoughts in righteousness, one's tongue in truth, and one's hands in doing good. (18) With all good men one must behave like a true Iranian. (19) (There must be) peace and concord in all one's virtuous undertakings. (20) With all good people one must act according to just laws and the pure religion. . . . (22) Virtuous acts done for justice's sake weigh more than those done for one's own sake, and through them salvation is more assured. (23) And (it should be) said: 'I am without doubt concerning the Good Religion which the Mazda-worshippers have accepted. Not for love of body or soul, not for better life or longer life, not for threatened death, will I renounce the Good Religion of the Mazda-worshippers. I am without doubt concerning it. I do not praise other religions, nor honour them, nor believe in them.' . . . (26) . . . Three paths are set in the body of man. (27) On these three paths three divinities have

their dwelling, and three demons make inroad. In thought Vahman has his dwelling and Eshm makes inroad. In speech Wisdom has his dwelling, and Desire makes inroad. In act the Holy Spirit has his dwelling, and the Evil Spirit makes inroad. (28) On these three paths a man must stand firm. He must not relinquish his heavenly reward for the sake of goods and chattels, or worldly desires. . . . (30) Further, he must be grateful; and by gratitude this is meant, that he should be thankful that he has it in his own power to save his soul from hell. (31) For when a man passes from the loins of his father into the womb of his mother, then Astvihad casts a noose invisibly around his neck. All his life long that noose cannot be taken off his neck, either by a good spirit or a bad one. (32) But after his death that noose falls from the neck of a just man because of his own good acts, but the wicked man is led away to hell by that same noose. . . . (34) A father and mother should teach a child these various duties before he is fifteen years old. And when these various duties have been taught him, then every duty which the child performs is as if the parents performed it. And if they have not been taught, the sins which the child commits (even) after he reaches maturity go to the parents' account. (From Chidag Andarz i Poryotkeshan, text in J. M. Jamasp-Asana (ed.), *The Pahlavi texts contained in the Codex MK*, Pt. II, 41–6; English translation of the whole text by R. C. Zaehner, *The Teachings of the Magi*, 20–8, and by M. F. Kanga.)

9.2 FROM SHKAND-GUMANIG VIZAR, THE 'DOUBT-DISPELLING EXPOSITION'

A book written in the ninth century A.C. by Mardanfarrokh, a Zoroastrian layman, 'for students and novices'. It survives only in a Pazand version with Sanskrit translation made by Neryosang Dhaval, an eminent Parsi scholar-priest, in the late eleventh or early twelfth century, cf. 1.1.1.18.

9.2.1 From SGV., ch. 1

(1–6) In the name of Ohrmazd the Lord, the most great and wise, all-ruling, all-knowing, all-powerful, who is in truth spirit among spirits. From His selfhood, single in unity, He created infallibly. And through His matchless power He brought into being the seven highest Amahraspands, and all the yazads, invisible and visible; and the seven physical creations, which are man, beneficent animals, fire, metal, earth, water, plants. And He created man to rule over the (other) creations in fulfilment of His will.

9.2.2 From SGV., ch. 2

(3–5) It was asked: 'Why did Ahriman assail the light, and how was it possible, when he is not of like nature with it, since we always see that whatever is not of like nature avoids what is of different nature, even as water fire?' The answer is this: Ahriman's assault on the light had his different nature for its actual cause: on account of the lust to destroy which was always part of his nature he smote what was of different nature.

9.2.3 From SGV., ch. 3

(1–7) As for the question 'Why did Ohrmazd the Creator not restrain Ahriman from doing and desiring evil, since He is able to do so? – and if we say He is not able to do so, then He is not perfect, for His power is limited', the answer is this: Ahriman's evil action comes from the evil nature and evil will which is his constant property, as the Druj. The omnipotence of Ohrmazd affects all that which can be and which is determined. As for what cannot be, there is no question of being able or not able to do it. (16–21) Were I to say that Ohrmazd the Creator had the power to restrain Ahriman from the wickedness which is his constant nature (this would mean that) it is possible to turn that devilish nature into a divine one, and the divine into a devilish; and that darkness can be made light, and light darkness. Those who say that essence itself can be changed know nothing of essence, and account wolf and reptile as beneficent.

9.2.4 From SGV., ch. 8

(1–14) Further, concerning the existence of a distinct contrary principle, this is manifest through good and evil existing in the world, and especially through the good agent having His own limitation. Thus there is darkness and light, knowledge and ignorance, fragrance and stench, life and death, sickness and health, justice and injustice, oppression and freedom, and other antagonistic factors which undoubtedly exist in every country and land at all times . . . And nowhere and never can it be said that good and evil can change their own nature essentially. . . . (18–23) The dissimilarity of good and evil, light and darkness, and other essentially different things is a difference not of function but of substance. This can be seen from the fact that their natures cannot combine and are mutually destructive, so that where goodness is, evil undoubtedly is not; and when light has entered, darkness is expelled. Similarly there are other antagonisms, incompatible and mutually destructive because of their different natures. Thus in the material world there is observable the essential antagonism and mutual destructiveness of things. . . . (35–6) Since we have seen in the material world contrariety of substance, and mutual toleration or destruction, there can be no doubt that it is the same in the things of the spiritual world, which are the root of what is material. . . . (39–40) The reason and cause for the wise activity of the Creator, who made visible the creating of creatures is the existence of the Adversary. . . . (49–51) Since the wise Creator, all-knowing and of perfect power, is wholly perfect in Himself, then He has no need to seek advantage or increase from without. Therefore we must recognise that the reason and cause for His actions is all of one kind, namely to repel and ward off the harm which there might be from the external Adversary and Destroyer, which is indeed the reason and cause for creation. (52–6) This too must be recognised, that the wise Creator wills only what is good, and His will is wholly good, and He created creation in accordance with His will. The fulfilment of the will of a wise Being who wills only what is good must be achieved through the destruction and annihilation of wickedness, for until wickedness is annihilated, He who wills what is good has not perfectly realised His will. . . . (59) Further, the goodness of the wise Creator is manifest through the fact that He creates, cherishes and protects, and has ordained and taught the way of repelling evil and the means of defending oneself against sin. . . . (64–8) Suffering and death are the destroyers of the body, not the Creator who wills what is good, and who preserves and cherishes the body. This is manifest from this, that the wise Creator neither repents nor regrets His acts, nor does He destroy His own creations or make them ineffective, for He is wise and aware of all. . . . (71–80) And He being wise plans with wise and skilful act to ward off from His creatures the one whose doings are stupid and who is ignorant of their outcome. He whose doings are stupid is enclosed and entangled and has fallen into the trap (of this world). For it is evident that a moving and living essence cannot be warded off or destroyed within a limitless void, nor can there be security from his assault until he is entangled and hedged in and made captive. In entanglement and captivity are the means to inflict pain and grievous punishment. But until he is fully conscious of his pain and fully aware of his own ignorant activity, his thoughts are falsely deluded as to what has befallen him. His realisation of suffering is (through) the complete power of the all-powerful Creator. And after his complete realisation of suffering and pain under the complete power of the wise Creator, (the Creator) casts him helpless into the limitless void. Then the good creation will have no fear of him; it will be immortal and free from harm. Perfect is the skill and wisdom of the omniscient Creator of good creatures, and (perfect) his foreknowledge of the means. . . . (89–102) The existence of evil as distinct in principle from good means that neither is the cause of the other, for both exist in their own essence, as is manifest from the continual assault from their mutual opposition. If someone were to say that since there is a multiplicity of contraries, such as good and evil, darkness and light, fragrance and stench, life and death, sickness and health, pleasure and pain, and many others, so there should be a multiplicity and diversity of principles, then the answer is that even if the contraries have many names and are of many kinds, yet all are comprised under two names, and these two names, the seeds comprising all the rest, are good and evil. The diverse names and species are developments from these two seeds, and there is nothing which is not comprised in these two names. There has not been, nor will be, anything which is neither good nor bad, or a mixture of the two. Hence it is abundantly clear that there are two principles, not more, and also that good cannot proceed from evil, nor evil from good. (103–10) And from this it must be recognised that what is perfect and complete in goodness cannot produce evil. If it could, it would not be perfect; for if a thing is said to be perfect, there is no room (in it) for another thing; and if there is no room in it for another thing, another thing cannot proceed from it. If God is perfect in goodness and wisdom, then ignorance and evil cannot come from Him. If they could come from Him, He would not be perfect; and if He were not perfect, He should not be praised as God and perfectly good. . . . (117–23) If someone should say: 'I constantly see both good and evil proceeding from a single substance, such as man, when he acts,' this is because man is not perfect in any single respect. Because he is not perfect in goodness, evil proceeds from him; and because he is not perfect in health, he falls sick, and therefore dies. For the cause of death is the conflict of two opposing propensities in one substance; and where there are two conflicting propensities in one substance, sickness and death result. (124–34) If someone should say: 'good and evil are actions, which do not exist until they are performed', then the answer is that an action can no more exist without an agent than a propensity without a substance, for it is acknowledged that its existence and disposition cannot be of itself. For when Wrath (Eshm) lays hold of a man, Vahman is far from there; and when Vahman is enthroned, Wrath is not there. And when a man utters a lie, truth is far from there, and that man is called a liar. And when he speaks the truth, falsehood is not enthroned there, and that man is called truthful. In the same way, when sickness comes, health is not there; and when health has come, sickness departs. For there can be substance which does not change, but there can be no change without substance. (Complete Pazand and Sanskrit texts published by H. J. Jamasp-Asana and E. W. West; pioneer English translation by E. W. West, *SBE*. XXIV; transcribed Pazand text with French translation by P. J. de Menasce.)

10 HISTORICAL TEXTS

10.1 FROM THE ACHAEMENIAN PERIOD

10.1.1 From the inscriptions of Achaemenian kings
See 1.1.2.1. These inscriptions are carved in Old Persian in cuneiform script. Behistun is a mountain near Hamadan; Naqsh-i Rustam is a sheer mountain cliff near Persepolis (the city founded by Darius) in which the tombs of the early kings of his line were hollowed out.
10.1.1.1 Darius the Great (522–486 B.C.), Behistun
(IV.61–9) Says Darius the King: 'For this reason Ahuramazda bore (me) aid, and the other gods who are, because I was not disloyal, I was not a follower of the Lie (Drauga, = Av. Drug), I did not do wrong – neither I nor my family. I walked in justice. Neither to the weak nor to the mighty did I do wrong. . . . You who shall be king hereafter, the man who follows the Lie or who shall do wrong – be not a friend to them, (but) punish them well.

10.1.1.2 Darius, Naqsh-i Rustam a

(1–8) A great god is Ahuramazda, who created this earth, who created yonder sky, who created man, who created happiness for man, who made Darius king, one king of many, one lord of many.... (31–4) When Ahuramazda saw this earth turbulent then he bestowed it on me, he made me king.... (48–60) This which has been done, all that by the will of Ahuramazda I did. Ahuramazda bore me aid, until I did the work. Me may Ahuramazda protect from harm, and my royal house, and this land. This I pray of Ahuramazda, this may Ahuramazda grant me! O man, that which is the command of Ahuramazda, let this not seem hateful to you. Do not leave the right path, do not rebel!

10.1.1.3 Darius, Naqsh-i Rustam b

(1–21) A great god is Ahuramazda, who created this excellent work which is seen, who created happiness for man, who bestowed wisdom and activity upon Darius the King. Says Darius the king: By the favour of Ahuramazda I am of such a sort that I am a friend to right, I am not a friend to wrong. It is not my desire that the weak man should have wrong done to him by the mighty; nor is that my desire, that the mighty man should have wrong done to him by the weak. What is right, that is my desire. I am not a friend to the wicked man. I am not hot-tempered. What things develop in my anger, I hold firmly in check by my thinking power.... The man who co-operates, him according to his co-operative action do I thus reward. Who does harm, him according to the damage do I thus punish. It is not my desire that a man should do harm; nor indeed is that my desire, if he should do harm, he should not be punished.

10.1.1.4 Darius, Persepolis d

(1–5) Great Ahuramazda, greatest of gods – he created Darius the King, he bestowed on him the kingdom. By the favour of Ahuramazda Darius is king.... (12–22) Says Darius the King: May Ahuramazda bear me aid, with all the gods. And may Ahuramazda protect this land from an enemy army, from famine, from the Lie! ... This I pray for as a boon from Ahuramazda, with all the gods!

10.1.1.5 Xerxes (486–465 B.C.), Persepolis h

(13–16) Says Xerxes the King: By the will of Ahuramazda these are the countries of which I was king.... (35–41) And among these countries there was a place where previously Daivas [= Av. Daeva] were worshipped. Then by the will of Ahuramazda I destroyed that sanctuary of Daivas, and I proclaimed: 'Daivas shall not be worshipped!' Where earlier Daivas were worshipped, there I worshipped Ahuramazda with due order and rites.... (46–54) You who shall be hereafter, if you shall think: 'Happy may I be when living, and blessed when dead,' respect that law which Ahuramazda has established. Worship Ahuramazda with due order and rites!

10.1.1.6 Artaxerxes III (358–338 B.C.), Persepolis a

(21–6) Says Artaxerxes the King: This stone staircase was built by me in my time.... Me may Ahuramazda and Mithra (and) the Baga protect, and this country, and what has been built by me.

(Translation, with minor changes, of R. G. Kent, *Old Persian*, 137–40, 135–6, 151–2, 156.)

10.1.2 From Greek writings of the Achaemenian period
10.1.2.1 From Herodotus' *History* (completed before 445 B.C.), Bk. I

Herodotus was born a Persian subject in Asia Minor c. 484. His informants on Persian religion were evidently Persian men of rank whom he knew in his homeland. There are small misunderstandings, e.g. 'the song of the birth of the gods' (132) may well represent an Avestan yasht. The magi (140) themselves offered the sacrifice of beneficent animals, and also tried to fulfil the general duty of killing creatures regarded as belonging to Ahriman, cf. 10.5.2.9. The mountain sacrifices described here have been maintained in their essentials down to the present century by Zoroastrians in rural Iran, see Boyce, Persian Stronghold, 243 ff.

(1) (131) As to the usages of the Persians, I know them to be these. It is not their custom to make and set up statues and temples and altars . . . ; but they call the whole circle of heaven Zeus [i.e. Ahuramazda], and to him they offer sacrifice on the highest peaks of the mountains; they sacrifice also to the sun and moon and earth and fire and water and winds. These are the only gods to whom they have ever sacrificed from the beginning. . . . (132) And this is their fashion of sacrifice to the aforesaid gods: when about to sacrifice they neither build altars nor kindle fire, they use no libations, nor music, nor fillets, nor barley meal; but to whomsoever of the gods a man will sacrifice, he leads the beast to an open space, and then calls on the god, himself wearing a crown on his cap, of myrtle for choice. To pray for blessings for himself alone is not lawful for the sacrificer; rather he prays that it may be well with the king and all the Persians; for he reckons himself among them. He then cuts the victim limb from limb into portions, and having boiled the flesh spreads the softest grass [i.e. the strewed baresman], trefoil by choice, and places all of it on this. When he has so disposed it a magus comes near and chants over it the song of the birth of the gods, as the Persian tradition relates it; for no sacrifice can be offered without a magus. Then after a little while the sacrificer carries away the flesh and uses it as he pleases. (2) (136) After valour in battle it is most reckoned as manly merit to show the greatest number of sons. . . . They educate their boys [i.e. noblemen's sons] from five to twenty years old, and teach them three things only, riding and archery and truth-telling. . . . (3) (137) . . . it is a praiseworthy law too which suffers not the king himself to slay any man for one offence, nor any other Persian for one offence to do incurable hurt to one of his servants. Not till reckoning shows that the offender's wrongful acts are more and greater than his services may a man give vent to his anger. . . . (4) (138) Moreover of what they may not do neither may they speak. They hold lying to be foulest of all, and next to that debt; for which they have many other reasons, but this in especial, that the debtor must needs (so they say) speak some falsehood. . . . Rivers they

chiefly reverence; they will neither make water nor spit nor wash their hands therein, nor suffer anyone so to do. . . . (5) (140) But there are other matters concerning the dead which are secretly and obscurely told – how the dead bodies of Persians are not buried before they have been mangled by bird or dog. That this is the way of the magi I know for a certainty; for they do not conceal the practice. . . . These magi . . . kill with their own hands every creature, save only dogs and men; they kill all alike, ants and snakes, creeping and flying things, and take much pride therein.

10.1.2.2 From Xenophon's Cyropaedia (written c. 365 B.C.)

Xenophon fought for Cyrus the Younger in his rebellion in 401 against his brother Artaxerxes II. In the 'Cyropaedia', a romance about Cyrus the Great, he appears to draw on what he learnt then about the Persians.

(1) (I.2.6) The boys go to school and give their time to learning justice and righteousness: they will tell you they come for that purpose, and the phrase is as natural with them as it is for us to speak of lads learning their letters. The masters spend the chief part of the day in deciding cases for their pupils: for in this boy-world, as in the grown-up world without, occasions of indictment are never far to seek. There will be charges, we know, of picking and stealing, of violence, of fraud, of calumny, and so forth. The case is heard and the offender, if shown to be guilty, is punished. (7) Nor does he escape who is found to have accused one of his fellows unfairly. . . . The culprit convicted of refusing to repay a debt of kindness when it was fully in his power meets with severe chastisement. They reason that the ungrateful man is the most likely to forget his duty to the gods, to his parents, to his fatherland, and his friends. . . . (8) Further, the boys are instructed in temperance and self-restraint. . . . Then they are taught to obey their rulers, and here . . . nothing is of greater value than the studied obedience to authority manifested by their elders everywhere. Continence in meat and drink is another branch of instruction.

10.1.2.3 From the Alcibiades (written some time after 374 B.C.)

A work emanating from Plato's Academy.

(I.121) When the (Persian princes) are seven years of age they are given horses and have riding lessons, and they begin to follow the chase. And when the boy reaches fourteen years he is taken over by the royal tutors, as they call them there: these are four men chosen as the most highly esteemed among the Persians of mature age, namely the wisest one, the justest one, the most temperate one, and the bravest one. The first of these teaches him the Magian lore of Zoroaster, son of Horomazes, and that is the worship of the gods: he teaches him also what pertains to a king. The justest teaches him to be truthful all his life long; the most temperate, not to be mastered by even a single pleasure, in order that he may be accustomed to be a free man and a veritable king, who is first master of all that is in him, not the slave; while the bravest trains him to be fearless and undaunted, telling him that to be daunted is to be enslaved.

10.1.2.4 A citation from Theopompus (born *c*. 380 B.C.)

And yet even Plato brings back Armenius in bodily form from Hades to the land of the living. And Zoroaster prophesies that some day there will be a resurrection of all the dead. Theopompus knows of this and is himself the source of information concerning it for the other writers. (Citation by Aeneas of Gaza, *Theophrastus*, 77; text in Jackson, *Zoroaster*, 248; trans. in Fox and Pemberton, 109.)

10.1.2.5 A citation from Aristotle (died 322 B.C.)

Aristotle in the first book of his work *On Philosophy* says that the magi are more ancient even that the Egyptians, and that according to them there are two first principles, a good spirit and an evil spirit, one called Zeus and Oromasdes, the other Hades and Areimanus. (*The Works of Aristotle*, trans. into English, ed. D. Ross, Vol. XII, *Select Fragments*, Oxford, 1952, p. 7, fragment 6.)

10.2 FROM THE PARTHIAN PERIOD

The Parthian kings left no long inscriptions. Business records recovered from their royal city of Nisa in the north-east of ancient Iran, now Soviet Central Asia, provide the earliest evidence for the secular use of the Zoroastrian calendar. On religious observances of their time see 4.1.3, 4.1.5, 4.4.3; for Parthian transmission of religious traditions see 5.3.2.

10.2.1 From 'Of Isis and Osiris' by Plutarch (lived *c*. 46–120 A.C.)

The following account contains a reference to occult practices, which presumably stood in relation to orthodox Zoroastrian observances as did the 'black mass' to accepted Christian rites.

(1) (46) This is the view of the majority and of the wisest; for some believe that there are two gods who are rivals, as it were, in art, the one being the creator of good, the other of evil; others call the better of these a god and his rival a daemon, as, for example, Zoroaster the Magian, who lived, so they record, five thousand years before the Siege of Troy. He used to call the one Horomazes and the other Areimanius, and showed also that the former was especially akin, among objects of perception, to light, and the latter, on the contrary, to darkness and ignorance, while in between the two was (Mithres) Mithras; and this is why the Persians call Mithres the Mediator. He also taught that votive- and thank-offerings should be made to Horomazes, but gloomy offerings to Areimanius, and those intended to avert evil. For they pound a certain herb called *omomi* in a mortar, invoking Hades and darkness, and then after mixing with it the blood of a slain wolf, they take it out to a sunless spot and throw it away. They believe that among plants too, some belong to the good god and others to the evil daemon, and that among animals some, such as dogs, birds and land hedgehogs, belong to the good god, whereas water-rats belong to the bad deity, and for this reason they regard as happy

whoever kills a great number of them. (2) (47) But they (the Persians) also relate many mythical details about the gods, and the following are instances. Horomazes is born from the purest light and Areimanius from darkness, and they are at war with one another. The former (Horomazes) created six gods, the first being god of good will, the second god of truth, the third god of good order, and the others gods of wisdom and wealth, the sixth being the creator of pleasure in beautiful things. The other (Areimanius) created an equal number as rivals to these. Then Horomazes, having magnified himself to three times his size, removed himself as far from the sun as the sun is distant from the earth, and adorned the heaven with stars; and one star, Sirius, he established above all others as a guardian and watcher. Twenty-four other gods were created by him and put into an egg. Those who were created from Areimanius were of equal number, and they pierced through the egg . . . and so it comes about that good and evil are mixed. There will come the destined time when Areimanius, the bringer of plague and famine, must needs be utterly destroyed and obliterated by these. The earth shall be flat and level and one way of life and one government shall arise of all men, who shall be happy and speak the same language. (Trans. J. Gwyn Griffiths, *Plutarch's De Iside et Osiride*, 191–3.)

10.3 FROM THE SASANIAN PERIOD

10.3.1 From the Letter of Tansar, third century A.C.
The core of this document appears to be a genuine letter written by the Persian high priest (herbad) under Ardashir I to a vassal king of the Parthian Ardavan V, whom Ardashir had overthrown. The letter was evidently revised in the sixth century under Khusrow I Anoshiravan, as a useful piece of propaganda. The legend that the faith had fallen into neglect under the Arsacids, and was restored by Ardashir, belongs to this later period. The letter was translated into Arabic in the ninth century, and from Arabic into Persian in the thirteenth century by Ibn Isfandiyar, an Iranian Muslim, who put it into his 'History of Tabaristan' (a mountainous region in north Iran). His version alone survives.

(1) (pp. 4–5) Long afterwards Ardashir son of Papak, son of Sasan, took the field. . . . Apart from Ardavan, the man of most might and dignity at the time was Gushnasp, king of Parishwar and Tabaristan. . . . When it became clear to Gushnasp that he could not avoid submitting and paying fealty, he wrote a letter to Tansar, chief herbad of Ardashir son of Papak. Tansar read the letter . . . and wrote the answer which follows: (2) (pp. 5–8) The chief herbad, Tansar, has received the letter of Gushnasp, prince and king of Tabaristan and Parishwar. . . . He has studied each point, good or bad, and is pleased with it. . . . Do not marvel at my zeal and ardour for promoting order in the world, that the foundations of the laws of the faith may be made firm. For Church and State were born of the one womb, joined together and never to be sundered. . . .

(3) (pp. 10–12) Now as to the question which you put concerning the decrees of the King of kings: ... you wrote, 'although the king seeks the truth of the ancients yet he may be accused of forsaking tradition; and right though this may be for the world, it is not good for the faith'. ... In the beginning of time men enjoyed perfect understanding of the knowledge of religion. ... Yet it is not to be doubted that even then, through new happenings in their midst, they had need of a ruler of understanding; for till religion is interpreted by understanding it has no firm foundation. ... (4) (pp. 16–17) You declared: 'There is much talk about the blood shed by the king and people are dismayed.' The answer is that there are many kings who have put few to death, yet have slain immoderately if they have killed but ten; and there are many who if they put men to death in their thousands should slay still more, being driven to it at the time by their people. ... Punishments, you must know, are for three kinds of transgressions; first that of the creature against his God ... when he turns from the faith and introduces a heresy into religion. ... For (this) the King of kings has established a law far better than that of the ancients. For in former days any man who turned from the faith was swiftly ... put to death. ... The King of kings has ordered that such a man should be imprisoned, and that for the space of a year learned men should summon him at frequent intervals and advise him and lay arguments before him and destroy his doubts. If he become penitent and contrite and seek pardon of God, he is set free. If obstinacy and pride hold him back, then he is put to death. (5) (p. 22) Next for what you said, that the King of kings has taken away fires from the fire temples, extinguished them and blotted them out, and that no one has ever before presumed so far against religion; know that the case is not so grievous but has been wrongly reported to you. The truth is that after Darius (III) each of the 'kings of the peoples' [i.e. the Parthians' vassal kings] built his own [dynastic] fire temple. This was pure innovation, introduced by them without the authority of kings of old. The King of kings has razed the temples, and confiscated the endowments, and had the fires carried back to their places of origin. ... (6) (p. 26) Then you said: 'He has exacted money from men of wealth and merchants.' ... The idea that the king of the day should seek help for the common people from the superfluity of the wealthy is a religious principle and clearly justified in reason. ... (7) (pp. 42–3) The King of kings has cast the shadow of his majesty over all who have acknowledged his pre-eminence and service and have sent him tribute. ... In the space of fourteen years ... he thus brought it about that he made water flow in every desert and established towns and created groups of villages. ... Good order in the affairs of the people affects him more than the welfare of his own body and soul. Whoever considers his achievements ... will agree that since the power of the world's Creator arched this azure sphere the world has not known so true a king. (8) (pp. 38–9) So that when the world is abandoned by the King of kings ... they will take up that prince [his heir] and seat him on the throne and place the crown on his head, and taking him by the hand will say: 'Do you accept the kingship from God ... according to the

religion of Zardusht, upheld by the King of kings, Gushtasp [= Vishtasp], son of Luhrasp, and restored by Ardashir son of Papak?' The king will accept that covenant. (Edited by M. Minovi, *Tansar Name*; trans. M. Boyce, *The Letter of Tansar*.)

10.3.2 From the inscription of Shabuhr I on the Ka'ba-yi Zardusht

The 'Ka'ba of Zardusht' is a tower-like Achaemenian building at the foot of Naqsh-i Rustam (see 10.1.1), whose smooth stone walls were used for Sasanian inscriptions. That of Shabuhr records his victories over the Romans between 243 and 260 A.C. His pious foundations (much abbreviated here) were in thanksgiving for these victories, the sheep, etc., being for sacrifices and offerings. The divine name Ohrmazd, which can be used still today as a personal one, appears from Parthian times onward in a variety of spellings, including (as here) Hormizd.

(1) I, Lord Shabuhr, Mazda-worshipper, King of kings of Iran and non-Iran, whose race is of the yazads, . . . am ruler of the land of Iran. . . . (2) And because with the help of the yazads we sought out and conquered these so many lands, there we have founded in each region many Vahram Fires, and have acted benevolently towards many priests, and have exalted the affairs of the yazads. (3) And in accordance with this record we founded one fire called 'Famed is Shabuhr', for our soul and our memorial; one fire called 'Famed is Adur-Anahid' for the soul and memorial of our daughter Adur-Anahid, Queen of queens; one fire called 'Famed is Hormizd-Ardashir' for the soul and memorial of our son Hormizd-Ardashir, Great King of Armenia. . . . (4) And the endowments we have made for these fires, and established as customary, all that we shall write in documents: and from every thousand sheep which by custom belong to us from the year's excess we order that there shall be brought daily for our soul's sake one sheep, one 'griw', and five measures of bread and four measures of wine. (5) And for the souls of Sasan the ruler, and King Papak, and King Shabuhr, son of Papak, and Ardashir, King of kings, and Khoranzem, Queen of the land, and Adur-Anahid, Queen of queens . . . for their souls (also) one sheep, one 'griw' and five measures of bread and four measures of wine. . . . (6) And . . . for Hormizd, Chief Scribe, . . . and Naduk, Warden of the State Prison, and Papak, Master of the Gate, . . . and Kirder the Herbad . . . and Mihrekhwast, Treasurer, . . . together (shall be brought) one sheep, one 'griw' and five measures of bread and four measures of wine. (7) Then even as we now are diligent in the affairs and service of the yazads, and are (ourselves) the *domain of the yazads, and even as we with the help of the yazads sought out and conquered these lands, and achieved deeds of fame and courage, so let him also who shall be ruler after us be of good service and good intent towards the yazads, so that the yazads may be his friends as they have been ours. (Text, with German translation, in M. Back, *Die sassanidischen Staatsinschriften*, 284–5, 328 ff.)

10.3.3 From the inscription of Kirder on the Ka'ba-yi Zardusht

Kirder, the second Sasanian high priest, lived through seven reigns. This inscription was composed under Vahram II, 276–293 A.C. The sacred fires in non-Iranian lands (8) were evidently founded there when these were part of the Achaemenian empire, and had been tended by local Zoroastrian communities through over 500 years of Greco-Roman rule, cf. 4.1.3.

(1) And I, Kirder the Mobad, have been acknowledged to be of good service and loyal to the yazads and to Shabuhr, King of kings. . . . Shabuhr, King of kings, made my position independent and authoritative over religious matters at court and in every province and place, and over the priesthood throughout the empire. (2) And at the command of Shabuhr, King of kings, and with the support of the yazads and the King of kings, religious services were multiplied in every province and place, and many Vahram Fires were founded. And many a priest became joyful and prosperous. And charters were sealed for many fires and priestly *colleges, and much benefit reached Ohrmazd and the yazads, and there was much confusion for Ahriman and the devs. . . . (3) And the documents, charters and records which were then made under Shabuhr, King of kings . . . were written upon thus: 'Kirder the Herbad'. And after Shabuhr, King of kings, had departed to the Place of the Gods, and his son Ohrmazd, King of kings, was in the land, then Ohrmazd, King of kings, bestowed on me cap and girdle, and increased my dignity and honour. . . . And I was styled 'Kirder the Mobad of Ohrmazd', in the name of Ohrmazd the Lord. . . . (4) And after Ohrmazd, King of kings, had departed to the Place of the Gods, and Vahram, King of kings, son of Shabuhr King of kings . . . was in the land, then Vahram also, King of kings, advanced and honoured me. . . . (5) And after Vahram, King of kings, son of Shabuhr, had departed to the Place of the Gods, Vahram, King of kings, son of Vahram, was in the land, who in rule is generous and upright and kind and beneficent and virtuous. And for love of Ohrmazd and the yazads, and for his own soul's sake, he increased my dignity and honour yet more. He gave me the dignity and honour of a nobleman; and . . . throughout the empire I was made more authoritative and independent than formerly over religious matters. And I was made Mobad and Judge of the whole empire, and I was made Master of Ceremonials and Warden of the Fires of Anahid-Ardashir and Anahid the Lady at Istakhr. (6) And I was styled 'Kirder by whom Vahram's soul is saved, Mobad of Ohrmazd'. And in every province and place of the whole empire the service of Ohrmazd and the yazads was exalted, and the Mazda-worshipping religion and its priests received much honour in the land. And the yazads, and water and fire and cattle, were greatly contented, and Ahriman and the devs suffered great blows and harm. And the creed of Ahriman and the devs was driven out of the land and deprived of credence. (7) And Jews and Buddhists and Brahmans and Aramaic and Greek-speaking Christians and Baptisers and Manichaeans were assailed in the land. And images were overthrown, and the dens of demons were (thus) destroyed, and the places and abodes of the yazads [i.e. fire temples] were established. . . .

(8) And from the first I, Kirder, underwent much toil and trouble for the yazads and the rulers, and for my own soul's sake. And I caused many fires and priestly *colleges to flourish in Iran, and also in non-Iranian lands. There were fires and priests in the non-Iranian lands which were reached by the armies of the King of kings. The provincial capital Antioch and the province of Syria, and the districts dependent on Syria; the provincial capital Tarsus and the province of Cilicia, and the districts dependent on Cilicia; the provincial capital Caesarea and the province Cappadocia, and the districts dependent on Cappadocia, up to Pontus, and the province of Armenia, and Georgia and Albania and Balasagan, up to the 'Gate of the Alans' – these were plundered and burnt and laid waste by Shabuhr, King of kings, with his armies. There too, at the command of the King of kings, I reduced to order the priests and fires which were in those lands. And I did not allow harm to be done them, or captives made. And whoever had thus been made captive, him indeed I took and sent back to his own land. And I made the Mazda-worshipping religion and its good priests esteemed and honoured in the land. (9) And heretics and harmful men, who being in the priesthood did not in their expositions further the Mazda-worshipping religion and the service of the yazads, them I punished and rebuked until through me they were amended. (10) And I drew up many documents and charters for fires and priestly *colleges. And with the support of the yazads and the King of kings, and by my act, many Vahram Fires were founded in the land of Iran, and many next-of-kin marriages were made, and many people who had not believed, became believers. And there were many who had held the religion of the devs, and by my act they abandoned the religion of the devs and accepted the religion of the yazads. (11) And many *seasonal observances were held, and many religious accountings, in various ways, and other services for the yazads too were greatly increased and exalted, which have not been written of in this inscription; for if they had been written of, then it would have been too much. And at my own cost I founded many Vahram Fires in different places. . . . And let whoever may see this record and read it aloud, be just and generous, even as I have been, for the sake of the yazads and rulers and his own soul, so that good fame and fortune may come to him in the flesh and blessedness attend his soul hereafter. (Text, with German translation, in M. Back, *Die sassanidischen Staatsinschriften*, 384 ff.)

10.3.4 A late Sasanian account of the transmission of the holy texts
Whether any Avestan texts were written down in other scripts before the invention of the Avestan alphabet (see 1.1.1.1) is debated; but thereafter the tradition quickly evolved that a complete written Avesta had existed from earliest times. The Achaemenian dynasty is represented here by the two 'Daray' (Darius), the Arsacid one by 'Valakhsh' (Vologeses), see 1.9.1. For Tansar cf. 10.3.1; for Adurbad, a later Persian high priest, cf. 5.2.6.5. The final writing down of the complete canon appears to have taken place under Khusrow I, son of Kavad, 531–579.

(1) Daray, son of Daray, commanded that two written copies of all Avesta and Zand, even as Zardusht had received them from Ohrmazd, be preserved: one in the Royal Treasury and one in the Fortress of Archives. (2) Valakhsh the Ashkanian commanded that a memorandum be sent to the provinces (instructing them) to preserve, in the state in which they had come down in (each) province, whatever had survived in purity of the Avesta and Zand as well as every teaching derived from it which, scattered through the land of Iran by the havoc and disruption of Alexander, and by the pillage and plundering of the Macedonians, had remained authoritative, whether written or in oral transmission. (3) His Majesty Ardashir, King of kings, son of Papak, acting on the just judgment of Tansar, demanded that all those scattered teachings should be brought to the court. Tansar assumed command, and selected those which were trustworthy, and left the rest out of the canon. And thus he decreed: 'Henceforth only those are true compositions which are based on the Mazda-worshipping Religion, for now there is no lack of information and knowledge concerning them.' (4) Shabuhr, King of kings, son of Ardashir, further collected the non-religious writings on medicine, astronomy, movement, time, space, substance, accident, becoming, decay, transformation, logic and other crafts and skills which were dispersed throughout India, Byzantium and other lands, and collated them with the Avesta, and commanded that a copy should be made of all those writings which were flawless, to be deposited in the Royal Treasury. . . . (5) Shabuhr, King of kings, son of Hormizd, induced men from all provinces to orient themselves towards God through disputation, and put forward all oral traditions for consideration and examination. After the triumph of Adurbad, through his declaration put to trial by ordeal, [in disputation] with all those sectaries and heretics who studied the nasks, he made the following statement: 'Now that we have gained an insight into the Religion in the worldly existence, we shall not tolerate anyone of false religion, and we shall be still more zealous.' And thus did he do. (6) His present Majesty Khusrow, King of kings, son of Kavad, after he had put down heresy and evil dominion with fullest antagonism, greatly promoted detailed knowledge and investigation in the matter of all heresy within the four estates, according to the revelation of the Religion. And at an assembly (of representatives) of the realm he declared: 'We have recognised the truth of the Mazda-worshipping Religion; and the wise can with confidence establish it in the world by discussion. But to be a bounteous propagator (of the faith) and a foremost sage lies essentially not so much in discussion as in purity of thought, word, act, the guidance of the Good Spirit and the worship of the gods, paid purely in conformity with the Holy Word.' (From *Denkard*, Book IV, ed. M. Madan, pp. 412.3–413.17; the translation (with a few superficial changes) is that of M. Shaki, *Archiv Orientalní* 49, 1981 114–25.)

10.3.5 Two citations from the utterances of late Sasanian kings
10.3.5a From the Karnamag i Anoshiravan

This work, attributed to Khusrow I, survives only in Arabic translation. The words 'equity and justice' clearly render the Zoroastrian concept of 'asha'.

I give thanks unto God . . . for all the favours which he has shown me. . . . Many benefits require in return a deep sense of obligation. . . . And since I hold that gratitude should express itself in both word and deed, I have sought the course of action most pleasing to God, and have found that it consists in that whereby sky and earth continue to exist, the mountains remain immovable, the rivers flow, and the earth is kept pure: that is to say, in equity and justice. (Text, with French translation, in M. Grignaschi, *Journal asiatique*, 1966, 26.)

10.3.5b From a letter by Hormizd IV (579–90) to leading magi

Even as our royal throne cannot stand upon its two front legs without the back ones, so also our government cannot stand and be secure if we incense the Christians and the adherents of other religions, who are not of our faith. Cease, therefore, to harass the Christians, but exert yourselves diligently in doing good works, so that the Christians and the adherents of other religions, seeing that, may praise you for it, and feel themselves drawn to our religion. (From the German translation of the surviving Arabic rendering by T. Nöldeke, *Tabari*, 268.)

10.4 PASSAGES CONCERNING THE ARAB CONQUEST AND THE EARLY CENTURIES OF ISLAM

10.4.1 From Baladhuri's *The Origins of the Islamic State* (ninth century A.C.)

(1) When al-Mughirah ibn Shu'bah came to al-Kufah as governor for 'Umar ibn-al-Khattab, he brought a letter to Hudhaifah ibn-al-Yaman giving the latter the governorship of Adharbaijan. . . . Hudhaifah advanced as far as Ardabil, the capital of Adharbaijan, in which city was the marzban [i.e. Persian governor] thereof, and where the payment of its tax was made. The marzban had gathered there the militia. . . . These resisted the Moslems fiercely for some days. Then the marzban made terms with Hudhaifah for all the people of Adharbaijan for 800,000 dirhams, the conditions being that he should not kill or enslave any of them, nor raze any fire temples, . . . nor hinder the people of ash-Shiz in their peculiar custom of dancing on their festal days nor in observing their usual observances. . . . 'Umar afterwards removed Hudhaifah and appointed as governor of Adharbaijan Utbah ibn-Farkad as-Sulami. . . . When he arrived at Ardabil he found its people in possession of a treaty, but some of them had broken it, so he raided them, defeating and plundering them. . . . (2) Then 'Ali ibn-abu-Talib appointed al-Ash'ath governor of Adharbaijan. . . . He established in Ardabil a number of Arabs who were enrolled in the pension lists and the register, and made it a capital city, and built

its mosque. (P. K. Hitti and F. C. Murgotten, trans., Vol. II, 19–20, 24.)

10.4.2 From Narshakhi's *History of Bukhara* (completed 943/4 A.C.)

(1) In the reign of Mu'awiya (661–680) Bukhara was conquered by Qutaiba ibn Muslim. . . . (2) In Bukhara there was a bazar called the bazar of Makh. Twice a year for one day there was a fair. . . . On the day of the fair, when the people had gathered, all went into the fire temple and worshipped fire. The fire temple existed to the time of Islam when the Muslims seized power and built a mosque on that place. . . . (3) The inhabitants of Bukhara became Muslims, but each time after the Muslims withdrew they apostatised. Qutaiba ibn Muslim converted them to Islam three times, but they (repeatedly) apostatised and became infidels. The fourth time he made war he seized the city and established Islam there after much difficulty. He instilled Islam in their hearts and made (their religion) difficult for them in every way. . . . Qutaiba thought it proper to order the people of Bukhara to give one half of their homes to the Arabs so that the Arabs might be with them and informed of their sentiments. Then they would be obliged to be Muslims. In this manner he made Islam prevail and imposed the religious laws on them. He built mosques and eradicated traces of unbelief and the precepts of the fire-worshippers. He laboured a great deal and punished everyone who broke the decrees of the religious laws. . . . Qutaiba . . . built a grand mosque inside the citadel of Bukhara in the year 712/3. That place (formerly) had been a temple. He ordered the people of Bukhara to assemble there every Friday, for he had it proclaimed that 'Whosoever is present at the Friday prayer, I will give him two dirhams.' . . . Outside the city were 700 villas where the rich people lived and they were very arrogant. Most of them did not come to the grand mosque. The poor wanted the two dirhams but the rich had no need for them. One Friday the Muslims went to the gates of the villas and called them to the Friday prayer and pleaded with them. The residents, however, threw stones at them from the roofs of the villas. They fought and the Muslims were victorious. (From R. N. Frye, trans., pp. 8, 20–1, 47–8.)

10.4.3 From a guide to Muslim officials, on how to collect poll tax (jizya) from non-Muslims (dhimmis)

The dhimmi . . . has to stand while paying and the officer who receives it sits. The dhimmi has to be made to feel that he is an inferior person when he pays. . . . He goes on a fixed day in person to the emir appointed to receive the poll tax. He sits on a high throne. The dhimmi appears before him offering the poll tax on his open palm. The emir takes it so that his hand is on top and the dhimmi's below. Then the emir gives him a blow on the neck and one who stands before the emir drives him roughly away. . . . The public is admitted to see this show. (Cited by A. S. Tritton, *The Caliphs and their Non-Muslim Subjects*, 227.)

10.4.4 A passage from the 'History of Sistan'

This is an anonymous Persian local history written about 1060 A.C. The following incident occurred in the reign of the Umayyad caliph Mu'awiya I, who made Ziyad ibn Abih governor of Basra, Khorasan and Sistan. In 671 Ziyad sent 'Obayd Allah to Sistan.

Before his departure, Ziyad gave him the following order: 'When you go there, kill Shabur, the chief of the priests of the fire temples, and stamp out their fires.' So 'Obayd Allah went to Sistan to carry out this assignment. Consequently, the small landlords and the (other) Zoroastrians resolved that they would rebel because of this. Whereupon the Moslems of Sistan said: 'If our Prophet (the blessings of God upon him!) or the first four Caliphs have done this to a group which have made peace with them, then we shall carry out the order; but if this has not been the case, then we must not act in this matter contrary to Islamic law and our peace (agreement).' So they wrote a letter to the court [in Damascus] in this regard, and the reply came, saying: 'You must not (harm them) because they have made a treaty of friendship with us and those places of worship are theirs. The Persians say: "We worship God and we have our fire temples and our sun. But it is not the sun and the fire temple we worship; on the contrary, they are ours in the same way that the altars [of mosques, i.e. the mihrab] and the Ka'ba are yours." In as much as this is so, you should not exterminate (their temples), since they have fire temples in the same fashion that Jews have synagogues and the Christians their churches. Since they are all Peoples of the Book, what difference does the place of worship make, since we worship God? . . . Furthermore they resent the destruction of any object or any building of ancient standing. If our Prophet (the blessings of God be upon him!) had so desired he would have permitted none of these to exist, but would have exterminated all the infidels and all religions other than Islam. However, he did not do so, and did not destroy them, but made peace with them on the basis of a capitation tax (jizya) . . .'. 'Obayd Allah did not carry out the orders, and acted in the capacity of both administrator and judge. (Milton Gold, trans., pp. 74–5.)

10.5 CONCERNING THE IRANI AND PARSI COMMUNITIES, FIFTEENTH TO EIGHTEENTH CENTURIES A.C.

10.5.1 Passages from fifteenth-century letters by Irani priests

In the late fifteenth century the Parsis, under the leadership of Changa Asa, also called Changa Shah (cf. 10.5.3.6) sought guidance from leading Irani priests on matters of ritual and observance. In 1478 a layman, Nariman Hoshang, travelled by trading vessel from Broach to the Persian Gulf, and thence overland to Yazd. The correspondence thus initiated was continued at intervals down to 1778. As well as the letters, the Iranis sent treatises (the 'Persian Rivayats', see 1.1.1.19), which are preserved with them at Navsari.

*The Parsis' neglect by then of Pahlavi (5) was due to their use of Pazand texts,
see 1.1.1.18.*

(1) In the name and with the praise and help of the Creator Ormazd, the
radiant and glorious, and of the invisible and visible yazads and of all fravashis
of the just, and of Mihr, Srosh and Rashn, and of the Glory of the pure and
good Mazda-worshipping religion! . . . May the lay leaders and behdins of
India, and Changa Shah, chief of the town of Navsari, and further the
athornans, high priests and herbads of Navsari, and also of Surat, Anklesar,
Broach and Cambay . . . abide with long life and health; may their names be
perpetuated and their souls be blessed! (2) Let (them) . . . know that during the
times which have elapsed since Gayomard, down to this day, there has been no
period more grievous and troublesome than this beginning of the millennium of
Wrath, not even the period . . . of the Greek Alexander . . . . (Yet) we hope that
by Ormazd's grace Ushedar son of Zardusht, Pishotan son of Vishtasp, and
mighty, victorious Bahram, the auspicious King of his time who will bring
*goodness, will very swiftly become the protectors and nourishers of the good,
and will destroy and annihilate the wicked, so that (prosperous) times may
approach for those of the Good Religion. (3) Nariman Hoshang, who came to
Yazd, did not know Persian for the first year. He spoke a few words, but we did
not fully understand their purpose. We said: 'If you want us to understand each
other, stay here for the length of a year.' Jamasp was informed of it, and he
(Nariman) learnt (from him). He lived in Yazd and did some trafficking in
dates. He learnt some Persian, and then put questions to us, saying that priestly
functions and acts of worship were carried on in Navsari and Surat, and that
there was an Atash Bahram. But we (had) pondered over this for a year from
the time (of his arrival), and we felt no confidence (about instructing him as a
layman), and were not over-hasty in allowing him (to learn) how to dispose of a
corpse with due rites; but we are writing a little of the niceties of such affairs,
and we are writing on several other subjects, e.g. . . . about a woman who bears
a still-born child. . . . Do not be remiss (in observing precautions) about a
woman who bears a still-born child, for you will be responsible for the harm
(arising). (4) . . . Nariman . . . helped to carry the bier of the dead; but he could
not enter the dakhma, as it is not permissible; but he learnt something of the
ritual and about (handling) the ceremonial apparatus. Going in and out of a
dakhma, or walking along the way in front of the corpse, is not allowed. (5) . . .
Again let it be known that it was so represented . . . that the head priests and
wise dasturs and herbads of India are not familiar with the script [i.e. Pahlavi]
in which are written the Zand of the Avesta and the judicial decisions and
rituals, and are quite unable to read it. . . . Since so much effort has already
been made by these wise men on behalf of the religion of Ormazd and Zardusht,
let a pair of herbads (from among them) come to this place, and refresh
themselves a little in the Zand and the religious decisions, until the time when
mighty Bahram and Pishotan son of Vishtasp shall arrive, and shall revive the
good laws and religion. (6) . . . It is difficult for us to send instructions about

these things, and we do not rely on this (sort of) instructions, for if we were to send (them verbally) we fear that there might be additions and omissions, and we should be responsible for the sin. (7) . . . Nariman Hoshang . . . has said: 'In Navsari there is a leader of the Zoroastrians who is called Changa Shah, and he has secured exemption for the Zoroastrians of Navsari from payment of the capitation tax (jizya).' All Zoroastrians here pronounced blessings on him. The mercy of God be upon that pious soul, and thanks be to God that there are such Zoroastrians in the land of Hindustan. Again, he should know that this great work (of leadership) should be very well performed, so that he may keep his soul vigilant, and protect the priests and laity. . . . If he suspects that a Zoroastrian does not cause his wife or child to be virtuous, or if any commits an offence, then indeed he must be as well informed of the circumstances as a master of a family in his own house. If a person marries a wife and she practises sorcery, or entrusts her children to unbelievers for instruction, and if that worthy (leader) does not inquire into it, it is a great sin, for it behoves him, as well as the priests, to prescribe punishment and retribution to the wrongdoers, so that they may become free from sin and may do as many meritorious acts as the Kayan kings. . . . (8) If (Hindu) servant boys and girls have faith in the Good Religion, then it is proper that they should tie the kusti, and when they become instructed, attentive to the religion, and steadfast, the barashnom should be administered to them. (Translation, with minor changes, of B. N. Dhabhar, *The Persian Rivayats of Hormazyar Framarz and others*, 598 ff., 276.)

10.5.2 From sixteenth and seventeenth-century letters by Irani priests to the Parsis concerning manuscripts

(1) From the city of Kerman, our abode and resting place, we send manuscripts of the Vishtasp Yasht and Visperad . . . so that the dasturs and those of the priestly class in Hindustan may make a copy thereof, and we also write to say that, if need be, a duplicate copy will be sent. Should you have duplicates of any books, please send them for this congregation, so that you will lay us under obligation, and all those of the Good Religion will share in the reward and recompense. . . . (2) Again, of every book, whether Avesta or Pahlavi, which there may be in Hindustan, show us (its contents) by copying out several sheets from the beginning, middle and end of it, so that it may be found out what books there are over there. . . . As you asked for religious books, we are sending . . . whatever was procurable, viz. . . . religious manuscripts on every subject, such as Saddar Bundahesh, Saddar-i Saddar, and a Viraf Namag [i.e. Arda Viraz Namag] illustrated with pictures, and several pages of religious decisions on every kind of allowable and non-allowable (actions), and a chapter on the enthronement of an Atash Bahram, and a chapter on surrounding a corpse with a ritually drawn furrow. We hope that they will be conveyed safely to you with our good wishes. . . . Everything which is sent is sent for the sake of the path of the religion of Ormazd and Zardusht. (Translation, with minor changes, of Dhabhar, *Persian Rivayats*, 591–2, 609, 618–19.)

E

10.5.3 Verses from the 'Qissa-i Sanjan'

See 1.1.2.5. The Parsi founding fathers, who appear to have landed at Sanjan in 936 A.C., apparently named this, their first settlement in India, after their home town in Kohistan, in Khorasan. Hormuz is a port on the Persian Gulf, Div an island off the Indian coast, see map.

(1) When sovereignty departed from Yazdegird (III), Unbelievers came and seized his throne.... Alas for the land of the faith, which was made desolate! ... Laymen and priests left their homes ... for their religion. For a hundred years they lived in Kohistan. When they were in this plight, a virtuous sage ... said to his companions: 'It will be hard to stay here, for fear of the Unbelievers.' So the peerless priests and laymen departed for the city of Hormuz. After fifteen years spent in that clime, each one of them had endured much trouble from the infidels. The wise Dastur who was with them said ... : 'It will be well if we leave this country ... and flee for fear of life and for religion's sake to India.' Then a ship was made ready for the sea.... When the ship came in sight of land, anchor was dropped at Div.... The people of the Good Religion stayed there for nineteen years.... The aged Dastur said ... : 'From here too we must depart for another place ...'. They set sail swiftly for Gujarat. When the vessel had made some way across the sea, a fearful storm approached.... (They prayed): 'Victorious Bahram, come to our aid and bring us out triumphant from this trouble! ... If we reach Hind ... we will kindle a great Atash Bahram.' By the blessing of the victorious Atash Bahram, all were saved from that danger.... Priests and laymen said the kusti prayers.... Then Providence so ordained that those people all arrived near Sanjan. (2) In that region was a virtuous Rajah who had opened his heart to holiness. His name was Jadi Rana. He was liberal, sagacious and wise. A Dastur renowned for learning and prudence went to him with gifts and, invoking blessings on him, said: 'O Rajah of Rajahs, grant us a place in this land! We are strangers seeking protection ... having come here solely for the sake of our religion ....' ... When that prince beheld them, a sudden terror filled his heart. Fears for his crown entered his mind, lest they lay waste his kingdom.... He questioned the Dastur about their religious mysteries. '... What are the customs of your creed? ... Let me first see what are your beliefs, and then we shall arrange for your abiding here. Second, if we give you shelter, you must abandon the language of your country, give up the Iranian tongue and adopt the speech of the realm of Hind. Third, as to your women's dress, they should wear garments like those of our females. Fourth, you must lay aside all your arms and swords and cease to carry them anywhere. Fifth, when your children wed, the marriage knot must be tied at night-time. If you first give a solemn promise to observe all this, you will be given places and abodes in my land.' When the Dastur heard all this from the Rajah, he could not but agree to all his demands. Then the old priest addressed him thus: 'O wise king, listen now to what I say of our creed.... Know that we are worshippers of God.... We strangers are of the seed of Jamshid, and reverence the sun and moon. Three other things also out

of creation we hold in honour, namely the cow, fire and water. . . . It is the Lord who has created all things which are on earth, and we pray to them, because He Himself has chosen them. Our sacred girdle is made of seventy-two threads, and when we tie it on we utter solemn professions of faith . . .'. All their other rites and customs he described one by one to the Rajah . . . and that good king forthwith commanded that they should dwell in his domain. . . . A place was chosen whose soil was excellent, and there they made their abode . . . . The Dastur gave it the name of Sanjan, and soon it was flourishing even as the realm of Iran. (3) One day they chanced to have business with the Rajah. . . . The Dastur then addressed him thus: 'O Prince, you have given us a dwelling place in this land. Now we wish to install in the Indian clime an Atash Bahram; but land should be cleared for three farsangs, so that the religious ceremonies may be properly performed. No stranger should be there, none but wise men of the Good Religion . . .'. The Rajah said: '. . . I rejoice with all my soul that such a Shah should be installed in my time . . .'. Straightway the Prince issued his commands and gave the Dastur a pleasant site. . . . For several days and months (the priests) recited yasnas and yashts and worked with great energy. The laymen too were concerned with the matter, and provided, out of their zeal for the faith, all the various things needful. The Prince Jadi Rana also sent offerings of every sort . . . Things were everywhere easy for them, for 'alat' [i.e. ritual objects and utensils] had been brought from Khorasan. With those 'alat' from Khorasan, they accomplished their task without trouble. The reason was that several (other) parties of priests and laymen of holy lives had also arrived in that place. . . . They had brought with them ample resources and they thus consecrated fire according to the dictates of the religion. Aged priests thus installed the Iranshah, a Light full of light. . . . All the laity and priests then celebrated in that land a special holy day with feasting. (4) In this manner some three hundred years passed, and people left that place in small or large groups. They scattered in all directions through the land of Hind, choosing places to their liking. . . . Some departed towards Broach . . . , some reached the town of Anklesar or strode proudly off to the city of Cambay. Others bore all their goods and chattels to Navsari. . . . Wherever each felt himself at ease, there he made his home. . . .

Islam eventually reached Gujarat, and a Muslim army approached Sanjan, probably in 1465 A.C., to 'wrest it from the Rajah'. The Rajah summoned the Parsis to his aid. They fought heroically and suffered heavy losses, but in vain. The Rajah was slain and Sanjan seized and sacked.

(5) The people of the Good Religion were also dispersed. There is . . . a hill named Bahrot. Many crept to it to save their lives. . . . Twelve years thus passed; they had carried the Iranshah along with them. After a time, at the Lord's command, they forgathered again with their kith and kin. Taking the Atash Bahram with them, they all arrived at Bansda. When the tidings reached that town, all came out with loving kindness. . . . They brought the Fire into the town with a hundred marks of reverence. Thenceforth Bansda flourished as if it

were perpetual spring there. Time passed this way; and those born into the Good Religion, old men even and women too, came to venerate the Iranshah from every district in which there were people of that pure creed. Just as in earlier times people used to go on special pilgrimage to far-famed Sanjan, so Parsis now came to Bansda from diverse places, with numerous offerings. (6) When fourteen years had passed . . . a layman . . . came forward to preserve the faith. . . . His name was Changa Asa. . . . He gave money from his own resources to those who had no sacred shirt or girdle. . . . No afflicted person went to him for whom . . . he did not provide some relief. . . . One year [he] went to the House of the Fire in pursuance of a vow.

On returning home to Navsari Changa Asa persuaded the Parsis there to invite the priests of the sacred fire to bring it to their town. The poem ends with its installation in a 'fine house' in Navsari. There it remained till the eighteenth century. It was then taken to Udwada, where it burns to this day, still an object of Parsi veneration and pilgrimage.

(Adapted from the translation of S. H. Hodivala, *Studies in Parsi History*, 92–117; Persian text in M. Unvala, *Rivayat*, II, 343–54.)

10.5.4 From the sixteen Sanskrit ślokas of Aka Adhyaru

These verses were probably composed before the Qissa-i Sanjan, but the oldest extant mss. belong to the seventeenth century. The text first became generally known to Parsis in the nineteenth century, and the verses were then popularly believed to have been recited before Rajah Jadi Rana (see 10.5.3.2); but clearly none of the first Parsi settlers could already have composed in Sanskrit. The origin of the text remains in fact obscure, as does the identity of its author, Aka Adhyaru. It has been much revised, and there are many divergences in mss. readings. – On the rule of silence, i.e. 'baj' (v. 2), cf. 4.3. On the need to offer as sacrifice all beneficent creatures which are slain (v. 10) cf. 3.1.

(1) Who at the three divisions of the day [i.e. dawn, noon and sunset] meditate with 'niyayesh' prayers on the sun and the group of five elements – fire, wind, earth, primordial space, water, . . . and on Hormazd, the Lord of the gods, mighty through many virtues, on him, the only merciful one – those are we Parsis, fair-skinned, brave, heroic abode of great strength. (2) Who in this world at the time of bathing, meditation, recitation (of the holy scriptures), offering to the fire, eating, answering calls of nature, keep the rule of silence mentioned in the scriptures (and) laid down by their own preceptors . . . those are we Parsis. . . . (3) Who wear against their bodies a fair garment of fine material, which has the qualities of a coat-of-mail, (and) at their waists a girdle, the good woollen 'kusti' . . . those are we Parsis. . . . (4) (Whose) young women celebrate their auspicious feast(s), accompanied by the singing of songs, at the marriage ceremony on auspicious days, and use sweet-smelling sandal and other scents on their bodies; who are pure in their behaviour, their conduct being of many virtues, attached to the precepts of the beautiful scriptures –

those are we Parsis. ... (5) In whose house(s) there is always (food), pleasant and delicious to the taste, and the giving of food; (whose) custom is to bestow in charity pools, wells and reservoirs here on the surface of the earth; who always practise the giving of things such as clothes to people with the virtues of Brahmins – those are we Parsis. ... (6) There is as much joy as sorrow, (there is) bliss and grief, knowledge and ignorance; and as much right as wrong, unfruitful and fruitful deeds, and malady and health, and high and low, and likewise the Creator and the Destroyer, consisting in light and darkness; on whose way(s) it is thus laid down as twofold – those are we Parsis. ... (8) Five times every day there should be an offering (to the fire) with pieces of aloe and sandalwood which has been dried for six months, with fragrance of wood and camphor (and) with recited words formed through sacred formulas; they (the Parsis), namely, help the fire with (their) efforts ..., who have the law of truth as principle ... – those are we Parsis. ... (9) For whose women there shall be purity in the menstrual period after the seventh night; and purity after one pure month at the time of a birth, thus (shall there be) purity of the body; (whose women) are of pleasing behaviour, sparkle like new gold ornaments, are vigorous and very strong, since (they are) exceedingly pure and have laughing faces – those are we Parsis. ... (10) There is no intercourse with courtesans; at the time of the offering to the ancestors there is special care of the fire ...; there is no meat (eaten) except in sacrifice [i.e. when the act of killing has been sanctified]; ... those are we Parsis. ... (11) A woman who has given birth to a child does not engage herself in the work of cooking for forty days, remains wholly silent, sleeps much, dedicates herself to murmuring prayers after bathing and to praising the sun; ... whose caste is not inferior, providing constant security – those are we Parsis. ... (12) Who always think of water, sky, moon, fire, wind, earth, sun and Hormazd, the wise, imperishable, immortal, who is to be reflected upon by the mind ... those are we Parsis. ... (16) May Hormazd protect you, the Lord of the gods, effecting complete victory, the giver of increase in children and grandchildren; may he, effecting abundant wealth and fortune, destroy the sin! (From the translation, with small changes, of H. P. Schmidt, *Bulletin of the Deccan College Research Institute*, 21, 1960–61, 157–96.)

10.6 FROM THE REPORTS OF EUROPEANS, SEVENTEENTH AND EIGHTEENTH CENTURIES

In the following extracts spelling and punctuation have been standardised where necessary.

10.6.1 From *L'ambassade de D. Garcias de Silva Figueroa*
Don Garcias was Spanish ambassador in 1618 at the court of the Safavid Shah 'Abbas the Great at Isfahan.

(Page 177) In the most eastern part of Persia, and in the province of Kerman, which forms its frontier to the east, there have remained a number of those ancient and true Persians who, although they have mixed with the others, and by identifying themselves with their conquerors, have become like one people, have nevertheless not ceased to hold steadfastly to their original way of life, their customs and their religion. Thus they venerate to this day the sun, as did the Persians of old when their empire was the greatest in the world, and, following their example, they keep fire always burning in their homes, maintaining it, so that it should never be extinguished, with as much care as did once the Vestal Virgins of Rome.

10.6.2 From J. B. Tavernier, in *Collections of Travels through Turkey into Persia*, Vol. 1

'Gaurs', or unbelievers, was the Muslim term for the Irani Zoroastrians. Their reticence about their faith, which this French traveller had to break through, had developed over generations of exposure to Muslim mockery. For their 'principal temple' (1), cf. 10.6.3 It was situated in the village of Sharifabad, near Yazd, where the ancient Atash Bahram still burns, see Boyce, Persian Stronghold, *2 ff.*

(1) (p. 163) There are no men in the world so scrupulous of discovering the mysteries of their religion as the Gaurs; so that I was forced to frequent their company very much ... to pick out what I have here to deliver. ... There are now above 10,000 in Kerman, where I stayed three months in the year 1654; ... four days' journey from whence stands their principal temple, where their chief priest resides; whither they are once in their lives obliged to go on pilgrimage. ... (2) (p. 165) (Their) Prophet perceiving that all the people had him in ... much veneration, withdrew himself, and would not be seen anymore. Nor do they fully know what became of him; which makes the greatest part of the Gaurs believe, that he was taken up into Paradise both soul and body together. ... (3) They allow their Prophet three children, who are not yet come into the world, though their names be already given them. ... The first child ... they call beforehand 'Ouchider'. He shall come into the world with authority, and shall cause his father's law to be received, and confirm it, not only by his eloquent preaching but by many miracles. ... The second, whose name is 'Ouchiderma' ... shall assist his brother. ... The third ... shall come with more authority than his two brothers, and shall perfectly reduce all people to the religion of their prophet. After which shall be the universal resurrection, at what time all the souls, either in Paradise or Hell, shall return to take possession of their bodies. ...

(4) (p. 166) So soon as women or maids perceive the custom of nature upon them, they presently leave their houses, and stay alone in the fields in little huts made of hurdles or wattlings, with a cloth at the entering in, which serves for a door. While they are in that condition, they have meat and drink brought them every day; and when they are free, they send, according to their quality, a kid,

or a hen, or a pigeon for an offering; after which they go to the bath, and then invite some few of their kindred to some small collation. . . . (5) They have . . . thirty Holy-days [i.e. the six gahambars] . . . , which they keep very strictly, no man daring to work. But the day of the Birth of their Prophet [i.e. the 'old' No Roz] is celebrated with an extraordinary pomp, besides that then they bestow large alms. (6) When the Gaurs are sick, they send for their priests, to whom they make a kind of confession; whereupon the priests enjoin them to give alms, and other good works, to gain pardon of their sins. (7) (p. 167) The Gaurs would not be thought to give honour to fire under the title of adoration. For they do not account themselves idolaters, saying that they acknowledge but only one God, Creator of Heaven and Earth, whom they only adore. As for the fire, they preserve and reverence it, in remembrance of the great miracle by which their Prophet was delivered [in infancy] from the flames. One day being in Kerman, I desired to see that fire, but they answered me, they could not permit me. For, say they, one day the governor of Kerman being desirous to see the fire, not daring to do otherwise, they showed it him. He, it seems, expected to see some extraordinary brightness; but when he saw no more than what he might have seen in a kitchen or a chamber fire, fell a-swearing and spitting upon it as if he were mad. Whereupon the sacred fire, being thus profaned, flew away in the form of a white pigeon. The priests considering then their misfortune, which had happened through their own indiscretion, fell to their prayers with the people, and gave alms; upon which, at the same time, and in the same form the sacred fire returned to its place; which makes them shy to show it again. (8) When they put any persons to their oaths, they swear them before this fire; for they think no person so impious, as to swear false before that sacred fire, which they take for the witness of their oath. Their priests put them in dread of very great punishments, and threaten them that the heavenly fire will forsake them, if they prove so wicked as to swear falsely before it. (9) (p. 168) There are some beasts which the Gaurs do mightily respect, and to which they give a great deal of honour. There are others which they as much abhor, and which they endeavoured to destroy as much as in them lies, believing that they were not created by God, but that they came out of the body of the Devil, whose ill-nature they retain. The beasts which they principally admire are the cow, the ox, and the dog. . . . The creatures which they abhor are adders, serpents, lizards, toads, frogs, crayfish, rats, mice, but above all the rest cats . . . ; so that they rather suffer the inconveniency of rats and mice, than ever keep a cat in their houses.

10.6.3 From John Chardin, *Voyages en Perse*, Vol. 2
Chardin, a French merchant-traveller, was in Persia during 1665–77.
(1) (p. 179) The Persian Fire Worshippers . . . work either as ploughmen or as labourers, fullers or workers in wool. They make carpets, caps, and very fine woollen stuffs. . . . Their chief occupation is agriculture; . . . they regard it not only as a good and innocent calling but also as meritorious and noble, and they

believe that it is the first of all vocations, that which the 'Sovereign God' and the 'Lesser Gods', as they say, approve of most and which they reward most generously. This opinion, made by them into a article of faith, causes them to turn naturally to work on the land. . . . Their priests teach them that the most virtuous action is to beget children, and after that to cultivate a piece of waste land, or to plant a tree. (2) These ancient Persians have gentle and simple ways, and live very peaceably under the guidance of their elders, from among whom they elect their magistrates, who are confirmed in their office by the Persian government. They drink wine, and eat all kinds of flesh. . . . But otherwise they are very particular, and hardly mix at all with other people, especially not with Mahometans. (3) (p. 177) Their principal temple is near Yazd, in a mountain eighteen leagues distant. This is their great 'atesh-gah'. . . . This place is also their oracle and academy. It is there that they communicate their religion, their maxims and their hopes. Their high pontiff lives there always, and without quitting it. He is called the 'dastur-dasturan'. This pontiff has with him several students, who form a kind of seminary. The Mahometans allow it, because it is inconspicuous, and generous presents are made to (their) officials. (4) (p. 182) They suppose that there are two principles of things, it not being possible that there should be only one because all things are of two kinds, or of two natures, that is, good or bad. These two principles are of the Light, which they call Ormous . . . and Darkness, which they call Ariman. . . . They hold that there are angels, whom they call subaltern gods, assigned to protecting the inanimate creations, each according to his own province.

10.6.4 From Henry Lord, *A display of two forraigne sects*
From 1624 to 1629 Lord was chaplain at the East India Company's factory at Surat.
10.6.4.1 From the Introduction to Lord's book
(1) (p. 1) I observed in the town of Surat . . . another sect called the Parsis; . . . (and) I thought it would not be unworthy of my labour to bring to the eyes of my countrymen this religion also. For this cause I joined myself with one of their churchmen, called their Daru, and by the interpretation of a Parsi, whose long employment in the company's service had brought him to a mediocrity in the English tongue, and whose familiarity with me inclined him to further my inquiry, I gained the knowledge of what hereafter I shall deliver.
10.6.4.2 From Lord, ch. 2
After a summary of Zoroastrian beliefs and traditional history, Lord describes the religious duties of Parsis. Some which he assigns to priests only were in fact required of all the community, e.g. maintaining an ever-burning fire.
(1) (pp. 29–31) The behdin [i.e. layman], . . . being by secular occasions drawn from the services of religion, had therefore a less difficult injunction laid upon him: (i) to have shame [i.e. self-respect] ever with them; (ii) to have fear always with them . . . lest they should not go to heaven; (iii) that whensoever

they are to do anything, to think whether the thing be good or bad that they go about; ... (v) whensoever they pray by day, they should turn their faces towards the sun, and ... by night they should incline towards the moon, for that they are the two great lights of heaven, and God's two witnesses – most contrary to Lucifer [i.e. Ahriman], who loveth darkness more than light. ... (2) (pp. 31–5) The (further) precepts ... to be observed by the ordinary ... churchman, called their Daru or Herbad ... : (i) to know in what manner to pray to God, observing the rites prescribed in the Zendavesta, for God is best pleased with that form of prayer that He hath given in His own book; (ii) to keep his eyes from coveting or desiring anything that is another's; (iii) to have a care ever to speak the truth, for all truth cometh from God ... but Lucifer is the father of falsehood; (iv) to be known only in his own business, and not to enquire after the things of the world, it belongeth only to him to teach others what God would have them do. Therefore the behdin ... shall see that he want nothing needful, but shall afford it him, and he shall seek nothing superfluous; (v) to learn the Zendavesta by heart, that he may be ready to teach it to the behdin. ... (vi) to keep himself pure and undefiled from things polluting, as from the carcasses of the dead, or touching matters unclean, for God is pure, whose servant he is, and it is expected he should be such, abhorring the sight of all things that are foul and loathsome; ... (ix) to give licence for marriage; (x) to spend the greatest part of [his] time in the temple, that he may be ready for all that come to him; (xi) upon pain of damnation, to believe no other law than that which was brought by Zardusht. ... (3) (pp. 35–9) Now their Dastur or high priest, whereof they never have but one [locally], to which all the herbads pay their observance, as he is above the rest in dignity so he is enjoined to be above the rest in sanctity ... ; (i) he must never touch any of a strange caste or sect, of what religion soever, nor any layman of his own religion, but he must wash himself, because God hath made him especially holy to Himself, for which cause he must not approach to God in prayer with the touch of others' uncleanness; (ii) he must do everything that belongeth to himself with his own hand ... , the better to preserve his purity, viz. to set the herbs in his own garden, to sow the grain of his own field, to dress the meat that he eateth, unless he have his wife to administer to him in that, which is not ever usual; (iii) that he taketh the tithe or tenth of all things from the behdin, as the Lord's dues, and employ it to such uses as he thinketh meet, since the Lord hath made him His almoner and dispenser of charity; (iv) that as he must use no pomp or superfluity, so of that great revenue that cometh yearly to him, he must leave nothing over-plus at the year's end that must not be bestowed in good uses, either in charitable contributions to the poor, or in building of the temples of God; (v) that his house be near adjoining to the church, where he must keep and make his abiding ... ; (vii) ... that (he) be acquainted with all the learning in the Zendavesta, both in that part which treateth of judicial astrology ... as also in that which concerneth the physician, and most especially in the book of the law ... ; (ix) that he stand in fear of nobody but God, nor fear anything but sin; (x) that . . . when any man sinneth he may tell him of it, be he never so great; and every man is to obey him, as one that speaketh not in his own cause, but God's; . . . (xiii) that he keep an ever-living fire that never may go out . . . and that he say his prayers over it.

Lord then proceeds to some general statements about communal observances.

(4) (pp. 40–2) Their law alloweth them great liberty in meats and drinks; but because they will not give offence to the Banyans [i.e. Hindus] amongst whom they live, nor displease the Moors [i.e. Muslims] under whose government they are, they especially abstain from eating of kine- and hogs-flesh, meats prohibited by the laws of the two former. It is observable also amongst them that they eat alone, as a means for greater purity and cleanness, for they suppose they participate of another's uncleanness by eating with them. They likewise drink everyone in several cups, proper and peculiar to their own uses, for the same cause, and if any chance to drink in another man's cup, they wash it three times, and abstain from the use thereof for a certain season after. . . . and whensoever they eat any fowl or flesh, they carry some part of it to the agiary or temple, as an offering to appease God, that for the sustenance of man they are forced to take away the life of His creatures.

He then tells of birth, initiation, marriage (omitted here) and death.

(5) (pp. 45–7) . . . The Daru or churchman cometh to the house and casteth the child's nativity . . . ; the mother in the presence of them all [i.e. relatives and friends] giveth the name to the child, there being no ceremony but the naming of the infant as then used. After this the kindred of the child together with the infant accompany the Daru to the agiary or temple, where he taketh fair water, and putting into it the bark or rind of a tree called 'hom' which groweth at Yazd in Persia . . . he thence poureth the water into the infant, uttering this prayer, that God would cleanse it from the uncleanness of his father and the menstruous pollutions of his mother, which done it departeth. . . . About the seventh year of the child's age . . . he is taught by the churchman to say some prayers and . . . instructed in religion, wherein, when he is prompt, he uttereth his prayers over the fire. . . . Then after the prayers be concluded, the Daru giveth him water to drink, and a pomegranate leaf to chew in his mouth, to cleanse him from inward uncleanness, so washing his body in a tank with clean water, and putting on him a linen cassock which he weareth next his skin, called 'shuddiro' [= sudra], which descendeth to his waist, as also a girdle of camel's hair called 'cushee' [= kusti], which he ever weareth about him, and is woven . . . by the preacher's own hand. He uttereth these prayers over him: that God would make him a true follower of the religion of the Parsis all the days of his life, of which those garments are the badge or sign. . . . (6) (pp. 51–2) They suppose the soul to be vagrant on earth for three days after the decease, in which time Lucifer molesteth it; for security from which molestation it flieth to their holy fire, seeking preservation there; which time concluded, it receiveth justice or reward, hell or heaven. Upon this opinion they all (as their business

will permit) assemble themselves for three days together, and offer up their prayers at morning, noon and evening, that God would be pleased to be merciful to the soul departed. After the three days are expired, and that they think the definitive sentence is passed, what shall become of him, they on the fourth day make a festival and conclude their mourning.

10.6.5 From John Ogilby's *Asia*, 1672

Ogilby's description, compiled from travellers' reports, partly concerns the purity laws. Thus the 'sin' in working for non-Parsis (3) was that unbelievers were necessarily unclean; and laying the dying on sand (5) was to insulate the good earth from what was soon to be a corpse.

(1) (p. 218) In most places of Surat dwell a sort of Persians . . . clothed like Indians, except for a girdle or sash of camel's hair or sheep's wool. . . . When accidentally they lose one of these girdles, they are not permitted to eat, drink, work, speak or stir before they have obtained another: and these girdles are to be bought of their priests. They live here like the natives, free and undisturbed, and drive what trade they please. They are very ingenious, and for the most part maintain themselves with tilling, and buying and selling all sorts of fruits, tapping of wine out of the palm-trees, which wine they sell in houses of entertainment. . . . Some also traffic, and are exchangers of money, keep shops, and exercise all manner of handicrafts, except smith's work, for they are not allowed to quench fire with water. (2) (p. 219) There are few amongst them that serve other people, alleging, that if any dies in another man's service, it will be very difficult for him to go to heaven, as having sinned against God; wherefore those that serve are accounted unclean. . . . They dwell in very dark houses, meanly furnished, in one street or ward by themselves. . . . They have no supreme governor amongst them. . . . (3) (p. 220) Their grand ceremonies of fire-worship are at present performed at Surat, or a place called Nuncery [i.e. Navsari], where the chief priesthood of this sect reside. . . . (4) (p. 222) One Twist tells us, that they take the sick from his bed and laying him on the ground, on a bed of sand, let him die there. . . . They account the bodies of men to be much more unclean than those of beasts.

10.6.6 From J. Ovington, *A voyage to Surat in the year 1689*

For Ovington's observations on communal charity (2) cf. 11.4.5. The 'solemn festivals' are evidently the gahambars. On the cock (1) cf. 11.4.1.10.

(1) (p. 216) The 'Persies' are a sect very considerable in India. . . . The cock is much esteemed by them, as the cow is by the Banyans. . . . (p. 217) . . . Active flame must be allowed to live, whilst there's any fuel for it to feed on. If the fire is once kindled, all care is taken that it comes to a natural expiration, and no violence allowed to bring it to a period sooner. (If buildings catch fire) they would sooner be persuaded to pour on oil to increase, than water to assuage the flame. (2) (p. 218) They own and adore one supreme Being, to whom, as he is the original of all things, they dedicate the first day of every month, in a solemn

observation of his worship. And enjoin, besides these, some others for the celebration of public prayers. At their solemn festivals, whither a hundred or two sometimes resort, in the suburbs of the city, each man, according to his fancy and ability, brings with him his victuals, which (are) equally distributed and eat in common by all those present. For they show a firm affection to all of their own sentiments in religion, assist the poor, and are very ready to provide for the sustenance and comfort of such as want it. Their universal kindness, either in employing such as are needy and able to work, or bestowing a seasonable bounteous charity to such as are infirm and miserable, leave no man destitute of relief, nor suffer a beggar in their tribe. . . . (3) (p. 219) In their callings they are very industrious and diligent, and careful to train up their children to arts and labour. They are the principal men at the loom in all the country, and most of the silks and stuffs at Surat are made by their hands.

10.6.7 From K. Niebuhr, *Travels through Arabia* . . . , Vol. 2
Niebuhr, a German scientific traveller, spent fourteen months in Bombay and Gujarat in 1762–64, returning home by way of Persia.

(1) (p. 429) At Bombay, at Surat, and in the vicinity of these cities, is a colony of ancient Persians. . . . Being beloved by the Hindus, they multiply exceedingly, whereas their countrymen in the province of Kerman are visibly diminishing under the yoke of the Moslem Persians. They are a gentle, quiet and industrious race. They live in great harmony among themselves, make common contribution for the aid of their poor, and suffer none of their number to ask alms from people of a different religion. . . . When a Parsi behaves ill, he is expelled from their communion. (2) (p. 430) Among them, a man marries only one wife, nor ever takes a second, unless the first happens to be barren. . . . (3) (p. 431) The religion of the Parsis enjoins purification as strictly as that of the Hindus. The disciples of Zardusht are not, however, obliged to abstain from animal food.

10.6.8 From J. S. Stavorinus, *Voyages to the East Indies*, Vol. 1
Stavorinus, a Dutch traveller, was in Surat in 1774.

(1) (p. 494) (The Parsis') number, in and around Surat, is at present estimated to amount to one hundred thousand souls, who almost all maintain themselves by agriculture and manufactures. . . . The greatest number of them, however, . . . live in the country, and along the sea-coast . . . , where they have several large and wealthy villages. (2) (p. 495) When Parsis die in distant places, their relations spare no expense in order to have the bones conveyed to their receptacles [i.e. dakhmas], and sometimes are at the cost of twenty thousand rupees, and more, to effect this purpose. (3) (p. 496) They . . . marry no more than one woman at the same time, and never any one but their own nation. . . . Adultery and fornication they punish among themselves, and even by death; but they must, however, give cognisance of any capital punishment to the Moorish government; the execution is performed in secret, either by lapidation,

drowning in the river, or beating to death, and sometimes by poison . . . (4) (p. 498) Murder, homicide and other crimes among them, which disturb the public tranquillity, are punished by the nabob, or governor of the city; he however acts very circumspectly in such cases, because he stands more in awe of the Parsis than the Moors or Gentoos, on account of their large numbers and greater courage, whereby they are left, in some measure, independent; such heavy crimes, I was told, are very seldom heard of among them; and besides, as they all live in separate wards in which they do not allow any strangers to reside, many things may remain hidden among them.

10.6.9 From H. Anquetil du Perron, *Zend-Avesta*, Vol. 2

This French scholar spent 1759–61 in Surat, studying Avestan and Pahlavi with a Parsi priest, Darab Kumana. He brought Zoroastrian mss. back to Europe, and himself published a pioneer translation of the whole Avesta and the Indian Bundahishn, as well as a very valuable, detailed account of the beliefs and customs of the Parsis. – Here he uses 'Zand' as a synonym for 'Avestan', cf. 1.1.1.13.

(1) (p. 616) The Zand and Pahlavi books present on the one hand a universe created by Ormuzd, and corrupted by Ahriman; on the other the restoration of Nature. Zoroaster appeared; the law which he proclaims strengthens the means whereby this great event is to be brought about. The Parsi, taught by this Law-giver, sees himself as a soldier whom Ormuzd sends under the leadership of the good Spirits to fight the Author of evil. The prayer which he says on waking brings before his eyes the end and cost of the battles in which he is going to engage, and the resurrection, and the glory of the Saints in Heaven. . . . (2) (p. 617) The girdle and the sort of shirt which are the mark of the true disciple of Zoroaster form his warlike apparel. For weapons he has prayer, by which he gains the protection of the heavenly Beings; the word which created the universe; the appointed ceremonies which maintain his physical purity; and an absolute obedience to him from whom he has received his being, who gives him purity of soul. (3) (p. 618) The precepts which he fulfils make the lands which he inhabits fertile, multiply people, trees and herds, increase riches and his own well-being, maintain peace and public security. Prepared for every eventuality, he accepts misfortunes without letting them cast him down. It would be to sin against Ormuzd and to make himself unworthy of the name of soldier of the good Principle if he were to show the signs of an excessive grief. Conversely, he enjoys without scruple, but always in moderation, all that Nature lawfully offers him, and thinks that he enters thereby into the plan of Ormuzd. To deviate from that plan is to increase the powers of Ahriman, to multiply his productions. So crimes, such as adultery, sodomy, theft . . . , lying, bad faith, (all) voluntary breaches of the Law, are visited by corporal punishment, and sometimes even death. The penalties are severe, because these sins . . . assail . . . the Divine Majesty by diminishing the glory of Ormuzd and by supplying his enemy with the means of destroying the universe.

11 THE FAITH IN MODERN TIMES: THE NINETEENTH AND TWENTIETH CENTURIES

11.1 FROM NINETEENTH-CENTURY EUROPEAN WRITINGS ON ZOROASTRIAN DUALISM

11.1.1 From John Wilson, *The Parsi Religion*

Wilson, a Scotsman, was a Christian missionary who strove to convert the Parsis. A scholar, he studied Anquetil's French translations of the Avesta and Bundahishn, as well as Greek, Latin, Armenian and Arabic works which conveyed the Zurvanite heresy (see 8). So although this had disappeared nearly 1,000 years earlier, he attacked both it and the living Parsi beliefs, to the bewilderment of the Bombay community.

(1) (pp. 26–7) When I commenced my missionary operations in Bombay in 1829, I found the Parsis a numerous and very influential portion of its varied community. . . . With a view to qualifying myself for . . . unfolding to them the truths of divine revelation, I considered it my duty early to embrace such opportunities as might be presented to me of becoming acquainted with their religious tenets and observances. . . . (2) (p. 149) According to the universal testimony of antiquity, the ancient Persians must be considered as Dualists, holding the existence of two independent principles, either secondary to another being from whom they are said to have originated [i.e. Zurvan], or themselves eternal in their own nature. The stress of the evidence . . . is in favour of their being viewed as secondary existences. Those who reject it will be obliged to admit the dualism of the Parsis in its most unmitigated form. Those who receive it, while they consider Hormazd and Ahriman the active lords of creation and providence, will still be held to be practical Dualists in the proper sense of the term. Whatever choice the Parsis may make in the case, most serious error must be laid to their charge, and secure their conviction before the bar of both reason and conscience. . . . (3) (pp. 170–1) . . . The doctrine of Two Principles . . . is both monstrous and supremely unreasonable. . . . It is a dogma, according to which God is robbed of his essential and peculiar glory. If it be true, God is not alone without a Creator; for the author of evil also exists without an origin. . . . (4) (p. 175) . . . We can of course have no dispute with them as to the fact that much evil exists in the world. Our controversy with them refers to the nature of evil, and the arrangements under which it is produced.

11.1.2 From Martin Haug, *Essays on . . . the Parsis*

Haug, a gifted German orientalist, was the first to discover for the West that the Gathas alone were the utterance of Zarathushtra. His monistic interpretation of Gathic doctrine, a modification essentially of Zurvanism, was reached at his own desk, and was subsequently expounded by him in public lectures in Bombay in the 1860s. This, the 'European heresy', was swiftly adopted by Parsi reformists as a defence against Christian attacks on Zoroastrian dualism.

(1) (p. 303) The opinion, so generally entertained now, that Zarathushtra was preaching a Dualism, that is to say, the idea of two original independent spirits, one good and the other bad, utterly distinct from each other, and one counteracting the creation of the other, is owing to a confusion of his philosophy with his theology. Having arrived at the grand idea of the unity and indivisibility of the Supreme Being, he undertook to solve the great problem which has engaged the attention of so many wise men ... viz. how are the imperfections discoverable in the world ... compatible with the goodness, holiness, and justice of God? This great thinker of remote antiquity solved this difficult question by the supposition of two primeval causes, which though different, were united, and produced the world of material things, as well as that of the spirit; which doctrine may best be learned from Y. 30 [= 2.2.2]. The one who produced the 'reality' is called vohu manah, 'the good mind', the other, through whom the 'non-reality' originated, bears the name aka manah, 'the evil mind'. . . . They are the two moving causes in the universe united from the beginning, and therefore, called 'twins'. They are present everywhere; in Ahuramazda as well as in men. (2) (p. 304) These two primeval principles, if supposed to be united in Ahuramazda himself, are ... called ... Spenta Mainyu, 'the beneficent spirit', and Angra Mainyu, 'the hurtful spirit'. . . . Spenta Mainyu was regarded as the author of all that is bright and shining, of all that is good and useful in nature; while Angra Mainyu called into existence all that is dark and apparently noxious. Both are as inseparable as day and night, and though opposed to each other, are indispensable for the preservation of creation. . . . (3) (pp. 305–6) Such is the original Zoroastrian notion of the two creative spirits, who form only two parts of the Divine Being. But in the course of time, this doctrine of the great founder was changed, and corrupted, in consequence of misunderstandings and false interpretations. Spenta Mainyu was taken as a name of Ahuramazda himself, and then, of course, Angra Mainyu, by becoming entirely separated from Ahuramazda, was regarded as the constant adversary of Ahuramazda; thus the Dualism of God and Devil arose. . . . After the sovereignty and independence of these two spiritual rulers was once acknowledged ... each of them was then supposed to have, like terrestrial rulers, his own council and court. The number of councillors was fixed at six, who were regarded as the actual governors of the whole universe, each ruling over a separate province assigned to him by his spiritual ruler. To Ahuramazda, or Spenta Mainyu, no other power was left but to preside over the celestial council. We often find him even included in the number of the celestial councillors who are then called 'the seven Ameshaspentas'. The several names by which we find the Ameshaspentas called ... are ... nothing but abstract nouns and ideas representing all the gifts which Ahuramazda ... grants to those who worship him with a sincere heart. . . . In the eyes of the prophet they

were no personages; that idea being imported into the sayings of the great master by some of his successors. ... (4) (p. 307) Quite separate from the celestial council stands Sraosha. ... While the Ameshaspentas in Zarathushtra's eyes represented nothing but the qualities and gifts of Ahuramazda, Sraosha seems to have been considered by him as a personality.

11.1.3 From E. W. West, *SBE*. V

West, an engineer on the Indian railways, and an outstanding scholar, was for Europe the pioneer of Pahlavi studies. His 'admitted even by Parsis themselves ...', written c. 1900, shows how rapidly Haug's ideas had influenced both Western-educated Parsis and other Europeans; but see in contrast 11.4.1.4.

(1) (pp. lxviii–lxx) The Parsi religion has long been represented by its opponents as a dualism; and this accusation, made in good faith by Muhammadan writers, and echoed more incautiously by Christians, has been advanced so strenuously that it has often been admitted even by Parsis themselves, as regards the mediaeval form of their faith. But neither party seems to have fairly considered how any religion which admits the personality of an evil spirit, in order to account for the existence of evil, can fail to become a dualism to a certain extent. ... (2) (pp. lxix–lxx) If it be necessary for a dualism that the evil spirit be omnipresent, omniscient, almighty, or eternal, then is the Parsi religion no dualism. ... (Ahriman's) powers are considerably less than those generally assigned by Christians to the devil, who is certainly represented as being a more intelligent and ubiquitous personage. On the other hand, Ahriman is able to produce fiends and demons, and the noxious creatures are said to be his; in which respects he has probably rather more power than the devil, although the limits of the latter's means of producing evil are by no means well defined. The origin and end of Ahriman appear to be left as uncertain as those of the devil, and, altogether, the resemblance between these two ideas of the evil spirit is remarkably close; in fact, almost too close to admit the possibility of their being ideas of different origin. The only important differences are that Zoroastrianism does not believe in an eternity of evil as Christianity does, and that Christianity has been content to leave all its other ideas about the devil in a very hazy and uncertain form, while Zoroastrianism has not shrunk from carrying similar ideas to their logical conclusion.

11.1.4 From Samuel Laing, *A Modern Zoroastrian*

Laing was appointed Finance Minister of the government of India, in 1861. He wrote several books for the educated Western public on religious questions in the light of contemporary science, his interpretation of Zoroastrian doctrine being essentially Zurvanite.

(1) (pp. 2–4) Electricity is itself subject to the law of polarity. ... In all cases a positive implies a negative; in all, like repels like and attracts unlike. Conversely, as polarity produces definite structure, so definite structure

everywhere implies polarity. The same principle prevails not only throughout the inorganic or world of matter, but through the organic or world of life, and specially throughout its highest manifestations in human life and character, and in the highest products of its evolution, in societies, religions, and philosophies. . . . But here let me interpose a word of caution. I must avoid the error . . . of confounding analogy and identity. Because the principle of polarity pervades alike the natural and spiritual world, I am far from assuming that the laws under which it acts are identical; and that virtue and vice, pain and pleasure, ugliness and beauty, are products of the same mathematical changes . . . as regulate the attractions and repulsions of molecules and atoms. All I say is, that the same pervading principle may be traced wherever human thought and human knowledge extend. . . . If I call myself 'a modern Zoroastrian' it is not that I wish or expect to teach a new religion or revive an old one, . . . but simply this. All religions I take to be 'working hypotheses', by which successive ages and races of men try to satisfy the aspirations and harmonise the knowledge which in the course of evolution have come to be, for the time, their spiritual equipment. The best proof of any religion is, that it exists — i.e. that it is part of the same evolution, and that on the whole it works well, i.e. is in tolerable harmony with its environment. When that environment changes, when loftier views of morality prevail, when knowledge is increased and the domain of science everywhere extends its frontier, religions must change with it if they are to remain good working, and not to become unworkable and unbelievable, hypotheses. (2) (pp. 4–5) Now of all the religious hypotheses which remain workable in the present state of human knowledge, that seems to me the best which frankly recognises the existence of this dual law, or law of polarity, as the fundamental condition of the universe, and, personifying the good principle under the name of Ormuzd, and the evil one under that of Ahriman, looks with earnest but silent and unspoken reverence on the great unknown beyond which may, in some way incomprehensible to mortals, reconcile the two opposites, and give the final victory to the good. . . . This, and this alone, seems to me to afford a working hypothesis which is based on fact, can be brought into harmony with the existing environment, and embraces, in a wider synthesis, all that is good in other philosophies, and religions. . . . (3) (p. 204) Admit that Christ is the best personification of the Spenta Mainyush, or good principle in the inscrutable Divine polarity of existence, and a man may be at the same time a Christian and a Zoroastrian.

11.2 PASSAGES FROM PARSI THEOSOPHICAL WRITINGS

In 1885 H. S. Olcott, a founder member of the American-based Theosophical Society, gave a series of lectures to Bombay Parsis. He praised their faith (of which his knowledge was only superficial) as 'one of the noblest, simplest . . . religions', but held that it rested on 'the living rock of Occult Science'.

F

Zarathushtra, he stated, having 'penetrated all the hidden mysteries of man's nature and the world', taught them 'under the safe cover of an external ritual'. So his followers should maintain and study this ritual. A number of Parsis joined the Theosophical Society, despite its basis in Vedantic Hinduism.

11.2.1 A theosophical interpretation of Zoroastrian ritual

(1) (p. xl) The Everlasting Life in its glorified state is represented in Mazdean Theology by Haoma. And the whole of the grander ritual of the Mazdayasnas centres round that holy idea. . . . The other essential in the holy ritual is the Holy Flame, the principle of Holy Vitality represented in all life and in all light, and comprising energy, health, and happiness. Ideally it is the glorified state of Divinity in its supremest splendour. . . . (2) (p. xliv) The glory of the Holy Flame ever strikes the mind and elevates the soul. Whereas its purifying energy not only rids the atmosphere of all impurities and fills it with life and animation for all breathing it, but it is also instrumental in creating pyro-electricity with all other kinds so apparently sought in the holy Mazdayasnan rituals. So that it also contributes to the concentration of all the nobler forces in Nature to help the beneficent effects of those grand and subtle operations. . . . (3) (p. xlv) . . . Alongside the sacred fire are also to be found in the holy precincts the sacred Fuel and the Sacred Incense; and these symbolize the fuel of good deeds which feeds and the incense of virtue which perfumes the Holy Fire of Life. . . . (4) (p. xlvi) The sacred Barsom draws our attention next. . . . The fact that the twigs have for a long time been replaced with metal rods, and that these are bound together in varying numbers and constantly held up and laid down on a special stand by the officiating divine during the sacred operations, at once suggests to us a purpose to generate a mild electrical current by the contact of heterogeneous metals. Indeed the idea of using the Barsom for the purpose of electrization need not be considered as a novelty latterly introduced into the service on the metal rods replacing the vegetable twigs: the ancients might have discovered a similar effect in certain vegetable twigs also. (From Sohrab J. Bulsara, *Aerpatastan and Nirangastan*.)

11.2.2 From a work of the 'Khshnoom' school

A purely Zoroastrian theosophical movement, 'Khshnoom', was founded in 1902 by a poorly educated Parsi of priestly family. The name is taken from the Gathic word 'khshnem', variant 'khshnum', cf. Y. 48.12, Y. 53.2 = 2.2.8.12, 17.2. The movement, which lays emphasis on orthopraxy, has a considerable following.

(1) (pp. 1–3) Though the great Zoroastrian Empire and Nations are non-existent, the Great Zoroastrian sages called 'Sahebe-Dilan' are still in existence in the mountain recesses of Persia, . . . having the old religion and its teachings intact with them. These sages have kept themselves secluded from the rest of the world. . . . Our late Ustad (Guru) Mr Behramshah Navroji Shroff, a Parsi

resident of Surat, was induced by them, at the age of eighteen years, by some inexplicable Law of Nature, to accompany them to their talismanic residence, where he was allowed to stay with them in their bountiful influence for three years and was taught about the Religion. Mr Shroff kept himself unknown for some years after his return from Persia and was out with his knowledge only in his last days. The knowledge of the Religion called 'Khshnoom' in Avesta was taught by him, which helped to explain the religion in its highly mystic development. The blessed word 'Khshnoom' is found in the Gathas, where it is venerated as the Word of God taught to the great prophet Spitama Zarathushtra. . . . The western mode of study has hardly enabled students to understand the Avestaic language, which abounds in words pregnant with technical interpretations, specially adapted to the special text, much less its philosophy and other mysticism. . . . (2) (pp. 6–8) Nature has in her working 'Mithra', i.e. the plan of creation and its redemption; 'Manthra', i.e. the basic foundation of the plan and its fulfilment; and 'Yasna', i.e. the creation of the universe according to the above plan and on the above basis. . . . Zoroaster through 'Haoma', i.e. Knowledge Divine of Ahura Mazda inspired in him by Ameshaspend Behman and Sarosh Yazat, had devised according to the . . . Divine Teachings . . . twenty-one Nasks . . . treating of the 'Mithra' (Planning Power), 'Manthra' (Sifting and Arranging Power), and 'Yasna' (Moving and Erecting Power), . . . the whole having been composed of 'Staota Vacha', capable of being understood by the developed heart powers with consequent growth of the third eye. . . . Authorised disciples and successors of the Prophet Zarathushtra . . . brought the 'Manthra' of such twenty-one Nasks called Fshusho-Manthra, into twenty-one Nasks of the talismanic Avestan language called Manthra-Spenta, the main part of which was written in Razengs. . . . The Razeng (cypher-codeword) style was meant only for the select few. The important part from these twenty-one Nasks . . . was put in the Avestaic language . . . capable of being understood by the laity. . . . The twenty-one Nasks of Fshusho-Manthra were kept unrevealed even in the Empire days. (3) (pp. 13–15) When in course of time and running of aeons materialism and ignorance of the spirit become established, the Saoshyants . . . will reestablish the 'daena' by the strength of the 'Patha' which is called in Gatha 53.2 the 'path of righteousness'. . . . Methods are devised called 'patha-tarikat', by which the lower self, the carnal desires, are subdued and the higher powers in the Self . . . are developed, which concentrate in a talismanic ring formed in the heart called 'Daena', a divine mirror which helps to see and feel the micro and the macro cosmos, i.e. the eternal universal consciousness. . . . The carnal desires and the invisible emanation due to the working of the carnal senses of the human body called 'Druj' obliterate the attainment of the occult heart powers. . . . As long as 'Druj' is triumphant in our body self-worth, self-recognition, self-appraisement, considering one's own reason competent enough to believe or disbelieve religious concepts of his birth, are prevalent in it with success, utterly forgetting with bleached-out faith the all-importance of Recognition of the One without a Second as the only Goal of the whole Universe. (From Framroze S. Chiniwalla, *Essential Origins of Zoroastrianism.*)

11.2.3 From another 'Khshnoomist' work

(1) (p. 137) Below the eighth heaven of the zodiac are the seven planetary heavens. . . . To the varied influences of the . . . planets on this earth races and individuals, their religions, cultures and civilizations, and all major upheavals of worldwide or nationwide magnitude, react in rise and fall, peace or war, weal or woe. . . . We have seen in the description of pre-cosmo-genesis world that souls possess varied degrees of Drvao, Evil. The rotations and revolutions of the planets being of varied velocities, the souls accommodated themselves in different planetary heavens suitable to their varied degrees of Drvao. Here a large mass of souls succeeded in eliminating their Drvao by self-effort, by a process somewhat akin to that of evaporation. However, there was another lot of souls which could not do so owing to their Drvao being very rigid or dense, and so for their purification Nature has created 'Dami' lit. creation (the Space), with which begins the mortal section of the Universe. (2) Before proceeding further it would be well to take a correct idea of the two terms 'Mazda-data' and 'Ahura-data', which are quite erroneously rendered in philology, and which relate respectively to the Infoldment of wicked souls into Matter, that is, investing them into physical bodies for their (spiritual) purification, and to the Unfoldment of saintly souls from Matter on their attaining complete purification. (3) (p. 138) 'The unfoldment of a soul is a process requiring ages after ages, and the Avesta word Urvan, with its derivation Uru, wide, and An, to breathe or exist, suggests that it is a principle always widening itself out, and thus expanding its consciousness', which means in other words that the consciousness of Urvans is not fully developed. In Khshnoomic parlance an Urvan up to the Lunar heaven at the bottom of the planetary world is a light with deficiency of divine knowledge, which is the cause of all Evil (Druj) in the world. Consequently, for effecting Reformation, that is, for transmuting this Druj, Evil, into Asha, holiness, for which the Universe is created, souls are exiled from their sidereal home in the eighth heaven . . . according to Mazda-data, the deified Law of Infoldment of Spirit (soul) into Matter, whereby the soul is invested with a physical body on this earth. Inversely, it may be stated that when a soul is on the path of righteousness, and after death advances upward to the paradisaical regions on its repatriating felicitous journey back toward the planetary world, though very very slowly, it (soul) is governed by Ahura-data, which is another law, also deified, but of Unfoldment of Spirit from Matter. It may be noted that Mazda-data and Ahura-data are both technical terms, where '-data' in both cases means 'law', and not 'made by', as erroneously rendered in philology (though etymologically correct) in the absence of Zoroastrian esoteric commentary knowledge. From the above it will be understood that a wicked soul trails down to this material world according to Mazda-data, and a holy soul ascends to the paradisaical regions according to

Ahura-data. (From Phiroz N. Tavaria, *A Manual of 'Khshnoom'*.)

11.3 WRITINGS BY MODERATE AND RADICAL REFORMISTS

11.3.1 From a catechism composed by a scholar-priest, *c.* 1910
This is based on Y. 12.8–9, which is part of the kusti prayers, see 3.4, 3.5. Since this part of the creed contains no reference to Anra Mainyu or the Daevas, the catechism could be composed without reference to an independent spirit of evil in the universe, in contrast to 9.1.1.

(4) Question. What does the Zoroastrian religion ask you to believe in? Answer. It asks us to believe in three things: . . . (i) the existence of Mazda, the all-wise Lord; (ii) the immortality of the soul, or life hereafter; and (iii) our responsibility for our thoughts, words and actions. (5) . . . Q. What does our religion say of God? A. . . . that God existed from all eternity. He always is, and will always be. . . . He has brought the whole universe into existence. . . . He is the Source of the existence of all. . . . (7) Q. What else does the Zoroastrian religion teach us about the Almighty? A. . . . that the Almighty is Mazda, i.e. Omniscient. . . . He governs the whole universe with wisdom. . . . (8) Q. What idea do we form of Ahura Mazda from the tenets of the Zoroastrian religion? A. The first and principal idea . . . is that He is omnipresent. . . . He has created the sun, the moon, the stars, air, water, the earth, together with other things whether animate or inanimate. . . . The second conception . . . is that of His Infinite Existence. . . . The third principal idea is that of His Omnipotence. He is perfectly capable of doing what He wishes in accordance with His fixed laws. . . . The fourth idea is that He . . . is Himself abounding in goodness and justice. (9) Q. (As to) the second thing we are to believe in . . . what do you mean by 'the life after death'? A. . . . All who are born will die one day and will have another life hereafter. . . . As, on birth, we came into existence from Ahura-Mazda, so after death we go back to Him. . . . (10) Q. What is the third . . . article of our faith? A. Our responsibility. . . . We shall be judged properly in the court of God, for all that we think, for all that we speak, for all that we do in this world. . . . If we do good in this world, Ahura-Mazda will do us good. . . . As Ahura-Mazda is the Lord of goodness and justice, if . . . we do not receive any reward due to our conduct in this life, we are sure to receive it in the hereafter. . . . (11) (Likewise) we are sure to be punished in one way or another for our bad conduct or the evil deeds we do. . . . Q. Then according to the teaching of our religion, there is no saviour for one, other than himself? A. Of course not. Every man is his own saviour. His deeds alone will bring about his salvation. . . . (12) Q. What do you mean by . . . 'I praise good thoughts, good words, good actions'? A. . . . Good thoughts, good words, good actions are the basis of our bearing in this life. It is these that lead us to salvation. . . . (15) Q. Then it is for its excellent moral teaching that a Zoroastrian praises the good Mazda-worshipping religion . . . ? A. Yes. (16) . . . In the Vendidad . . . it is said:

'Purity is best for man from his very birth, because purity is the same as the Mazda-worshipping religion.'... Purity is of two kinds, physical and mental.... Physical purity consists in always keeping our body clean and sound.... Mental purity consists in entertaining good thoughts and dispelling evil thoughts.... (21) The first principle of conduct should be this: We should do as much good to others as lies in our power. We should never harm others. We should do no harm even to our enemy.... We should act towards all in an upright way.... (22) ... We should treat all animals with kindness. Q. What about noxious creatures ...? A. ... Such a state of existence should be produced for them as would not permit of their doing harm. (23) Q. To whom else, besides our fellow men and animals, do we owe a duty? A. ... to all the objects of God's creation. . . . Ahura-Mazda expects us to promote the growth and development of the whole of His creation, whether animate or inanimate.... It is man's duty to engage himself in some sort of work. Work is a kind of worship.... (24) We must make good use of all the objects of God's creation.... Take for instance fire.... If an upright man prepares, on fire, his meal out of things bought of money acquired by honest means, he makes a good use of fire. The fire is, as it were, pleased with it.... That man ... is said to have done his duty towards that object of Ahura-Mazda's creation.... If a dishonest person prepares his meal on his household fire, out of things bought out of his ill-gotten gains, ... he makes a bad use of fire.... The Archangel Ardibehesht presiding over fire is displeased. (25) ... If a man prepares metallic tools to promote thereby agricultural or other industrial pursuits, the metal – or more properly speaking ... the Ameshaspand Shehrivar presiding over metal in general – becomes pleased. But if a thief, a robber, or a murderer prepares any metallic weapon, whereby he may kill others and rob them of their property, the Ameshaspand Shehrivar becomes displeased. (26) ... Our first duty towards ourselves is to keep our body and mind sound and healthy ... and then make such a good use of them as would lead us thereby to do good.... We should not enfeeble or enervate our body by unnecessary pain or exertion (nor) indulge in over-gratification of the senses and appetites. We must lead a simple life and maintain our body in good order.... Keeping fasts, leading a useless and idle life like that of the common class of ascetics and recluses, ... are wrongful acts.... (28) ... the path of Nature, wherein is generally observed harmony, system, law or order, is the path of asha, i.e. righteousness. (29) Q. The excellence of the sublime objects of Nature ... is recognised in our scriptures and a reverential regard is shown therein towards them. All this then, is ... to direct our thoughts from Nature to Nature's God? ... Is it also with the same object in view that ... we hold fire in reverence and erect fire temples ...? A. Yes.... We look to fire generally with reverential feelings, as the manifested form of the power of heat and light permeating this world, and also as a symbol of the splendour and glory of the Creator. Then, in the case of the sacred fire of the fire temples, the religious ritual in its consecration adds some elements of moral thoughts. (30) ... It is said in the Vendidad that the Zoroastrian religion is as much greater than all other religions, as the sea Vourukasha is greater than all other waters. . . . Those who wish to be called Zoroastrians must make an open declaration that their religion is the best of all. . . . Q. How are we to act towards other religions and (their) professors? A. With a firm and earnest belief in our own religion, we must behave with forbearance and toleration towards the professors of other religions. (31) Q. . . . what more do you declare in your confession of faith? A. 'I ascribe all good to Ahura-Mazda.' . . . We must express our thankfulness to the Creator for the good that we enjoy. . . . Q. On the other hand, if any evil happens to us . . . what are we to think of that? A. If that evil is the result of our own faults, we should repent . . . before God and should correct those faults. . . . Q. If we are involved in affliction not through our own faults or transgressions . . . what view are we to take of that? A. We should affirm our faith in God, and bear those sufferings with a confident hope that those sufferings are a trial for us and that everything will be right in the end. . . . We should . . . believe that everything is intended by Ahura-Mazda for our good. (From J. J. Modi, *A catechism of the Zoroastrian religion.*)

11.3.2 From a devotional work by a high priest

(1) (pp. 1–2) Thou art all in all to me, Ahura Mazda . . . my creator and nourisher, my guardian and protector, my guide and friend. . . . In my heart I will raise thee a sanctuary. There will I seek thee and find thee . . . there will my soul commune with thee. . . . Ill do I requite thy grace, when I desert thee and go over to Angra Mainyu, the Evil Spirit, and live for him. My footsteps slide on the path of wrong. . . . Let me faithfully and steadfastly range myself on thy side. Let me be steady in the performance of the task that thou dost assign me to do. . . . (2) (p. 3) Creation is the free act of thy divine goodness, Ahura Mazda. When nothing was, thou alone didst live in thy sublime self-sufficiency. Thou art the father of the Amesha Spentas and the Yazatas, and the Fravashis are thine. . . . (3) (p. 6) Thou, Ahura Mazda, didst say unto Zarathushtra that to see a righteous person was like seeing thee. I will then strive to see thee in the righteousness of righteous persons around me. But I pray to thee for more. Inspire me to act righteousness and own righteousness and be righteousness, that, steeped in righteousness, and being righteousness myself, I can see thee in my righteous self. . . . (4) (p. 17) The Fravashis represent thee, Ahura Mazda, and keep the living united with the dead. . . . The Fravashis bring to us from heaven the united blessings of the dead and take our thanksgivings heavenward in turn. . . . Nearer in time to Zarathushtra than we are, they have set the pattern of our conduct. . . . They have laid the foundation upon which our communal greatness is built. . . . With reverence and affection, let us so live that our living may be an honour to our departed dead. . . . (5) (pp. 21–2) Thou, Ahura Mazda, hast made Zarathushtra the lord and overseer over mankind. . . . He is the light of man's life. . . . To follow him is to follow thee. To be like him is to be like thee. I will assimilate Zarathushtra's teachings into my life. I will live devoted to him. . . . With Zarathushtra as my guiding spirit,

sustaining energy and driving will, fearlessly and courageously I will face whatever befalls me.... Zarathushtra is ever the same to us as he was to our ancestors.... He moulded the lives of our fathers and so may he mould and make our lives today and make our dear community patterned after his sublime life, Ahura Mazda.... (6) (pp. 24–5) In fire as the sublime symbol of my faith, I glory, O glorious Lord.... When I bow before the fire, I worship not the fire but thee alone, Ahura Mazda. Fire is but a sacred symbol that stands for thee and reminds me of thee.... In the enlightenment of the fire I will see thee, in its inspiration I will know thee. Verily it is said that fire is thy son, and through the son will my soul soar to thee, the Father.... The fire temple is the symbol in stone of the Mazdayasnian religion, and the fire priest feeds the consecrated fire with fresh fuel at every watch of the day and night. I shall raise an altar to thy divine fire burning in my heart and make it thy sanctuary. I will be my own fire priest and I will tend the holy fire within.... I will burn incense of the good thoughts of Vohu Manah and the righteousness of Asha, with the full-hearted devotion of Armaiti.... May my soul rise upward to thee, Ahura Mazda, as the flame on the altar leaps heavenward.... (7) (pp. 186–7) Spenta Mainyu, the Good Spirit, and Angra Mainyu, the Evil Spirit, are inveterate foes. With the advent of man upon earth the warfare between them has begun. It will end in the defeat of the Evil Spirit, when human life upon earth will end. The Evil Spirit deranges what the Good Spirit has arranged, frustrates what he has willed, levels down what he has raised.... Human nature likewise is based on the law of contrast and conflict. Irreconcilable opposites exist side by side in human nature. Vohu Manah, the Good Mind, and Aka Manah, the Evil Mind, are the two principles poised against each other in man.... Man has to fight evil within himself and in the world without. He has to seek the enemy, shake his fist at him, wage war with him, bravely face his attacks, intrepidly risk his all, and subdue the evil in his nature.... With a purpose higher and nobler than my own self-interest will I live my life upon earth. Daily will I fight to weaken the power of the Evil Spirit and to hasten his defeat. I will live the life of good thoughts and good words and good deeds. I will strive to convert Zarathushtra's ideal of life into the practical.... I will live pure life, Zoroastrian life, that thy life may pervade my inner life, Spenta Mainyu, thou Good Spirit of Ahura Mazda.... (8) (pp. 254–6) All communities are hydraheaded. They have their orthodox and their reformers, fanatics and soberminded persons, visionaries and men of commonsense, mystics and rationalists, hypocrites and sincere persons. The orthodox do not see the absurdity of remaining in bondage to the customs of infant humanity, when it was in swaddling clothes. They are wedded to the beliefs and practices, good and bad, that have come down to them through a long past and whose origin lies buried in obscurity.... Save me, my Saviour, from bigoted narrowness.... Let me not take the form for the substance. Let me not live according to the letter of religion, but according to its spirit.... Zarathushtra, the wisest priest of my religion, does not forcibly exact implicit, mechanical obedience from me to his teachings. He . . . leaves me freedom of thought to exercise my will freely. May the breath of Vohu Manah, Good Mind, blow the mists of superstition and credulity . . . from my mind and illumine it with the gleams of sunshine of needful reform. May he, the premier archangel of Ahura Mazda, so guide me that I may not be impervious to the light of the new age. . . . Let me not forget the debt I owe to the past, yet let me discern the signs of the age I live in. Let me be in harmony with it. (From M. N. Dhalla, *Homage unto Ahura Mazda.*)

11.3.3 From a public address by a radical lay reformist
For the extreme rejection, by some western-educated Parsis, of tradition in doctrine and observance cf. 1.1.1.20, 1.4.2 and 3.

(1) I therefore beg of you with all the earnestness I am capable of to set about the business of reform in religious matters. The first and most imperative need of the times is to have a simple creed of the Zoroastrian religion. When the fundamental beliefs are formulated, it will be seen how singularly free from all dogmas the Zoroastrian creed is. The one dogma which is often hurled at the heads of Zoroastrians by the enemies of our faith, namely, the doctrine of two independent self-created deities, Spenta Mainyu and Angra Mainyu, continually fighting with each other, is not accepted by the best exponents of our faith, these opposing so-called deities being only the good and evil motives or feelings in our mind which are opposed to each other, before a man endowed with free will decides in favour of the good motives and bases his action upon them alone. If this dogma is discarded, there is nothing like a dogma left in the articles of our faith, which can be reduced to a very simple belief in an omniscient, all-bountiful and omnipotent God, who insists on good thought, good word and good action, and ordains evil to the evildoer and blessings to the pure both in this world and the next, according to their thoughts, words and deeds. If our creed is thus authoritatively formulated by an ecclesiastical council formed of the best religious experts in our community, it will stand out in most favourable contrast to the creeds of other religious systems. . . . (2) I would dwell for a moment on this aspect of our religion. It is singularly free from dogmas, and is so simple in its tenets that it differs but little from Unitarianism or Rationalism. Its system of morality is extremely simple, straightforward and practical, like the practical morality of Freemasons. It is not overlaid with metaphysical distinctions and disquisitions such as are found in the Hindu schools of philosophy, which, however ingenious and subtle they may be from an academic point of view, have led to harassing and unpractical observances. The progress and prosperity of the Parsis are not a little indebted to their religion, which enjoins righteousness in thought, word and deed, vigorous activity of body and mind, a hatred of asceticism, purity of conduct, cleanliness of habits, stern punishment and suppression of all evildoers, love of all mankind, and charity without distinction of caste or creed. (From the presidential address to the Fourth Zoroastrian Conference, 1913, given by Mr H. J. Bhabha; cited by J. H. Moulton, *The Treasure of the Magi,* 174–5.)

11.4 TRADITION IN BELIEF AND PRACTICE

11.4.1 From a Parsi account of Parsis in rural Gujarat, 1898

Much of this account would still have been true at that time of many Bombay Parsis. The use of 'nerang' (more exactly, 'gomez') in (1) is to make a barrier between the impurities of the body and the pure creation of water, see further 11.6.2.4.

(1) (p. 208) . . . both men and women are early risers. The religious, who make a point of reciting prayers between three in the morning and dawn, at which the Parsi day begins, leave their beds between three and four, and most others are up a good while before sunrise. All, on rising, standing at the foot of their bed, loosen their sacred cord, 'kusti', and recite the 'kusti' prayer. When the prayer is finished they take some cow's urine, 'nerang', in the palm of the left hand, and while reciting a short prayer, rub it on their face, hands and feet and afterwards wash with water the parts rubbed. The devout and those who have leisure bathe at once daily after the 'nerang' prayer. The poor bathe once in three or four days. Every time they take a bath, that is, before they commence to wash the body with water, they rub the urine three times over their whole person. After washing the body they clean the mouth and again recite the sacred-cord prayer. They are now ready either to recite further prayers or to take a light breakfast, and go to work or visit friends or the fire temple. . . . (2) (p. 209) Traders, shopkeepers and clerks stay at their offices or shops till about seven. On returning home they wash their face, hands and feet, recite the sacred-cord prayer, and sup either at once or after reciting the night prayers, beginning with a short prayer before the lamp. After supper they play chess or cards or chat for an hour or two, or at once go to bed. After every call of nature all Parsis wash the face, hands and feet and recite the sacred-thread prayer. In places where palm liquor is plentiful . . . 'tadi' or palm liquor parties of men and women are often arranged, those who join them going to the palm gardens about three and making merry till after sunset. (3) Parsi women rise about four, go through the sacred-thread and cow-urine prayers, wash, sweep the house and part of the street in front of the house, clean the vessels to be used during the day, bring the day's supply of fresh water from the well, sprinkle with water the whole house, the entrance, and the street in front of the house. . . . By seven they have prepared tea and breakfast for the house, and cooking and other housework keeps them busy till about noon. . . . After the male members of the family have dined, the women dine, clean the dishes, rest or bathe, and spin or weave till about three. At three the house is again swept and cleaned and sprinkled with water, and about five those who did not bring water in the morning go to fetch it. On returning home they light the lamps and carry over the whole house a small metal urn of burning frankincense, and, especially on new-moon day, hang garlands of sweet flowers round the lamp. They next bake bread and make ready the other articles which have to be cooked for supper. . . . (4) (p. 212) The leading beliefs which as a Zoroastrian

the ordinary Parsi holds, are the existence of one God, Ahuramazd, the creator of the universe, the giver of good, the hearer and answerer of prayer. Next to Ahuramazd the name most familiar to a Parsi is that of Ahriman, Angromanyus, or Satan, to whom he traces every evil and misfortune that happens to him, and every evil thought and evil passion that rises in his mind. He thinks of Ahuramazd and Ahriman as hostile powers and in his prayers he often repeats the words 'I praise and honour Ahuramazd; I smite Angromanyus'. He believes that every man has an immortal soul which after death passes either to a place of reward . . . or of punishment. (5) (p. 213) The reward or punishment of the soul depends on its conduct during life. At the same time the due performance by its friends of certain rites helps the soul to reach the abode of happiness. . . . He believes in Zoroaster or Zarathushtra as the Prophet who brought the true religion from Ahuramazd. He believes that when the world becomes overburdened with evil, Soshios [= the Saoshyant], the son of Zarathushtra, will be born and will destroy evil, purify the world, and make the Mazdayasnian religion supreme. . . . (6) Fire is the chief object of Parsi veneration and the Fire Temple is the public place of Parsi worship. Gujarat fire temples . . . include an outer and an inner hall. In the centre of the inner hall is a small domed room, and in the centre of the room on a solid stone stool stands an urn of copper-brass or of silver in which burns the sacred fire fed with sandal and other commoner woods. . . . The hearth fire . . . a Parsi never allows to go out. If he changes his place of residence in the same town or village he carries his fire with him to his new abode. If he goes beyond the town or village he gives his fire to his neighbours or relations who mix it with their own fire. . . . (7) (p. 215) Religious Parsis visit the fire temple almost daily, and on four days in each month, the 3rd, 9th, 17th and 20th, which are sacred to fire, almost all Parsis go and offer prayers. Men and women come to the same part of the temple and worship the fire in the same way. On reaching the fire temple the worshipper washes his face, hands and feet and recites the 'kusti' . . . prayer. Then carrying a piece of sandalwood and some money for the officiating priest, he passes through the outer hall. On entering the inner hall where a carpet is spread he takes off his shoes and goes to the threshold of the central fire room, kneels, and again standing begins to recite prayers. The worshipper is not allowed to pass the threshold of the fire room; the priest alone is allowed to enter. . . . (8) (p. 216) The day of the month that bears the same name as the month is a holiday. . . . The high priest, priests and leading men meet in the hall of the fire temple. They sit on a carpet with trays of fruit and flowers before them and with a small fire urn which one of the priests feeds with sandal and frankincense, and recite hymns of praise and thanksgiving in honour of the guardian angel [i.e. yazad] of the month. When the prayers are over the fruit is handed round and all present are bound to taste it. This rite is called 'Jasan', that is, feast. . . . All Soul's Feast . . . is performed in honour of the . . . Fravashis. . . . Parsis go to the Towers of Silence, offer prayers for dead relations and friends, and in the large yard round the Towers . . . spread carpets and hold private 'jasans'. . . . The 'Avan Ardvisur Jasan' . . . is held in honour of the . . . angel who presides over water. On this day Parsis go to the seashore or to the river bank and pray. . . . Many throw into the sea or river coconuts, sugar and flowers. . . . (At) the Fire Feast, 'Adar Jasan', . . . almost all Parsis go to the fire temple with offerings of sandalwood and pray before the fire. The rich and well-to-do distribute money in charity to priests and to poor Parsis. . . . During the whole month of Bahman all try to show kindness to animals, feeding street dogs with milk and cattle with grass. The devout abstain from animal food during the whole month. . . . Besides the monthly 'jasans' . . . other festivals called Gahambars . . . are held in great veneration among the Parsis. . . . They are held six times a year, each lasting five days, when the whole community meet on terms of equality and offer prayers and thanks and join in a common feast. . . . (9) (p. 218) Naoroz the New Day . . . (is) a day of universal rejoicing. . . . Both men and women rise earlier than usual, put on their best clothes, and deck their children with ornaments. After offering prayers of repentance in their houses [for the sins of the past year], they go to the fire temple with offerings of sandalwood. In the streets and in the temple they give alms to the poor. In the fire temple they offer their prayers before the sacred fire and then go visiting friends and relations, the hosts offering the guests the choicest wines, fruits and sweets. . . . After the visits are over they spend the rest of the day in feasting with their families or in attending garden parties. . . . As among Parsis eating and drinking are considered religious acts and fasting and penance are forbidden, all holidays are spent in feasting, rejoicing and prayer. . . . (10) (p. 219) . . . Parsis have many minor practices and observances to which more or less of a religious sanction is supposed to attach. A Parsi must always keep his head and feet covered, he must never be without the sacred shirt and cord, must never smoke. . . . He must return thanks to God before every meal and keep silence while he is eating. The Parsi prayer before meals is [the Itha aat yazamaide, cf. 3.1, 3.1.3.1]. After shaving his head a Parsi should bathe before touching anything. Similarly on leaving his bed, before he can touch or do anything, a Parsi is required to perform the smaller ablution, that is to wash his face hands and feet, and to perform the larger ablution, that is to bathe his whole person, if he has had impure dreams or has cohabited. In practice, though they know they are laid down in their religion, Parsis neglect many of these rules. Parsis are very careful regarding the ceremonial uncleanness of a woman in her periods. . . . She has to sit apart on an iron bed placed in a corner of the house, her food is served to her from a distance, and all clothes which she has worn during her period must be washed before they can be used again. After sneezing or yawning old Parsis generally say, 'Broken be Ahriman,' apparently believing that the spasm of breath in sneezing or yawning is the work of an evil spirit. When a tooth is drawn or when the nails or hair are cut, texts should be said over them and they should be buried four inches under ground. Temple priests are careful to observe this practice. The cock is held sacred [to Srosh] and is never killed or eaten after it has begun to crow. The widespread belief (is) that the crow of the cock scares evil spirits and defeats their wiles. . . . Strict old women never let people sleep with the head towards the north, because the north is the home of Ahriman and his evil spirits. (From K. N. Seervai and B. B. Patel, *Gujarat Parsis*.)

11.4.2 Inauguration of the Anjoman Atash Bahram, Bombay, 1897

For the preparatory ceremonies of consecration cf. 4.1.2 and see Modi, Religious Ceremonies and Customs, 200 ff. One reason for their length is that lightning fire is needed among the fires purified to create an Atash Bahram. Swords are carried by the processing priests (2) as a symbol of the unceasing fight against evil.

(1) Yesterday was a red-letter day in the history of the Parsees of Bombay. . . . The fire temple which was opened . . . with great . . . ceremony on the Girgaum Road . . . was constructed and endowed out of the funds of the Anjuman or the Community residing not only in Bombay, but in some of the distant parts of India, and also in China and Persia. . . . The enthusiasm of the community for their new fire temple may well be judged by some thousands of them paying visits to the new building, which was constructed after the Persepolitan style. . . . From an early hour in the morning hundreds and thousands of Parsees were seen wending their way from all parts of the city to their new Atash Bahram, where the sacred fire, the preparation and purification of which involved long and elaborate ceremonies and took no fewer than twelve years, was to be installed, or as the Parsees would say 'enthroned', in the sanctum sanctorum of the fire temple, where no one but the officiating priest can enter. The Parsees eschewed their English or semi-English costume for the day, and attended the ceremony in white coat and trousers, which are considered their full dress, many of the leading citizens putting on their 'jama' (a long flowing gown) and 'pitchori' (waist band), being the dress worn on festive occasions. By 9 a.m. the Atash Bahram was full of Parsees, the two halls on the ground floor and the upper spacious hall being full to overflowing. The congregation . . . inside the fire temple numbered about ten thousand persons. . . . The Shenshais and the Kadmees, the orthodox and the advanced party, all drowned their . . . differences for the time being, and graced the occasion by their presence. (2) About 9 a.m. before the gates were opened for the general public . . . a procession was formed of priests, some of them armed with swords, with the high priest walking in front, followed by members of the committee, and the sacred fire was transferred from the 'Dar-i Mihr', where it had been kept, to the new fire temple, and enthroned there with appropriate ceremonies. The public were then admitted into the new premises, and thousands of them, each carrying in his hands his contribution of pieces of sandalwood for feeding the sacred fire, appeared before the new sanctum sanctorum to offer up prayers. The premises were decorated throughout with flowers and evergreens. . . . The grand 'jasan' ceremony was then commenced by Dastur Jamaspjee Minocherjee and Dastur Kaikobad of Poona, who sat in

the middle of three parallel rows of priests on the carpeted floor, having in front of them large trays filled with fruits, flowers, sacred bread, milk, rose water, etc. . . . (3) These thanksgiving ceremonies . . . lasted about an hour. . . . Mr Jalbhai Ardesir Sett, Chairman of the Managing Committee, then declared, amid prolonged cheering, that . . . the new 'Atash Bahram' was now open for worship to the members of the community. . . . The Chairman also alluded to the zealous care evinced in the performance of the many difficult and complicated religious ceremonies which were absolutely necessary for the purification of the 101 fires, a combination of which constituted the sacred fire which was installed that morning. . . . A large number of Parsee ladies visited the fire temple during the day, and made offering of pieces of sandalwood. The entire street in which the fire temple is situated was illuminated in the evening, and the Parsees throughout the city held high feast in commemoration of the inauguration of the fire temple. (From the report, slightly rearranged, in the *Times of India*, 18 October 1897; cited by B. B. Patel, *Parsi Religious Buildings*, 489–93.)

11.4.3 Texts concerning dakhmas (towers of silence)

Cf. 4.2. For the liturgies of preparation and consecration of a dakhma see Modi, Ceremonies and customs, *ch. 10. Parsis living far away from their oldest communities necessarily bury their dead (with special precautions against contaminating the earth), or use electric cremation. The continuance of the rite of exposure, strongly upheld by traditionalists, is currently a subject of controversy within the community. Cf. 11.6.2.4.*

11.4.3.1 The foundation ceremony for a dakhma, Navsari, 1877

(1) This morning between six and ten o'clock the inaugural ceremony connected with the foundation work of a new Tower of Silence at Navsari was performed in accordance with the ancient rites of Zoroastrianism, in the presence of an assembly of about five thousand Parsees. . . . About one-half came from Ahmedabad, Surat, Broach, Anklesar and other places in Gujarat; more than a fourth from Bombay; while the remaining portion might be placed to the credit of Navsari and adjacent villages. . . . The mail train which left Bombay last night and arrived here at 3.30 a.m. this morning . . . was 'a purely Parsee train' . . . ; for the driver was a Parsee, the guard was a Parsee; and the whole of the passengers were Parsees. . . . Shortly before the special started, the platform of the station was more densely crowded than it has ever been known to have been in the recollection of the oldest railway traveller. There were Parsee mammas with babes held in their arms, and young Parsee ladies by their side, who had been taught by their family priests to regard attendance at the performance of ceremonies connected with a Tower of Silence as an act of exemplary piety; there was the old orthodox Parsee, with a growing dimness in his eyes, with a faltering voice and a tottering step, leaning heavily upon his crutch, who looked upon attendance at the ceremony as a talisman which would help to open the gates of paradise to him; there was the gaily dressed young

Parsee of the period, who entertained as the best an equivocal sense of the piety or value attached to the ceremony; and there were little Parsee boys and girls who cared little for, and understood less of, either its piety or efficacy. . . . During the journey the women sang favourite gurbees (ditties) in chorus, while the young men amused themselves by singing Hindustani and other songs . . . from midnight until the train steamed into Navsari station. . . . (2) The gentleman at whose expense the Tower of Silence is to be built, Mr Nusserwanjee Ruttonjee Tata, had engaged from 300 to 400 bullock carts for driving the visitors from the station into the city, a distance of about two miles. . . . In Navsari nearly all the Parsee residents possess houses of their own, and all these, numbering about 1,800, afforded accommodation to the friends and acquaintances of the owners. To provide . . . accommodation for the rest, several temporary hotels had been improvised. . . . Chief among these were four hotels opened in Khurshed Varree, where long mandaws (marquees) had been put up. . . . Khurshed Varree presented a novel spectacle. The approach to it had been decorated with strings of paper bannerets, while a company of native musical instrument beaters, who were stationed in the entrance, were meant to remind the people that the day was sacred to feasting and public rejoicing. . . . A long passage decorated on each side with evergreens, and supporting coloured lanterns, led you to the spacious, well protected mandaws, which were kept cool with festoons of leaves and flowers. Here on the ground, covered with matting . . . meals were served on fresh plantain leaves. Some of the principal Parsee streets in the city were decorated with flags and bannerets . . . , which contributed their share to the public rejoicing; crowds of sightseers and tomtom beaters wandered from place to place, and their presence in the streets added to the general liveliness of the occasion. . . . (3) From six o'clock in the morning the carts, which had carried the visitors from the station into the city, were again put into requisition to take them to the high ground on which the Towers of Silence are situated, . . . about two miles from Navsari and four from the railway station. . . . Two roads lead to the Towers, one a raised footpath for the use of and accessible to Parsees only, the other a public road full of ruts and hollows and a deep coating of dust. The private road is raised on masonry arches in places which, in the monsoon, are filled with large sheets of water which rendered access to the Towers impossible except by boats, in which the dead bodies had formerly to be carried. . . . (4) Outside the enclosure wall of the Towers, several booths had been erected for the sale of sweetmeats and refreshments, while on the other side of the gateway is a room containing chatties [pots] filled with drinking water for the use of Parsees. Here also the pious Zoroastrian washes his hands, feet and face before he enters the enclosure and commences to say his prayers for the dead. . . . There are already three Towers of Silence built within the enclosure, which is about 30,000 square yards in extent, one of which is said to be 350 years old. . . . Only one of the three is in use at present; and the fact is pretty clearly evidenced by a number of vultures which had perched over the top of the wall. (5) The foundations of the

Tower to be built at Mr Tata's expense have been laid on a high piece of ground within the enclosure. . . . The building of the Tower is likely to occupy a year and a half, and its estimated cost amounts to Rs. 70,000. A circular mandaw had been erected over the mouth of the circular hollow dug for the foundations of the Tower. Benches had been placed in the mandaw for the accommodation of the visitors, who were protected from accidents by a bamboo railing fixed over the hollow. . . . The Tower is to be $70\frac{1}{2}$ ft in diameter with the surrounding wall being $4\frac{1}{2}$ ft. The inner diameter will be $61\frac{1}{2}$ ft. In the middle of the Tower is a well, 20 ft in diameter, in the north-east, south-east, north-west, and south-west, corners of which are cut four outlets, . . . each $4\frac{1}{4}$ ft wide, which will communicate with four wells to be dug at equal distances from the Tower [and lined with charcoal or sand]. The four outlets divide the inner space into four oblong blocks, which stand at each corner of the well, and are intended to contain slabs for the exposure of dead bodies. Matter issuing from the dead bodies trickles down into the well, and is carried down by the outlets into the four wells, which are covered up. Looking at the [foundations] of the Tower today, you saw the surface of the four blocks three feet lower than the surface of the ground, the bottom of the well three feet lower than the surface of the blocks. . . . (6) The two priests, who officiated today, got on to the top of one of the blocks, then got down into the well, and by means of one of the outlets . . . got finally to the foundations of the outer wall. They then fixed in the ground four huge iron nails, each about a maund in weight, facing each of the four outlets, . . . and a similar nail in the centre of the well. In the foundations of the outer wall, they then fixed thirty-six smaller nails, crossways, at a short distance from each other, there thus being nine nails to each of the four blocks. They next fixed a large nail in the entrance of each of the outlets from the well; also sixty-four nails on both sides of each outlet, that is, thirty-two on each side, making in all 301 nails, large and small. With a large bundle of yarn, the priests [reciting Avesta continually], went the round of the nails three times and interwove a warp round the nails, giving three threads to each nail. A communication was thus established by means of the yarn between all 301 nails, and the ceremony concluded about 9.15 a.m., when the priests got out. The spectators, each according to his means, then threw silver and copper coins into the well. . . . (7) Mr Byramjee Jeejeebhoy, C.S.I., addressing Mr Nusserwanjee Tata, wished success to the pious work which had been begun that day. . . . Mr Tata deserved the thanks of the Zoroastrian community for having taken upon himself the expense and trouble of building a Tower, a work in the successful completion of which, even when assisted by the subscriptions of the entire community, many obstacles had to be encountered. Mr Byramjee wished every success to the work, and prayed for God's blessing upon it, and that it might be brought to a successful close. (From the *Bombay Gazette*, 10 March 1877, cited by B. B. Patel, *Parsi Religious Buildings*, 231–6; some of the material has been slightly rearranged.)

11.4.3.2 From public notices concerning the consecration of a Bombay dakhma, 1832

Framjee Cowasjee begs to inform his friends and the public, that he has erected a 'Tower of Silence' or Cemetery on the Malabar Hill, which he will leave open for such of the Ladies and Gentlemen as may be desirous of inspecting it, till the 15th of April next – after which day, the ceremonies will commence. . . . There will be a general assemblage of Parsees, . . . the Cemetery will be consecrated, and a solemn feast [jasan] held by all assembled; no admission will be allowed to any other caste from and after (that day). . . . Framjee Cowasjee will . . . feel particularly obliged if such of the Ladies and Gentlemen as have Parsee Clerks and Servants will be pleased to grant them leave on this day. As the road leading to the Hill will be literally covered with conveyances of every description on the above day, Framjee Cowasjee begs to state that the passage will be attended with some delay, if not inconvenience, and he trusts the cause will be considered as an excuse. (From the *Bombay Gazette*, April–May 1832; cited by B. B. Patel, *Parsi Religious Buildings*, 66–7.)

11.4.3.3 From a description of a completed dakhma

It is a circular platform about 300 ft in circumference, entirely paved with large stone slabs, and divided into three rows of exposed receptacles, called pavis, for the bodies of the dead. As there are the same number of pavis in each concentric row, they diminish in size from the outer to the inner ring, so that by the side of the wall is used for the bodies of the males, the next for those of the females and the third for those of the children. These receptacles or pavis are separated from each other by ridges which are about one inch in height, and channels are cut into the pavis for the purpose of conveying all the liquid matter flowing from the corpses, and rainwater, into a bhandar, or deep hollow in the form of a pit, the bottom of which is paved with stone slabs. This pit forms the centre of the tower. When the corpse has been completely stripped of its flesh by the vultures, which is generally accomplished within an hour at the outside, and when the bones of the denuded skeleton are perfectly dried up by the powerful heat of a tropical sun and other tropical influences, they are thrown into the pit where they crumble into dust – the rich and the poor thus meeting together after death in one common level of equality. (From D. F. Karaka, *History of the Parsis*, Vol. 1, 200–1.)

11.4.3.4 A European reaction

When the Secretary had finished his defence of the 'Tower of Silence', I could not help thinking that however much such a system may shock our European feelings and ideas, yet our own method of interment, if regarded from a Parsi point of view, may possibly be equally revolting to Parsi sensibilities. The exposure of the decaying body to the assaults of innumerable worms may have no terrors for us; but let it be borne in mind that neither are the Parsi survivors permitted to look at the swoop of the heaven-sent birds. Why then should we be surprised, if they prefer the more rapid to the more lingering operation! and

which of the two systems, they may reasonably ask, is more defensive on
sanitary grounds? (From Monier Williams, *Modern India and the Indians*,
88–9.)

11.4.4 A gathering for the sunset prayers

*The description belongs to the late nineteenth century; but this evening
gathering of Bombay Parsis continued to attract the notice of travellers well
into the twentieth.*

A shrewd Scotch-American ironmaster, Andrew Carnegie ... gives the
following description of the worship of the modern Parsees, as actually
witnessed by him in Bombay: 'This evening we were surprised to see, as we
strolled along the beach, more Parsees than ever before, and more Parsee ladies
richly dressed, all wending their way towards the sea. It was the first of the new
moon, a period sacred to those worshippers of the elements; and here on the
shore of the ocean, as the sun was sinking in the sea, and the slender silver
thread of the crescent moon was faintly shining on the horizon, they
congregated to perform their religious rites. Fire was there in its grandest form,
the setting sun, and water in the vast expanse of the Indian Ocean outstretched
before them. The earth was under their feet, and wafted across the sea the air
came laden with the perfumes of 'Araby the blest'. Surely no time or place could
be more fitly chosen than this for lifting up the soul to the realms beyond
sense. ... How inexpressibly sublime the scene appeared to me, and how
insignificant and unworthy of the unknown seemed even our cathedrals 'made
with human hands', when compared with this looking up through nature unto
nature's God! I stood and drank in the serene happiness which seemed to fill the
air. I have seen many modes and forms of worship, ... but all poor in
comparison with this. Nor do I ever expect in all my life to witness a religious
ceremony which will so powerfully affect me as that of the Parsees on the beach
at Bombay'. (Cited by S. Laing, *A Modern Zoroastrian*, 219–20.)

11.4.5 On the practical charity of the Parsis

For traditional usages behind these activities cf. 10.6.6.2.

Wherever in India or abroad there lived five to ten Parsis or more, a
Panchayat or Anjoman soon grew up and collected funds for common religious
and charitable purposes. Their activities soon expanded to meeting other needs
as of relief of poverty, assistance for education, providing medical care, housing
and other social needs. The apex of these local Anjomans has been the Parsi
Panchayat of Bombay, the custodian of the funds of most of the Panchayats in
India and a few from abroad. This great co-operative pyramid of the Parsis has
been a bulwark of strength, representing a modest structure of a unique Social
Security system. ... Although all the wants of the needy members may not be
met adequately, one can say that no deserving Parsi need starve or grow
hungry, no Parsi child need grow up without minimum education, and no sick
Parsi need suffer from want of medical care. (J. F. Bulsara, *Bird's Eye Picture
of the Parsis*, 9.)

11.5 MATTERS OF CONTROVERSY

11.5.1 On the conversion question among Parsis

Irani Zoroastrians have never been opposed to conversion (cf. 10.5.1.8), though, historically, seeking to convert Muslims would have meant death. There has been much controversy concerning the matter among Parsis. Most of the orthodox maintain today the traditional position, that blood and faith are a linked heritage, which can be transmitted through the male line alone. The strictest go further, and refuse to accept as a co-religionist the child of a Zoroastrian father and a non-Zoroastrian mother. The question is of considerable practical importance, since it affects admission to fire temples and to all major religious observances.

11.5.1.1 From two concurring judgments delivered in the Bombay High Court by a Parsi and an English judge in a twentieth-century lawsuit

The lawsuit was brought by a group of Parsis against members of the Bombay Parsi Panchayat, which had ruled not to accept as one of the community the foreign wife of a Parsi who had converted to Zoroastrianism.

11.5.1.1a From the judgment of Mr Justice Davar. A Zoroastrian need not necessarily be a Parsi. Any one who professes the religion promulgated by Zoroaster . . . becomes a Zoroastrian the moment he is converted to the faith; but . . . a Parsi born must always be a Parsi, no matter what other religion he subsequently adopts and professes. . . . There are three categories of Parsis: Parsis who are descended from the original Persian emigrants, and who are born of both Zoroastrian parents, and who profess the Zoroastrian religion; the Iranis from Persia professing the Zoroastrian religion, who come to India, either temporarily or permanently; and the children of Parsi fathers by alien mothers who have been duly and properly admitted to the faith. . . . [Be it noted] (i) that the Zoroastrian religion not only permits but enjoins the conversion of a person born in another religion and of non-Zoroastrian parents. (ii) That, although such conversion was permissible, the Zoroastrians, ever since their advent into India . . . have never attempted to convert any one into their religion. (iii) That there is not a single instance proved before the Court of a person born of both non-Zoroastrian parents ever having been admitted into the Zoroastrian religion professed by the Parsis in India.

11.5.1.1b From the judgment of Mr Justice Beaman. I am quite ready to start with the assumption that the Plaintiffs make, namely, that when the Zoroastrian exiles fled from the Mussulman persecution, they brought with them to India as their common bond . . . their ancient religion. I will go further and add that, at that remote time, they would probably have not only approved but welcomed Converts if – to use the phrase that has so often been repeated – those Converts would do no harm to the good religion. They needed help, they needed countenance, they needed, above all things, powerful allies. . . . They were then not a dominant, but a . . . scattered people, the mere remnant and straggling fugitives of an overturned kingdom ..., in a strange land, surrounded by strange peoples, professing an unknown religion. In these circumstances, it is easy to understand that while they dared not proselytise, they would have been only too glad to welcome influential Converts from Hinduism and Mahomedanism. ... But two main causes must have been steadily at work to re-mould, and by degrees altogether to transform, the attitude of the community towards conversion. The first, and no doubt the most powerful of these, was the immemorial Indian caste sentiment, with which the whole atmosphere in which they lived was charged. The second was their own growing prosperity. This had a natural and inevitable tendency to reinforce the pressure of the caste principle and to accelerate its growth. Caste must always be more acceptable to a high, than to a low, order in its organisation. In proportion as the Indian Zoroastrians were able to compare themselves and their circumstances freely, without apprehension, with the peoples about them with whom they came into the most direct and frequent contact ... it is almost certain that the caste idea must have struck a deeper and deeper root, and coloured all their relations with the indigenous Indians in their neighbourhood. ... While theoretically adhering to their ancient religion and consistently avowing its principal tenets – including, of course, the merit of conversion as the theological dogma, they erected about themselves real caste barriers, and gradually fell under the influence of the caste idea, till, in modern popular language, it has found current expression in the term Parsi, which now seems to me to have as distinctly a caste meaning ... as that used to denominate any other great Indian caste. This, of course, by analogy only; but yet by an analogy that was forced upon the Indian Zoroastrians by the circumstances and conditions in which they found themselves, and by adaptation to which their corporate existence was alone made possible. ... The first glance at the Defendants' definition of members of the Parsi community professing the Zoroastrian faith satisfied me ... that we were not really concerned with a religious, but with a caste question. ... The Defendants, expressing as we now know the orthodox Parsi view, are ready to admit any and every Irani Zoroastrian ..., but they will not admit the purest, most blameless foreigner. Why? Because a foreigner is outside the caste, and caste is an institution into which you must be born. (From Suit No. 689 of 1906, Sir Dinsha Maneckji Petit and others *v.* Sir Jamshetji Jeejeebhoy and others, *Indian Law Reports*, XXXIII, Bombay Series, 1908, 538 ff.)

11.5.1.2 From an address by a Parsi reformist

This concept of 'purity of blood' should certainly not transcend the inner core of our belief which is pure thoughts, pure words, pure deeds. In fact I am of the opinion that the present controversy on whether the children of Parsi women married to non-Parsis can take on the faith or not is too timid. ... I am for more robust reforms. I believe all those who are even remotely connected by blood to the Parsis should be ordained into the community through a Navjote ceremony at any time in their life ... through their own free will and preference. I would go further and recommend that all those who voluntarily practise the Zoroastrian faith and subscribe to the Zoroastrian ethic should be taken into the fold. . . . I should like to re-emphasise the need to vitalise the community genetically. (Mr Piloo Mody, M.P., in R. B. Pastakia (ed.), *Treatise on Zoroastrian Tradition* . . . , p. i.)

11.5.2 Two writers on the reincarnation controversy
11.5.2.1 From a theosophical exposition
For the remote date given to Zarathushtra in (4) cf. 1.4.1.3.

(1) Reincarnation or rebirth . . . is a most controversial doctrine amongst Parsis. . . . We must remember that throughout the scriptures there is nothing explicit to denounce the doctrine of rebirth. At the most, there is a lack of emphasis on this point; either because during the earlier Avestan age, it was too well known and needed no reiteration; or perhaps it was thought preferable to shift the focus on the present precious life, rather than speculate on the distant future. The life after death, as narrated in Pahlavi times, took a sudden jump from the Judgment-scene to resurrection; and hence the intervening series of incarnations were not reviewed in detail. . . . (2) After having emphasised the law of retribution, one cannot patch up several glaring doubts that arise. . . . If God is just, each must start with equal opportunities, uniform longevity and equal abilities. . . . God has certain attributes in the Avesta . . . , such as 'Accountant of all living beings', 'Supervisor of all deeds', 'never liable to be deceived', 'an upright judge', etc. Then surely there can be no anarchy, no favouritism and no arbitrary punishment! . . . (3) The truth is patent, that Zarathushtra even in [his] sacred hymns, does mention the law of reincarnation. Gatha 49.11 [= 2.2.10.11] is explicit, though for so long European scholars followed the Pahlavi version [i.e. the Zand], without examining the original Avestan text. Dr Tarapore . . . translated the stanza differently: 'Those souls who ruled badly, who perpetrated bad deeds, who spoke evil words, do come back (paiti-yeinti) on account of their evil record. Verily they are dwellers in this abode of untruth.' This is how it should be translated. . . . (4) It is easy to accuse a Parsi believing in the law of rebirth of being a theosophist or a Buddhist. But I discovered this doctrine in Gatha 49.11 many years before I joined the Theosophical Society. . . . Besides, the society is barely eighty years old, while Zarathushtra's message has had its influence for 8,000 years. Buddhism is comparatively a modern religious message, with an entirely different theology. But granting that other religions uphold this doctrine, there is no reason why a Parsi should reject it, simply on (that) score. . . . Comparative religion reveals several such points of mutual similarities, where all Teachers and Prophets are in agreement. . . . (5) Having said that 'all good thoughts, propounded anywhere and at any time, would deserve our allegiance', how can we exclude any true and good idea from the field of Zoroastrianism? . . . If eternal verities constitute all religions, the fact of reincarnation must pertain to all faiths. . . . (6) When we question any doctrine,

due to its non-inclusion among religious books, we have to remember that we have barely saved the contents of about three volumes out of twenty-one; and what has been retrieved, has been connected with sacred rituals, and rubrics of prayers. Philosophical books have been lost, and it therefore does not behove anyone to ask us to point out chapter and verse. (From Khurshed S. Dabu, *Message of Zarathushtra*, 54–61.)

11.5.2.2 From an orthodox refutation

Note: *Taraporewala, in (4), is identical with Tarapore in 11.5.2.1.3.*

(1) In recent years there has been a periodic increase in interest among Parsis in their religion. This has naturally brought to the fore a question which has interested and agitated the Parsis for several decades: is reincarnation compatible with Zoroastrianism? ... Dabu opines that 'the doctrine of reincarnation has to be a natural corollary to the Law of Justice.' ... (He) then sets out to show that reincarnation is mentioned in the Gathas and quotes the key verse Ys. 49.11 ... in Taraporewala's interpretation.... The two key phrases (are) 'Abode of Untruth' (drujo demane) and 'do come back' (paiti-yeinti).... 'Paiti-yeinti' ... can mean either 'go (forth) to meet' or 'come back'. Taraporewala admits that there is no specific mention of the place to which the Souls 'do come back' except in the words 'drujo demane', but he finds indications to it being 'our earthly environment'.... (This) cannot be accepted. 'Druj', 'lies, deceit', has at all times in Zoroastrian literature been the attribute of the Evil Spirit; to say that this Earth is the Abode of the Evil Spirit is to repudiate all the good creations of Ahura Mazda with which this earth is full.... If 'drujo demane' means Hell, as all other scholars agree, then the souls of the wicked must go forth to Hell, and the correct meaning of 'paiti yeinti' in this context must mean 'go forth' and not 'come back'.... (2) From the 'Gathas' to the 'Persian Rivayats' there is a consistent picture of the fate of the soul: at death the soul is judged at Chinvat Bridge and then goes to heaven or hell. At no time during a span of 3,000 years has there been any other picture but this. The inference is obvious: the possibility of the soul returning to this world ... was never envisaged in the Zoroastrian religion. An argument that proponents of the reincarnation theory often use is that twenty of the twenty-one Sasanian 'nasks' are now lost and therefore we cannot make a dogmatic statement that Zoroastrianism rejects reincarnation; ... while twenty 'nasks' are now lost to us, the contents of nineteen of them are known, thanks to the extensive summaries in the 'Denkard'; also some parts of these lost 'nasks' are ... included in the extant Avesta. It is significant that the summaries of the nineteen 'nasks' do not contain even a hint of reincarnation.... (3) The weakness of the 'lost nasks' argument can be illustrated by an example. Suppose a heretical Parsi were to say that cannibalism formed part of Zoroastrian ritual, and to the horrified objections of the Parsis he replied: 'How can you be so dogmatic that this is not so? It might well be mentioned in some of the twenty lost 'nasks'.' It is doubtful if this argument would be accepted by anyone, because cannibalism is so alien to all that Zoroaster worked for and preached,

to the whole ethos of the religion, that under no circumstances can we conceive of it being part of the ritual. The real test is whether a doctrine is compatible with the rest of the religion, and it is this test that we must ... apply to reincarnation. (4) The problems created by the existence of suffering and evil have been tackled by all the great religions, and Zoroastrianism has supplied its own answers. . . . Dabu . . . asks: 'Why should a Zoroastrian not believe in the Law of Reincarnation?' The answer is best given by J. E. Sanjana . . . : '. . . Faith in this dogma is so incompatible with the letter and spirit of traditional Zoroastrianism that it can be said without any exaggeration, and with the most perfect reason and justice, that a man who believes in reincarnation is no true Zoroastrian. . . . Whoever believes in this dogma . . . cannot logically and honestly believe in God as a creator and ruler of this universe, of this world and of man. He must put "karma" or blind destiny in the place of God; he must become a fatalist to whom all action and volition, whether bad or good, is a means of creating bad or good "karma", and thus entailing future births and future evil in countless incarnations on this earth.' (From H. E. Eduljee, in *Supplement to Zoroastrian Studies, News Letter*, Vol. III, No. 1, April 1982, 1–5.)

11.6 RESTATEMENT AND REAPPRAISAL

11.6.1 Of doctrine
11.6.1a The 'latent omnipotence' of God
God in Zoroastrianism is deemed to be totally good and perfect. Hence that which is imperfect (evil) cannot emerge from God, for if it did, then God would no longer remain totally good and perfect. In Zoroastrianism therefore God cannot be held to be the bringer of imperfections such as misery, pain, suffering, poverty, disease or death. Here lies the intellectual strength of Zarathushtra's teachings. . . . God is latently omnipotent. A temporarily non-omnipotent God should not be seen to be a weak or powerless Being, for in the Zoroastrian tradition God is recognised to be the strongest (Y. 28.9), the mightiest (Y. 45.6) and indeed invincible (Yt. 1.8) at the end of time. A distinction should be made, however, between a Being who is all-powerful at all times and a Being who is very powerful . . . , but yet not all-powerful to prevent the onslaught of evil, eventually culminating in death. . . . Man by recognising God to be temporarily non-omnipotent in no way implies that evil is equal to, and therefore as powerful as God. . . . The will of Ahura Mazda continues to overwhelm the imperfections and inequalities in this world. The process of 'creative evolution' is an ongoing one. . . . Man in Zoroastrianism is the soldier who has been chosen to spearhead this evolution, through the recognition of a strongly contrasted ethical dualism. . . . This ethical dualism in no way lessens the . . . greatness of God; nor does it preclude a monotheistic belief in one God whose eventual supremacy at the end of time is unquestionable in

Zoroastrianism.

11.6.1b The doctrine of the Heptad

The task of a Zoroastrian is to imbibe the attributes of the seven Amesha Spentas in order that one may consciously integrate into one's own life each quality of Ahura Mazda, as represented through each of His seven Bounteous Immortals. Every man requires the Wisdom and the Spirit of God (Spenta Mainyu) in order to be aware of the Good Mind (Vohu Manah). The Good Mind is God's greatest gift to man, for it is from the Good Mind that man learns to develop a perception of the Best Truth (Asha Vahishta). . . . A combination of God's wisdom balanced by the Good Mind and the Best Truth gives man the strength or the Sovereign Kingdom (Khshathra Vairya) to implement the will and goodness of God in this world. Man, however, must learn to accept this will through Piety and Devotion (Armaiti), in order that he may experience an inexplicable moment of cosmic harmony. The experience of this harmony lies in the Perfection (Haurvatat) of whatever one does. Every thought, word and deed must be created to bring to fruition the final goal of creation, which is the defeat of evil, resulting in the state of undyingness (Ameretat). The duty of man is to realise the nature of . . . (these) abstract principles, which when personified take on the role of becoming the guardians of the seven good creations. An awareness of the sensate world enables man to gain . . . an extension of consciousness from the physical to a subtler dimension of reality. This subtler state is not to be seen as being more important than the physical one. . . . The true realisation that everything good in this world is the affirmation of God is perhaps the kernel of Zoroastrian spirituality. . . . A Zoroastrian is encouraged to live life to its fullest, in order that he may learn to preserve and enjoy the goodness of the seven creations. . . . It is through an existential perception of the Bounteous Immortals that a Zoroastrian learns to formulate an ethical policy of 'good living'. This awareness brings about a gnosis of what is indeed the right thought, the right word and the right deed – the key unquestionably to becoming an 'ashavan', the possessor of truth. (From Khojeste Mistree, *Zoroastrianism*, 28–9, 18–19.)

11.6.2 Of ritual and observance

(1) The problem of the ritual ceremonies still remains to be considered. The earliest to appear in the history of Zoroastrian ceremonials is undoubtedly the Haoma ceremony . . . ; in the . . . Younger Avesta we find a whole series of hymns of request and praise, and also other rituals of veneration and commemoration. . . . These prayers and . . . rituals . . . are part of the hieratical acts in the Zoroastrian tradition. Now suppose a present-day believer asks why, i.e. for what religious reason should we perform these hieratical acts, what would be a reasonable response to give in terms . . . of the religious vision . . . of Zarathushtra? . . . Our view of the world has been markedly changed by the development of scientific thought in the last two hundred years. We think of disease, pollution and the physical condition of our environment no longer in

demonic or angelic terms. . . . The conception of how the world works which prevailed when hieratical acts were taken to be the efficient means of promoting our welfare has been changed for ever. Does this imply that they have lost significance . . . ? The answer is: No; but it entails interpreting (their) significance differently. . . . (2) We distinguish three notions of 'Hieratic Religious Acts' . . . : those where it is believed that the hieratic agent (i.e. the performer of the act), by interaction with some divine entity or force, produces effects either in the physical or spiritual domain, either in this world or the next. . . . This is the view of ritual as a technological operation . . . ; 2. those . . . which are expressions of the devotion of the agent; and which by their performance generate in (his) consciousness a communion with a reality beyond, or at least an elevation from the web of mundane existence . . . ; 3. those . . . which by the antiquity and continuity of their practice generate in their practitioners a . . . sense of belonging to an ancient yet living tradition and of sharing with generations past a belief in a religious view reflected in the ritual. . . . The function here focuses on the traditional and historical aspect of spiritual awareness, which is an aspect of the life of every religious tradition . . . (and) is the life-blood of (its) social existence and continuity. . . . This is not the sort of hieratical act which would be in conflict with an ethical religious act. One who rejects the traditional pietistic form of a hieratical act is not an immoral person (although perhaps asocial), nor even irreligious; he fails to appreciate the vital, socially cohesive character of religion, and lacks the awareness of the collective power of religious faith. . . . A hieratical act of (the second) type needs no justification, nor, indeed, can it be argued for. To a believer in whose consciousness (its) performance generates a sense of spiritual communion or upliftment, the act is thereby justified. And for one in whom this is not the case, the justification is absent. . . . There is, however, a genuine value to the experience. For . . . communion with a greater reality beyond de-emphasises the self's exclusive concern with itself and releases it from the vicissitudes of social abrasion, facilitating the selfless life of good thoughts, good words and good deeds. But there is danger too. If the conscious experience, no matter how uplifting, becomes an end in itself, it may fail to motivate the individual to a life of action. Indeed, it may stand in the way of a life of striving to bring about the good, a state which can be described as the indolence of spirituality. (The first is) the most complex notion: hieratical acts of transnatural technology. This view, completely dominant in ancient religions, and widely prevalent in most religions until the last century, has waned steadily in the last hundred years, . . . and fails to be of persuasive justification in this . . . age. (3) Consider first the total set of religious beliefs and practices of a religious tradition. The beliefs incorporated into the 'religious vision' constitute the 'central core' of that religion . . . (which) will contain a fusion of a view of the world's destiny and a way of life. Alongside the 'core' there will be certain 'associated practices' which are part of the religious tradition, some . . . ritualistic, others, prescriptions concerning social, communal or personal life.

The associated practices, unlike the 'core', may . . . change from time to time
. . . ; a religious practice is justified if it achieves or promotes some goal or value
contained in the 'core', and our knowledge of the world is required to establish
that it does or does not. . . . (4) Let me illustrate: purificatory and cleansing
ritual practices which use purified bull's urine as a cleansing agent were
justifiable in antiquity when such urine was one of the very few antiseptic
agents available. But with far better antiseptics available now the practice
cannot be justified. . . . Of course, bull's urine is not used for this purpose any
more, it is only ritually employed on special rare occasions. If one who uses it as
a hieratical act justifies it by an appeal to 'traditional piety' he may, but he has
missed the point of its original use. And anyone who fails to use better
antiseptics when they are available is acting contrary to the injunctions in the
'core' of the religion. A similar problem is the practice of the disposal of the
dead. Exposure in the tower of silence is justified as a method of disposal which
is non-polluting to the elements of divine creation, and generally diminishing
the hazards of contamination. If, however, one can provide a non-polluting,
non-contaminating method different from the present and . . . more efficient
and effective, one would have to evaluate it to see if it does not implement the
concept of the religious 'core' better. To strive for the better implementation of
the values in the 'core' is itself a religious obligation. . . . To hold to a traditional
practice merely because it is traditional is an insufficient reason, particularly
for a Zoroastrian, who, enjoined to think good thoughts through the gift of the
Good Mind (Vohu Manah), is under a religious obligation to reflect, reason and
then choose. (5) The Zoroastrian community, if it is to be responsive to the
message of the prophet, must clearly formulate and articulate the religious
vision he preached to this world and then apply its ethical principles to the
complex and varying conditions of modern existence. . . . There have been
historians who have concluded that Zoroastrianism, like so many ancient
religions, has outlived its significance and is quietly passing away. This
misconception arises because Zoroastrianism is viewed as a cultic religion of a
particular tribe or people. The religious concepts in the message of
Zarathushtra are completely universal, and the ethical imperative of good
thoughts, good words and good deeds is utterly timeless. Seeing this world and
human life therein in radically moral terms, and giving significance to human
life in the moral endeavour to perfect this world, is as relevant and meaningful
today as it was when Zarathushtra preached it. (From Kaikhosrov D. Irani,
'Reflections on the Zoroastrian religion . . .', *Parsiana*, August 1980, 23,
43–51.)

BIBLIOGRAPHY

Section A contains details of the works excerpted in this anthology, and their translations. Sections B and C list general and background books, with preference being given, following editorial policy, to those in English. Section B especially names books which illustrate the diversity to be found in modern studies of Zoroastrianism (cf. 1.4. 2 and 3). *Note:* Greek and Latin texts have been quoted from the Loeb edition, except where another reference is given. Spelling variations occur in the transcriptions of titles of Pahlavi works.

A TEXTS EXCERPTED AND THEIR TRANSLATIONS

Al Biruni, *The Chronology of Ancient Nations*, ed. E. Sachau, text, Leipzig, 1923, trans. London, 1879, repr. 1969.

Anklesaria, B. T. (ed.), *Vichitakiha i Zatsparam*, Pahl. text with almost complete Eng. trans., Bombay, 1964.

— *Zand-Akāsīh, Iranian or Greater Bundahishn*, Pahl. text with Eng. trans., Bombay, 1956.

— *Zand i Vohuman Yasn*, Pahl. text with Eng. trans., Bombay, 1957.

Anklesaria, T. D. (ed.), *The Datistan-i dinik*, Bombay, n.d.

Anquetil du Perron, H., *Zend-Avesta, ouvrage de Zoroastre*, 2 vols., Paris, 1771.

Antia, E. K. (ed.), *Pāzand Texts*, Bombay, 1909.

Asmussen, J. P., *Xuāstvānīft, Studies in Manichaeism*, Copenhagen, 1965.

Avesta. The text of all Av. passages is to be found in the edition of K. F. Geldner, see below.

Back, M., *Die sassanidischen Staatsinschriften*, Acta Iranica 18, 1978.

Bartholomae, C., *Die Gatha's des Awesta*, Strassburg, 1905.

Benveniste, E., 'Le Mémorial de Zarēr',

Journal asiatique, 1932, 245–93.

Beroukhim (ed.), *Shahname-yi Firdausi*, 10 vols., Tehran, 1935.

Bidez, J., and F. Cumont, *Les mages hellénisés*, Vol. II, Paris, 1938.

Boyce, M. (trans.), *The Letter of Tansar*, Istituto Italiano per il Medio ed Estremo Oriente, Rome, 1968.

Bulsara, J. F., *Bird's Eye Picture of the Parsis*, Bombay, 1969.

Bulsara, S. J., *Aērpatastan and Nīrangastān*, Bombay, 1915.

Chiniwalla, F. S., *Essential Origins of Zoroastrianism, some glimpses of the Mazdayasni Zarathoshti Daen in its original native light of Khshnoom*, Parsi Vegetarian and Temperance Society of Bombay, Bombay, 1942.

Clemen, C., *Fontes historiae religionis persicae*, Bonn, 1920.

Cumont, F., see under J. Bidez.

Dabu, Khurshed S., *Message of Zarathushtra*, Bombay, 1956.

Darmesteter, J. (trans.), *The Zend-Avesta*, Pt. I, *The Vendīdād*, 2nd ed., SBE. IV, Oxford, 1895, repr. Delhi, 1965; Pt. II. *The Sirozahs, Yashts and Nyayesh*, SBE. XXIII, Oxford, 1883, repr. Delhi, 1965.

— (trans.), *Le Zend-Avesta*, Annales du Musée Guimet, 3 vols., Paris, 1892–1893, repr. 1960.

Dhabhar, B. N. (trans.), *The Persian Rivayats of Hormazyar Framarz and Others*, Bombay, 1932.

— *Translation of Zand i Khūrtak Avistāk*, Bombay, 1963.

— (ed.) *Zand i Khūrtak Avistāk*, Bombay, 1927.

Duchesne-Guillemin, J., *The Hymns of Zarathushtra*, Eng. version by M. Henning of his French trans., Wisdom of the East series, London, 1952.

Eduljee, H. E., 'On the reincarnation theory', an article in *Supplement to Zoroastrian Studies* (Bombay), *News Letter*, Vol. III, No. 1, April 1982, 1–5.

Figueroa, G. de Silva, *L'ambassade de D.*

Garcias de Silva Figueroa, trans. into French by A. de Wicquefort, Paris, 1669.

Fox, W. S., and R. E. K. Pemberton, 'Passages in Greek and Latin literature relating to Zoroaster and Zoroastrianism rendered into English', *Journal of the K. R. Cama Oriental Institute* (Bombay), XIV, 1929.

Frye, R. N. (trans.), *Narshakhi's History of Bukhara*, Cambridge, Mass., 1954.

Geldner, K. F. (ed.), *Avesta, The Sacred Books of the Parsis*, 3 vols., Stuttgart, 1886–96, repr. 1982.

Gershevitch, I., *The Avestan Hymn to Mithra*, text with Eng. trans. and notes, Cambridge, 1959, repr. 1967.

Gold, Milton (trans.), *The Tārikh-e Sistan*, Istituto Italiano per il Medio ed Estremo Oriente, Rome, 1976.

Griffiths, J. Gwyn (ed. and trans.), *Plutarch's De Iside et Osiride*, Cardiff, 1970.

Grignaschi, M. (trans.), 'Quelques spécimens de la littérature sassanide . . .', *Journal asiatique*, 1966, 1–142.

Haug, M., *Essays on the sacred language, writings and religion of the Parsis*, 1st ed., 1862, 3rd ed., London, 1884, repr. 1971.

— see also under H. Jamaspji Asa.

Hitti, P. K., and F. C. Murgotten (trans.), *Baladhuri's The Origins of the Islamic State*, Part II, New York, 1924, repr. New York, 1969.

Hodivala, S. H., *Studies in Parsi History*, Bombay, 1920.

Hoffman, G., *Auszüge aus syrischen Akten persischer Märtyrer*, Leipzig, 1880, repr. 1966.

Humbach, H., *Die Gathas des Zarathustra*, 2 vols., text with German trans. and notes, Heidelberg, 1959.

Insler, S., 'The Ahuna Vairya prayer', *Monumentum H. S. Nyberg*, Acta Iranica 4, Leiden, 1975, 410–21.

—, *The Gāthās of Zarathushtra*, text with Eng. trans. and notes, Acta Iranica 8, Leiden, 1975.

Irani, K. D., 'Reflections on the Zoroastrian religion: the philosophy of belief and practice', *Parsiana* (Bombay), August 1980, 13–23, 43–51.

Jackson, A. V. W., *Zoroaster, the prophet of ancient Iran*, New York, 1899, repr. 1965.

Jamaspji Asa, H., and M. Haug (ed. and trans.), *The Book of Arda Viraf, with . . . an appendix containing the texts and translations of the . . . Hadhokht Nask*, Bombay and London, 1872.

Jamasp-Asana, H. J., and E. W. West (ed.), *Shikand Gūmānīk Vijār*, Bombay, 1887.

Jamasp-Asana, J. M. (ed.), *The Pahlavi texts contained in the Codex MK*, Pt. II, Bombay, 1913.

Kanga, M. F. (trans.), *Chitak Handarz i Poryotkeshan*, Bombay, 1960.

Karaka, F. D., *History of the Parsis*, 2 vols., London, 1884.

Kent, R. G., *Old Persian, Grammar, Texts, Lexicon*, 2nd ed., New Haven, 1953.

Laing, S., *A modern Zoroastrian*, London, 1890.

Lincoln, B., 'Mithra(s) as Sun and Savior', *La sotériologie dei culti orientali nell' impero romano*, ed. U. Bianchi and M. J. Vermaseren, Leiden, 1982, 505–26.

Lommel, H., *Die Gathas des Zarathustra*, German trans., ed. B. Schlerath, Stuttgart, 1971.

— *Die Yäšt's des Awesta*, German trans. with notes, Göttingen and Leipzig, 1927.

Lord, H., *A Display of Two Forraigne Sects in the East Indies*, London, 1630.

Madan, D. M. (ed.), *Dinkard*, 2 vols., Bombay, 1911.

Mahjub, M. (ed.), *Vis u Ramin*, Tehran, 1959.

Menasce, P. J. de, *Škand-Gumānīk Vičār*, transliterated text with French trans. and commentary, Fribourg-en-Suisse, 1945.

Mills, L. H. (trans.), *The Zend-Avesta*, Pt. III, *The Yasna, Visparad, Afrīnagān, Gāhs and Miscellaneous Fragments*, SBE. XXXI, Oxford, 1887, repr.

Delhi, 1965.

Minovi, M. (ed.), *Tansar Name*, Tehran, 1932.

— (ed.), *Vis u Ramin*, Tehran, 1935.

Mistree, K. P., *Zoroastrianism, an ethnic perspective*, Bombay, 1982 (printed privately).

Modi, J. J., *A Catechism of the Zoroastrian religion*, Bombay, 1911.

— *Dr. J. J. Modi Memorial Volume*, Bombay, 1930.

Molé, M., *La légende de Zoroastre selon les textes pehlévies*, transliterated texts with French trans. and commentary, Paris, 1967.

Monchi-Zade, D., *Die Geschichte Zarēr's*, Uppsala, 1981.

Morrison, G. (trans.), *Vis and Ramin*, New York and London, 1972.

Moulton, J. H., *The Treasure of the Magi, A Study of Modern Zoroastrianism*, Oxford, 1917, repr. 1971.

Murgotten, F. C., see under P. K. Hitti.

Narten, Johanna, *Die Aməṣa Spəṇtas im Avesta*, Wiesbaden, 1982.

Niebuhr, K., *Travels through Arabia and other countries*, Eng. trans. by R. Heron, Vol. II, Edinburgh, 1792.

Nöldeke, T. (trans.), *Geschichte der Perser und Araber zur Zeit der Sasaniden aus der arabischen Chronik des Tabari*, Leiden, 1879.

Ogilby, J., *Asia*, London, 1673.

Ovington, J., *A Voyage to Surat in the year 1689*, ed. H. G. Rawlinson, Oxford, 1929.

Pastakia, R. B. (ed.), *Treatise on Zoroastrian tradition* ..., 2nd ed., Jamshedpur, 1982 (printed privately).

Patel, B. B., *The Religious Buildings of the Parsis*, Bombay, 1906.

— see also under K. N. Seervai.

Pavry, J. C., *The Zoroastrian Doctrine of a Future Life from Death to the Individual Judgment*, New York, 1929.

Pemberton, R. E. K., see under W. S. Fox.

Sanjana, P. B. and D. P. (ed. and trans.), *Dinkard*, 19 vols., Bombay, completed 1928.

Schmidt, H.-P., 'The sixteen Sanskrit ślokas of Ākā Adhyāru', *Bulletin of the Deccan College Research Institute*, 21, 1960–61, pp. 157–96.

Seervai, K. N., and B. B. Patel, 'Gujarat Parsis', *Gazetteer of the Bombay Presidency*, Vol. IX, Pt. 2, Bombay, 1899.

Shahname, for text see under Beroukhim; for Eng. trans., under Warner.

Shaki, M., 'The Denkard account of the history of the Zoroastrian scriptures', *Archiv Orientalní*, 49, 1981, 114–25.

Stavorinus, J. S., *Voyages to the East Indies*, trans. from the Dutch by S. H. Wilcocke, Vol. II, London, 1798, repr. 1969.

Taraf, Zahra, *Der Awesta-text Niyāyiš mit Pahlavi- und Sanskrit-übersetzung*, Munich, 1981.

Taraporewala, I. J. S., *The Divine Songs of Zarathushtra*, Bombay, 1951.

Tavaria, P. N., *A Manual of 'Khshnoom', the Zoroastrian occult knowledge*, Bombay, 1971.

Tavernier, J. B., *Collections of Travels through Turkey into Persia, and the East-Indies*, Eng. trans., Vol. 1, London, 1784.

Tritton, A. S., *The Caliphs and their Non-Muslim Subjects*, London, 1930, repr. 1970.

Unvala, M. R. (ed.), *Dārāb Hormazyār's Rivāyat*, 2 vols., Bombay, 1922.

Warner, A. G. and E. (trans.), *Firdausi's Shahname*, 9 vols., London, 1912–25.

West, E. W. (trans.), *Shikand Gumanik Vijar*, SBE. XXIV, 1885, repr. Delhi, 1965.

— (trans.), *The Book of the Mainyo-i Khard*, Stuttgart and London, 1871.

— (trans.), *The Bundahesh*, SBE. V, Oxford 1901, repr. Delhi, 1965. This is a translation of a shorter recension of this work, now known as the Indian Bundahishn.

— (trans.), *Zand i Vohuman Yasht*, SBE. V, 1880, repr. Delhi, 1965.

— (trans.), *The Dādistān-ī dīnīk*, SBE. XVIII, 1882, repr. Delhi, 1965.

— see also under H. J. Jamasp-Asana.

Williams, Monier, *Modern India and the*

Indians, London, 1878.

Wilson, J., *The Parsi Religion . . . unfolded, refuted and contrasted with Christianity*, Bombay, 1843.

Wolff, F., *Avesta, Die heiligen Bücher der Parsen übersetzt auf der Grundlage von Chr. Bartholomae's Altiranischem Wörterbuch*, Strassburg, 1910, repr. 1960.

Wüstenfeld, F. (ed.), *Qazvini's Kosmographie*, Vol. II, Göttingen, 1849.

Zaehner, R. C., *The Teachings of the Magi, a compendium of Zoroastrian beliefs, Ethical and Religious Classics of East and West*, London, 1956, repr. 1975.

— *Zurvan, a Zoroastrian dilemma*, London, 1955.

B ADDITIONAL WORKS CONCERNED WITH ZOROASTRIAN DOCTRINE, RITUAL, LITERATURE AND HISTORY

Bailey, H. W., *Zoroastrian problems in the ninth century books*, Ratanbai Katrak Lectures, Oxford, 1943, repr. 1971.

Boyce, M., *A history of Zoroastrianism*, Handbuch der Orientalistik, ed. B. Spuler, I.8.1.2, Leiden, Vol. I, *The early period*, 1975; Vol. II, *Under the Achaemenians*, 1982.

— *Zoroastrians, their religious beliefs and practices*, Library of Religious Beliefs and Practices, ed. J. R. Hinnells, London, 1979; paperback, 1984.

— 'Middle Persian literature' in *Handbuch der Orientalistik*, ed. B. Spuler, 1.4.2.1, Leiden, 1968, 31–66.

Dhalla, M. N., *Zoroastrian Theology*, New York, 1914.

— *History of Zoroastrianism*, New York, 1938.

Duchesne-Guillemin, J., *La religion de l'Iran ancien*, Paris, 1962, Eng. trans. by K. M. Jamasp Asa as *Religion of Ancient Iran*, Bombay, 1973.

— *The Western Response to Zoroaster*, Ratanbai Katrak Lectures, 1956, Oxford, 1958.

Gershevitch, I, 'Old Iranian literature', in *Handbuch der Orientalistik*, ed. B. Spuler, 1.4.2.1, Leiden, 1968, 1–30.

Gnoli, Gh., *Zoroaster's Time and Homeland*, Istituto Universitario Orientale, Seminario di Studio Asiatici, Series Minor VII, Naples, 1980.

Jackson, A. V. W., *Zoroastrian Studies*, New York, 1928.

Kotwal, F. M. P. (ed. and trans.), *The supplementary texts to the Šāyest nē-šāyest*, Copenhagen, 1969.

Lommel, H., *Die Religion Zarathustras nach dem Awesta dargestellt*, Tübingen, 1930, repr. 1971.

Mirza, H. K., *Outlines of Parsi history*, Bombay, 1974.

Modi, J. J., *The religious ceremonies and customs of the Parsees*, 2nd ed., Bombay, 1937.

Moulton, J. H., *Early Zoroastrianism*, The Hibbert Lectures, 1912, London, 1913, repr. 1972.

Nyberg, H. S., *Die Religionen des Alten Iran*, trans. from Swedish into German by H. H. Schaeder, Leipzig, 1938, repr. 1960.

Schlerath, B. (ed.), *Zarathustra, Wege der Forschung*, Bd. CLXIX, Darmstadt, 1970.

Shaked, Shaul (ed. and trans.), *The Wisdom of the Sasanian sages (Dēnkard VI)*, Boulder, Col., 1979.

Zaehner, R. C., *The Dawn and Twilight of Zoroastrianism*, London, 1961, repr. 1975.

C ADDITIONAL WORKS CONCERNED WITH RELIGIOUS ART AND WITH COMMUNITY MATTERS

Boyce, M., *A Persian Stronghold of Zoroastrianism*, based on the Ratanbai Katrak Lectures, 1975, Oxford, 1977.

Browne, E. G., *A Year amongst the*

Persians, Cambridge, 2nd ed., 1926, repr. 1927, chs. 13–15.

Desai, S. F., *History of the Bombay Parsi Punchayet 1860–1960*, Bombay, 1977.

Dhalla, M. N., *Autobiography*, trans. from Gujarati into English by G. and B. S. Rustomji, Karachi, 1975.

Ghirshman, R., *Persia from the origins to Alexander the Great*, Eng. trans. by S. Gilbert and J. Emmons, London, 1964.

— *Persian Art: the Parthian and Sasanian Dynasties*, London and New York, 1962.

Godard, A., *The Art of Iran*, London, 1965.

Hinnells, J. R., *Persian Mythology*, London, 1973.

— *Zoroastrianism and the Parsis*, London, 1981.

Jackson, A. V. W., *Persia Past and Present*, New York, 1910, chs. 23, 24.

Kulke, E., *The Parsees in India. A Minority as Agent of Social Change*, Munich, 1974.

Lukonin, V. G., *Persia II*, trans. J. Hogarth, Archaeologia Mundi, Geneva, 1967.

Menant, Dauphine, *Les Parsis, Histoire des communautés zoroastriennes de l'Inde*, Paris, 1898, repr. Osnabrück, 1975.

Molé, M., *L'Iran ancien*, Religions du Monde, Paris, 1965.

Murzban, M. M., *The Parsis in India*, 2 vols., Bombay, 1917.

Nanavutty, P., *The Parsis*, New Delhi, 1977, 2nd ed., 1980.

Porada, E., *Ancient Iran, the Art of Pre-Islamic Times*, Art of the World Series, London, 1965.

Schmidt, E., *Persepolis*, Vols. I–III, University of Chicago Oriental Institute Publications LXVIII, LXIX, LXX, 1953, 1957, 1971.

Stronach, D., *Pasargadae, A Report on the excavations conducted by the British Institute of Persian Studies from 1961–1963*, Oxford, 1978.

GLOSSARIAL INDEX